Travels of a Texas Poet

Travels of a Texas Poet

A Memoir / Volume Two

Dave Oliphant

ALAMO BAY PRESS
SEADRIFT•AUSTIN

Copyright © 2021 by Dave Oliphant

All rights reserved. No part of this book may be reproduced in any form without permission in writing from the publisher, except by a reviewer who may quote brief passages in a review.

Cover: Scanned illustrations by Elisa Oliphant De Faria
Photo on page 273 by David Leonnig, 2015

Book Design by ABP

For orders and information:
Alamo Bay Press
Pamela Booton, Director
825 W 11th Ste 114
Austin, Texas 78701
pam@alamobaypress.com
www.alamobaypress.com

ISBN 978-1-943306-21-3

In Memory of My Beloved Soulmate
María Isabel Jofré Aguirre de Oliphant

Travels of a Texas Poet

Brazil (December 1998-January 1999)	1
Chile (May-June 2006)	93
Chile / Chiloé (March 2007)	149
Chile (March-April 2009)	203
Chile (March 2011)	231
María In Memoriam (1944-2020)	273
About Dave Oliphant	293

Travels of a Texas Poet

Brazil (December 1998-January 1999)

No journey begins with the scheduled departure time; it starts rather with the experiences or events that led up to the motivation for travel. The most immediate reason for our flying to São Paulo was simply to see our daughter Elisa, our granddaughter Isabella, and our son-in-law Newton, and hopefully to be present for the birth of our granddaughter Annabella. Some ten days before leaving for Brazil on December 27th, 1998, we drove to Fort Worth to see my mother, and while there we visited the Amon Carter Museum, where I saw a painting that had been on display there for a number of years but to which I had not paid much attention: a depiction of "Two Hummingbirds Above a White Orchid" (the title of the artwork), the flower larger and more brilliant than the hovering pair of *beija-flores* (hummingbirds in Portuguese; literally, "kisses-flowers"). The artist of the work was Martin Johnson Heade (1819-1904), and according to the caption below the painting, he had traveled to Brazil to study and draw what was said to be the country's national bird.

Once we had arrived in Brazil and were going by car to Jundiaí (both the "j" and "d" pronounced like the English "j" in June and "iaí" like "eye-ee"), the city where our daughter's family lived, I asked Newton about the hummingbird, but he did not think Brazil had a national bird. He then remembered that pictured on the one *reai* bill is a hummingbird, but since other denominations of the country's paper currency carry other fowl, he was sure that the hummingbird was not the nation's symbolic bird. I later learned that the rufous-bellied thrush had become the national bird, after it had been the bird of the State of São Paulo, in which Jundiaí is located. Some Brazilians, I was told, think the golden parakeet should be the national bird, since its colors of yellow and green are the same as those on the national flag. But the pair of hummingbirds that I had seen in Fort Worth had started me thinking, even before we left, about how it had come about that we would be traveling to Brazil. Heade's 19th-century painting, from circa 1875-1890, had led me to retrace in my own life the reasons for our trip to a land that I had known only through literature.

When Elisa met Newton by chance on a flight that he was taking to Brazil and his hometown of Anapolis and in which she was flying to Santiago to see her Chilean relatives, Newton was studying at the University of Texas at Austin toward a doctorate in biomedical engineering. After they met, we learned a bit about Newton's country, which María knew only through her father, who had won a magazine design award in Brazil and had traveled from their home in Santiago to Rio de Janeiro to receive the prize. At that time, María was about thirteen, and she wrote to her father and asked him not to come back to Chile because his unfaithfulness had ruined her mother's life and had also made her own life miserable. After receiving the letter, her father never returned to Chile, and María never had the least desire to visit such a reportedly hot, humid, tropical place.

How things change through time and circumstances. Despite the heat that María hates, she and I were both eager to see our daughter and her family, and so made our reservations months in advance. Only at the last minute did Newton ask if I had a visa. Never having needed one in my previous travels, I had not thought that it was necessary, but had asked early on about María, since in 1975 when we moved to Mexico, it had been problematic for Chileans to enter the country following the military coup in Chile, since many leftist supporters of the Allende regime had been exiled and were not welcome in Mexico. I had failed to ask about myself because I assumed that I could go anywhere without a visa.

Once I was told that U.S. citizens were required to have a visa for Brazil but not Chileans, María made fun of my presumption. My then current passport was still valid for five more months, but the Brazilian Consulate required that it be good for at least six months. After we had driven to Houston to expedite a new passport, and then sent it off with all the forms, copies of airline tickets, and driver's license, the visa did arrive in time, but all the trouble with the visa made me dread the trip. Knowing very little of the language and fearful of all the bureaucracy, I began to have cold feet, and yet this always happens to me on going to another country, and as María says, even outside Texas and in another state of the U.S., I am paranoid. Nevertheless, I have traveled more than I ever imagined that I would, and the reasons for this go back in part to my introduction to Spanish in grade school and high school.

The closest that I had ever been to Brazil was through novels and poetry. In my last year of high school, I had read W.H. Hudson's novel *Green Mansions*, set in southeastern Venezuela and the Guyana jungle, both of which share borders with Brazil. Decades later I would read a number of novels set in other countries bordering Brazil: *Yo el supremo* by Augusto Roa Bastos of Paraguay; *Sobre héroes y tumbas* by Ernesto Sábato of Argentina; *La casa verde* by Mario Vargas Llosa of Perú; and *Cien años de soledad* by Gabriel García Márquez of Colombia. Only in 1978, on writing *Civilization and Barbarism: A Guide to the Teaching of Latin American Literature,* did I finally read works by or on Brazilian authors, including Machado de Assis' "The Psychiatrist"; Mario de Andrade's *Hallucinated City*; a bilingual collection of poetry, entitled *An Anthology of Twentieth-Century Brazilian Poetry,* translated by Elizabeth Bishop and W.S. Merwin; and parts of a literary study, *The Modernist Movement in Brazil*, by John Nist, published by the University of Texas Press.

As we flew toward Brazil and watched a movie on the plane's video screen, I thought how easy it was to reach our destination, even though the eight and a half hours from Miami to São Paulo seemed interminable. Compared with those who first settled the country, sailing for weeks on treacherous seas, we were making the trip in style while viewing *The Mark of Zorro,* starring Antonio

Banderas, Anthony Hopkins, and Catherine Zeta-Jones. This film reminded me of how not only California and New Mexico had been taken from Mexico by the U.S. but that Mexico, Brazil, and all the Americas had been seized by the conquerors from Spain, Portugal, and England. But there is no going back, as Newton commented as we were driving through São Paulo, alongside the completely polluted Tietê River, crossed over by various bridges that connect the different sections of the city founded some five hundred years before. As Newton explained, because the sewage system of São Paulo is so ancient, little has been done or, it seems, can be done to treat the raw sewage before it empties into the Tietê. In the same way, how can one change the past that has produced the present moment. I certainly would not have changed anything in my life that had led to our coming to the land of Brazilian composers Heitor Villa-Lobos and Ernesto Nazareth, whose music I had heard and loved prior to our trip, and of the writings of Brazilian poets like Mario de Andrade, Mario, Osvaldo, and Carlos Drummond, and American Elizabeth Bishop, whose poems on Brazil I had admired for years.

But back behind the more recent memories of listening to compositions like Villa-Lobos' *Bachianas Brasileiras* and *The Little Train of the Caipira* or Nazareth's piano pieces like "Odeon" and "Confidências" (the latter performed at Elisa and Newton's wedding) and of my readings in literature lay the first glimmerings of another world beyond that of English. In grade school, we were taught a few Spanish words: *gato* and *leche* being the ones I still remember. Later in high school I signed up for the language, but came to dislike my old-maid teacher Miss Rachel Dean, and regrettably did not continue with Spanish when I went on to college. An interest in Spanish would resurface with my first year of teaching in the south-Texas town of Hebbronville, where almost all my students were Mexican-American. On working on the M.A. degree the following year, I read for a course on the economic and social history of Latin America a textbook entitled *Latin American Civilization*, by Benjamin Keen, which further piqued my interest in the southern continent. The following year I would apply to an exchange program between the universities of Texas and Chile, and would be selected as one of fifteen UT students for a five-week stay in Chile. It was Miss Dean who had given me the fullest taste for Spanish American culture when she would tell of her time in Mexico when a young man had serenaded her and sent her a bouquet of roses that filled her bathtub. She never tired of recounting that romantic episode, and even though I would ridicule her fond memory, it had its effect in picturing to my mind another life in a distant place with an entirely different way of speaking. The desire to know more about Spanish culture was instilled in me from that high school course and Miss Dean's nostalgic tale of perhaps the one romantic encounter of her unmarried life. Eventually I would write a tribute to my old-maid teacher as part of my sequence of poems entitled "Teachers at South Park High," included in my 2004 collection, *Backtracking*.

The love of my life came about on my second trip to Chile, not with the University group but when I returned alone and would meet and marry my María Isabel. The journey to Brazil was but one of many outcomes of that second Latin American adventure. More than anything, each visit, especially the first to Chile, was to reveal the rich literature in Spanish that is now so much a part of my essential being. Not knowing Portuguese well, however, has kept me from immersing myself as deeply in Brazilian writings as I would like, other than through translations. From time to time, by using my less-than-fluent Spanish and the little that I learned from sitting in on Portuguese classes at the University, I have dipped into a Brazilian poet or prose writer, but the languages are to me so different that Spanish does not help that much with Portuguese, at least in terms of speaking. When María and I lived in Mexico for a year, we both attended for a while a class in Portuguese, but she found it so laughable when we were asked to talk to one another in Portuguese that she stopped going and without her continuing I dropped out as well.

On finding how easily Elisa had picked up Portuguese, partly because she was already fluent in her mother's Spanish, it stirred in me both pride and frustration. It was so wonderful to find her conversing with everyone, the first instance coming when she took Isabella to have her bangs trimmed. This was in a barber shop for children, where one attraction for the kids was the seating arrangement. In place of a regular barber chair, a child could choose a brightly-colored automobile to sit in and to entertain him- or herself by turning the steering wheel and squirming from side to side as the lady barber tried to trim his or her hair. When Isabella's moving around became too much or she wanted to stand up in the car, the barber would take a candy from one of the round jars filled with lollipops and other goodies and give it to her so she could finish the job. During the entire operation, Elisa and the barber carried on a commentary on the haircut, on other barbers who had done Isabella's hair, and various topics that I could not understand. The barber seemed to enjoy talking with Elisa, as both were quite animated in their conversation, which made me wish more than ever to be able to join in, or at least to comprehend more of what they were saying.

Later we went to a fruit stand, where Elisa spoke with the young manager, who was also quite animated in his conversation about all the types of produce. He handed María what he called a *roma* (the "r" in Portuguese pronounced like an aspirated "h" in English) and María identified it as a *granada* in Spanish, or a pomegranate in English. Obviously *roma* had something of the same root as pome in pomegranate, or so I thought when I first saw the fruit and the sign on its box. Later, on looking up the fruit's name, I found that *pome* comes from Middle French (for seedy apple) and that the root *pom* in Latin has to do with fruit in general. In the same stand I saw a newspaper and could read fairly well an article on an elevator accident that had killed two workers. A photo of three fellow workmen carried a caption that seemed to say that they were mourning their loss. But again, reading and speaking are two entirely different activities, and listening to Elisa speak with the people left me understanding very little. Now and then a word would come through from the closeness of Portuguese to Spanish, despite the different sound of the two languages. Perhaps with time, I hoped, I would manage to make out more of what was being said and could even take part in a conversation. Being dropped in the middle of another culture is always a shock, yet stimulating even if in the beginning so disheartening. I think of all the people who came to Latin America to start a new life, many after World War Two; without knowing the languages or customs, they had made the change successfully and had become a vital part of largely homogeneous cultures.

Looking from a 10th-floor window of Elisa and Newton's 12-floor apartment building, Edificio Solar, at Rua Bela Vista 395, I could see quite a different type of architecture from the one that I knew in the States. Outlined against tiers of white- and gray-toned clouds, with below them in the distance tree-covered hills, the colors of some of the high-rises were striking in contrast to the rather bland shades of U.S. buildings. Prominent were the walls of mauve, with the roofs of houses in tones of burnt orange that reminded me of the tiled roofs of the University, which were influenced by the Spanish style that originated with the Arabs. The two-toned gray steeple of a Catholic church, with a white-faced clock, stood next to a park near the local bus station. Newton said the area around the church was dangerous, due to the fact that passengers from everywhere showed up at the station and had been known to kidnap children, so he did not want Elisa taking Isabella there without him.

The wind was blowing and banana leaves swayed in the spaces between the houses, as did the branches of other trees like the ligustrum that we had seen the day before at the barber shop. We knew the ligustrum bushes from our backyard in Austin when we lived on Irma Drive, where Elisa played as a young girl, with our Chilean Araucana chickens clucking to one another and scratching for bugs among the bushes' fallen leaves. Each morning in Jundiaí we were treated to a nearby rooster crowing, just as we had been on Irma Drive when our own cocky Chester would "wake the dead." Such sights and sounds do unite the various locales of the different parts of the globe and make one feel at home in spite of the lack of a common tongue. As Claude Levi-Strauss argues in *Tristes Tropiques*, his study of primitive Brazilian societies, the "savage" mind has the same structures as the "civilized" mind and human characteristics are everywhere the same.

Our routine, however, had changed radically. We went to bed past midnight and got up around nine, whereas at home we rose at 5:15 and hit the sack by 10:30. Meals were, as a result, much later than usual, and the schedule differed almost entirely, for we did not have to go anywhere until it was time for lunch at the vegetarian café, named Vida Natural. But my days did begin, as ever, with exercises, in an almost futile attempt to avoid the middle-age spread. After breakfast I would sit down to write, recalling the events of the day before. December 29th was marked by our second visit to the vegetarian café, since María was on a strict non-meat, non-dairy diet. The food was delicious every day that we went and always included beans and rice. The day before there had been pizza slices, which María could not eat because of the cheese; eggplant fried in soy oil, which she preferred not to eat because this vegetable contains solanine that can cause joint pain; some type of soy meatballs, which she loved; okra, which I always like; and beets, carrots, salad, and more. Vida Natural was on the second floor of a building on the corner of Rua Senador Fonseca, above another establishment, and operated as a kind of cafeteria, with each person serving him- or herself and eating as much as he or she liked. A young couple ran the place, and their child, a bit younger than Isabella at age three, wandered around and passed through the strings of beads hanging from the door frame and separating the dining area from the kitchen. Every now and then a man parted the strings and carried in fresh platters of various veggies. Visible through the open windows and across the street was a park with a newsstand, flowering azaleas, and among other trees a lovely pine distinct from our Texas variety, similar to a mimosa but with a trunk larger around and leaves differing from the fern-like foliage of the mimosa, and with no sign of its gaudy, flamingo-colored blooms.

After we ate, Newton drove us to a health center where Elisa would be given another in her series of tetanus shots. Since she was expecting in less than a month, her visit to the center was part of the precautionary measures taken during her pregnancy. The street leading to the center was paved with bricks of pink granite, and the center itself was a small house converted into a type of clinic for vaccinations, blood samples, urine tests, and minor care. One poster on a wall in a type of porch area described the effects of mosquito bites on dogs and children: loss of weight and hair, elongated eyelashes, and a swollen belly, among others. I could not understand what illness this was—not yellow fever but some other infirmity. My limited Portuguese in many cases was not enough to read such information on walls or packages. I later asked Elisa what the sickness was and she said that she thought it was dengue, which is a tropical mosquito-borne virus.

The young mothers who brought their children to the center held them in their arms, and the variety of skin colors, facial shapes, and hair textures was strikingly distinctive to me, and seemed characteristic of the Brazilian population. This was evident as well in the supermarket where we went shopping in the late afternoon. The African influx, involuntary I should add, was apparent both in pure blacks and in mixed black and Italian, Indian, and so many other immigrant groups. The grocery store itself was like any other, whether in the U.S., Chile, or England; it was the people who differed from those in any other country that I had known. Of course, each section of Brazil must have its own particular racial traits, but perhaps there is something in the physical characteristics and the style of dress that is common to all Brazilians. It may be that the most typical feature in terms of dress is the Brazilian tendency to go casual, which struck me as also true of their whole way of life.

In the evening I listened to Elisa speak of her maid, Marinalva, who was from a farm family of ten children. She lived near Jundiaí with two sisters, who also worked as maids. Marinalva was eighteen and had only completed the fifth grade but was attending classes in the evening to finish a high school equivalency, our GED. Elisa told María about a conflict between Marinalva and Newton's mother, Maria do Carmo, who lives in Anapolis, some eight hours away, but who visits on occasion. It seems that the maid went to pick up Isabella at school when Maria do Carmo had come to Jundiaí expressly to do so. Maria do Carmo was totally crushed because Marinalva had already gone for Isabella and so she had to return home without having another opportunity on that particular trip to fetch her grandchild at school. Elisa had threatened to replace the maid but could not bring herself to do so, for various reasons, including Marinalva's honesty, her not having missed a single day of work, and her sweetness with Isabella. Elisa had had to become sterner with Marinalva, which Newton had warned her that she should be, but Elisa is so very kind-hearted and the role of a mistress was foreign to her nature. She often praised Marinalva and even took her out on her birthday, which apparently is never done for maids. All of this is typical of Elisa and certainly endears me to my "favorite" daughter.

While mother and daughter talked of the difficulties of having a maid and other household trials, Elisa worked at cross-stitching a design on a frame, in which she was going to place a photograph of Isabella with her Brazilian grandmother. She mentioned that Newton had told her that such needlework was for people who had nothing better to do. Elisa objected to his attitude, partly because she really enjoys cross-stitching and partly, as she told Newton, because it can be a kind of art. She had taken classes locally and learned to finish the stitches so that the reverse side would be perfectly smooth and even. While I was proud of her handiwork, I remained most impressed by her language facility, and her vocabulary in English, Spanish, and Portuguese, which to me was downright amazing, especially since she had never been a big reader. She would use words that I knew from my constant reading but that I had never myself employed in conversation or on the written page.

Shortly before noon we began to hear firecrackers, very near and extremely loud, and also from other parts of the city. Elisa said that Isabella had at first been frightened by this frequent form of celebration but that now she was accustomed to it. She suspected that it was caused in this case by a soccer game, and when Newton returned from having taken his nephew Aldo to play video games, he informed us that the Brazilian national team had won a competitive cup. Elisa said that she disliked the tradition, especially since the people only exploded firecrackers rather than skyrockets, which at least at night would be something pretty to watch. Meantime, I went on reading in Adrian Johns' *The Nature of the Book: Print and Knowledge in the Making*, which our son Darío had given me for Christmas. An almost 800-page study of the impact of printing on the creation or production of knowledge, the book had interested me most, up to the point that I had reached in my reading, from its description of English booksellers' houses. Johns' book describes perfectly the arrangement in the childhood home of Dr. Samuel Johnson, which María and I had visited in Lichfield in 1997. The ground floor served as the bookshop of Johnson's father, the second floor as the family's living quarters, and the third floor as garrets for apprentices or servants. Although I was pleased to have time to read, I was more interested in meeting and conversing with Brazilian writers. Elisa laughed to think that there were any in Jundiaí, but I suspected that there were and hoped that perhaps I would discover them.

On the 30th I continued with the same ritual: 60 sit-ups, a large glass of water, bathing, shaving, a glass of freshly made juice (usually carrot and apple but on this day collard greens and orange), cooked bran cereal with honey, and then writing up of the previous day's activities. This day, before reading more in *The Nature of the Book* and also in *Swingin' the Dream*, a study of the Swing Era by Lewis Erenberg, I worked on some of the piano music that I had brought along, since I had known in advance that Newton had an electric keyboard. It was a Kawai with headphones that María loved because she did not have to hear me go over and over the same passage, repeating the same wrong notes and driving her nuts; I, however, never tire of trying to play correctly a piece like the Bach prelude, number 12, BWV 857, from his *Well-Tempered Clavier*. Even though I made the same mistakes, could never get the trills quite right, and did not balance the two hands properly, I was constantly in awe of Bach's ear. Despite my very low performance level, I enjoyed just being able to play such a piece well enough to hear the composer's marvelous note combinations and relationships. Lewis Erenberg reveals that a friend convinced him to take up the piano, even though his teachers "might not be as thankful" as he would be, which I can say must be true of my long-suffering Taiwanese teacher, Jennifer Feiereisel. I had started taking lessons on the instrument after Elisa gave it up, since her mother felt that her ballet and track were not leaving her time for another extracurricular activity. Trying to play has been for me a source of deep personal pleasure, even though I have made such painfully slow progress—more painful to those who have had to listen to me practice.

After our customary nap, María, Elisa, and I walked in a leisurely fashion to the center of town. In her ninth month, Elisa felt fine, even though the weight of the baby was quite evident from her distended stomach. She needed to purchase a pair of zippers for a piece of clothing, and so she and María looked over the offerings in a small notions shop. In the store's single aisle, replacement heads for childrens' dolls filled a container and a larger head with clown-like painted cheeks sat on a shelf behind the shop's one long counter. From reading some of the signs, I learned that doll in Portuguese is *boneca*, which is close to the Spanish *muñeca*. Meanwhile, a shop girl was showing Elisa the shades of thread to match the fabric of the zippers she was buying. Although this was not exactly my idea of a walking tour, which was what I had expected, it had proved "a learning experience," and it was good as well to be with my girls and watch them "doing their thing." Also, seeing the dolls' heads recalled María's doll Paula, who utters her opinionated views in my poem, "María's Voices." Paula's head is broken and she now gathers dust in our garage, but through María's witty imitation baby voice Paula still makes her know-it-all pronouncements on whatever burning issue of the day. So even a visit to a notions shop had its value for a chauvinist, and as with every occasion for writing, this one led to words and memories that it called up and gave meaning to. Like the purchased zippers, such little events can reveal the mind's *roupa íntima* (intimate clothing) or the unexpected connection between here and there, now and then.

Continuing up Rua Bernandino de Campos, we came to a church in the Plaza Governador Pedro de Toledo, which it seemed was in the Parish of Our Lady of Exile. María immediately identified the style of the painted arches as African because of the bright colors: blues, orange-browns, with red crosses and etched leaves at the tops of the arches. Two angels over the rounded arch of the nave were in greens and held a banner in Latin that read: *Gloria in Excelsis Deo et in terra Pax Hominibus*. Inside, the altar was painted white, with three panels above it depicting, to me, the flight of Mary and Joseph into Egypt. In the center panel were palm trees against green and blue skies, the holy parents in blue and gray, the Christ child held by the Virgin Mother as she knelt, while in the two outer panels, figures in pink robes also knelt, one with a silver halo around his head. A few people in the church sat scattered about on the wooden benches, facing the altar. No service was in progress, but people in the Sacristía to the right seemed to be discussing church business. In all, the contrast with most Spanish or U.S. Catholic churches was striking in terms of the bright colors on the pillars and for the scenes depicted, and yet the atmosphere was as spiritually charged as any, regardless of the exotic outer appearance.

Unlike the respectful silence inside the church, the surrounding plaza bustled with shoppers going in and out of shops. On the side away from the plaza, a street lined with shops was named Rua Barão de Jundiaí and was restricted to pedestrians. One kiosk on the street displayed a life-sized poster with a half-naked woman, her right hand over her right breast, a long tattoo in black running down from her left shoulder and over her breast, and at her stomach a snake-like head gazing toward her black bikini-style panty barely covering her *mons veneris*. The tattoo again brought to mind Lévi-Strauss's book, where he describes and illustrates with photos the fantastic geometrical designs inscribed by Brazilian aborigines on their faces and bodies, incorporating their lips and nipples into the elaborate lines and angles of their permanent make-up. Nothing of that practice was apparent on the citizens of Jundiaí, and even in the period of the late 1930s (I believe it was), tattooing was becoming something of a lost art among the native peoples. It was not clear to me whether or not the natives mixed to any degree with the European and African immigrants. Once again, Jundiaí is just a small part of Brazil, which takes up almost half of the South American continent, so that such a vast country cannot be characterized by one small section. Not knowing much about life in Brazil made it endlessly fascinating, and I said to myself that I could live here. María, however, has always reminded me that anywhere outside of Texas I am totally paranoid, impatient, and always think the worst.

As we strolled up Rua Barão, we passed a building named for a Count (*Conde* as in Spanish). Witty María thought of Count

Dracula, the moppet character on *Sesame Street* who could and would count everything in sight. As I had noticed before, streets were named for a Senator and a Governor, and now on Rua Barão, for a Baron. One of the shops on the street specialized in American jeans and another in shoes and sneakers; in the latter, salespeople stood about waiting for a customer, the way I did for many years as a "shoedog," the trade term in the States for a shoe salesman. I could empathize with the sales personnel while at the same time I enjoyed immensely my freedom from the retail grind. At the end of Baron Street we found another plaza where trinket vendors were closing up their little stands for the day. There were huge trees that María found repellent because of their parasitical plants and their jungle-looking appearance—one in particular with ferny, cypress-like leaves. She has never approved of tropical vegetation and heat, and especially not the tropics' snakes of every kind, which in Chile are rare and none there is deadly. Toward the back of the plaza was a monastery of São Bento (Saint Benito), which to María was more appealing. (I was reminded of Melville's novella, "Benito Cereno," with its setting off the coast of Chile, its human cargo of rebellious African slaves, and the monastery where the title character dies from trauma and/or remorse.) From there we descended on a street with walls bearing graffiti that Elisa recognized must have been scrawled by the same person whose commentary she had seen elsewhere around the city; it declared that the worthless U.S. should get out of Africa.

After picking up a few items at a grocery store named Super Box, we ascended the hill to Elisa's apartment building where we found Newton sitting in its beautifully-landscaped gardens while Isabella ran and screamed with other children, one boy doing cartwheels on black and white tiles. The view of the city from the back of the building by the swimming pool was scenic and peaceful, for in general Jundiaí was a quiet, uncongested metropolis. We were pleased that Elisa was in such a tranquil setting, with friendly shopkeepers and neighbors who knew and treated her well. All the people that we had met or come across seemed extremely pleasant and attentive, their dress casual, their manner relaxed and unpretentious. Seen at least from the perspective of a foreigner on vacation, Jundiaí appeared a place even a dyed-in-the-wool Texan could love.

On New Year's Eve, we looked out from the balcony of the living-dining room on a fireworks display. From the tops of a number of high-rise buildings, skyrockets and various types of candle-launched explosions punctuated the sky, which was already lit by a full moon. Elisa wondered out loud how people in Iraq could endure the aerial bombardments when she could hardly stand all the fireworks noise that was at times so much like mortar or machinegun fire. This brought back the world of television coverage that we had left behind, for we had not once watched TV in Brazil, until this evening, when I tried to understand the São Paulo newscast and found it virtually impossible to follow the words of the commentators. I caught only a word or phrase here or there but could see from the on-the-scene reporters that they were presenting the story of a traffic jam on the São Paulo route to the Atlantic beach. Cars had been stuck for five hours when the trip normally took one hour. Those interviewed in autos were taking it with good humor, it seemed. One young woman sat with her door open, revealing her uncovered, pregnant belly as she rested back in her seat.

María and Elisa had gone earlier in the day to a nearby video store to rent a movie. They reported that one of the two very friendly brothers who ran the store had asked María if she thought the U.S. would get rid of President Clinton. María said she had no idea, that it was now up to the Senate to determine his fate. The brother said that the U.S. economy was doing great, so the U.S. could send Clinton to Brazil and they could send this guy—meaning President Cardosa—to the U.S. The impeachment was another news story that we had no longer been following. In fact, we had been completely cut off from the constant bombardment of such political reportage. When Newton informed us that the Iraqis had shot down a U.S. war plane I was saddened to think that the conflict was still going on, but I had not in the least missed knowing of such news or of the Clinton scandal. Saddam Hussein's policies seemed to me to bring endless suffering on his people, while Clinton's private peccadillos and obvious evasion of the truth had inflicted on his family a senseless embarrassment. Certainly the two men were not to be compared, since one was given to violent rule and the other to sexual indiscretions. But because of both, it was clear that 1999 would see more of the same frenzy feeding in the media to satisfy the public's rabid appetite for revenge, recrimination, and partisan politics as usual.

Before the midnight celebrations, we had watched the rented film, which was *The Eighth Day*—a French movie with Portuguese subtitles. The mongoloid Georges, the central character, misses his mother and leaves the institution in which she had placed him, walking with a dog and his suitcase until the other main character, Harry, hits the dog with his car, from having steered with his eyes closed in hopes of committing suicide. In finding one another, Harry and Georges discover a certain form of happiness. It was easy enough to follow the subtitles (and necessary since I know no French) because the written Portuguese is enough like Spanish that I could figure out the meanings of words slightly different in spelling within the larger context. Also, the same situations were repeated often (as well as a song sung by Luis Mariano, Spanish-Basque film and operetta singer of the 1940s and '50s), and the dialogue was quite simple, with frequent pictured imaginings by Georges of his mother having told him that he was the best gift she had ever received. Fireworks also figure in the film—rockets shot off by Harry win back his estranged wife and daughters. The most famous fireworks in music are those of Handel's *Music for the Royal Fireworks*. (Charles Ives' *Decoration Day*, with its musically cinematic "explosion of the first rocket, which falls in a shower of sparks," as described by music critic Jan Swafford, is clearly not well known.) Earlier in the day I had been playing on the electric keyboard a bourrée from Handel's *Water Music*, and before that I had been reading more in *The Nature of the Book*, living in both cases in the 18th century. Time moves on but I am drawn back constantly to the past. On the other hand, I looked forward to 1999, since I had several publishing projects in the offing.

January 1st was a fruit and flower day. At lunchtime Elisa had me try several different Brazilian fruits. What I took to be a persimmon—called *caqui*—set my teeth on edge. The meat had the consistency of mango and almost the same color, but it was not as sweet or satisfying. Another fruit was called *caju* and was from the cashew tree, with the pod or nut attached to the bottom of the pear-shaped fruit. According to Elisa, the pod or cashew nut can be poisonous if not cut away from the fruit, the shell removed, and the nut washed and roasted before being eaten. Neither fruit appealed to me that much; not having been raised on such fruits, they would have to be an acquired taste, as they say. Large figs were more to my liking, along with grapes, bananas, apples, and plums. There were several varieties of grapes, with or without seeds. The local Jundiaí grapes reminded me of the Texas A & M grapes in our arbor at home—the skins were rather tough and bitter, the pulp too full of bitter seeds. At a fruit stand in Jundiaí, the owner approached me with his crowbar in hand, seeming to think that I wanted to buy some grapes in a crate that I was standing beside. I explained in my few Portuguese phrases that I did not speak the language, but tried to ask if the grapes in the crates were from Jundiaí and he answered yes. I then told him that I knew Chilean grapes, so he pointed out another crate nearby with the printed name Copiapó, a city in northern Chile. That was my first attempt at conversation, and the two of us managed to understand one another well enough, but in general I could say very little and usually understood even less. Isabella insisted on speaking Portuguese exclusively, even though she understood English and Spanish perfectly. It made me feel like the baby in the family.

In the afternoon I wanted to take a walk, but since the day before Elisa had discouraged me from going out alone to the Plaza, for fear I would be mugged, I decided just to walk around in the grounds of the apartment building, which was beautifully landscaped on three sides. Many of the plants, trees, and bushes were familiar, but a number were unknown to me. I asked the groundskeeper about the name of a particularly beautiful flowering bush with violet and light-purple blooms, but neither he nor the gardener knew what it was called. The plants that I could recognize included the variegated lantana, nasturtiums, different types and colors of roses, a yellow lily, petunias, azaleas, and various herbs and vegetables, among them rosemary, mint, tomato, onion, eggplant, and salvia. The most fragrant flower turned out to be from Chile—*boldo de Chile*. Like lamb's ear, *boldo* has soft, fluffy leaves which when rubbed are deliciously aromatic. The red flowers of one bush were similar to red blooms with long pistils that I had seen before but could not identify by name. The most exotic plant was a small coconut tree, and Newton told me later that it did bear small edible coconuts. Its ringed trunk was smooth green and its leaves palm-like. Fern-like plants were scattered here and there, along with a few cedar-type bushes—what my grandmother Keetch called dog-peeing trees. I walked the area half-a-dozen times, including around the swimming pool where a neighbor's overhanging tree dropped its leaves in the water.

Elisa had explained earlier that the apartment owners had tried to convince the neighbor to cut down his tree, which was rather non-descript and not in the least attractive. The owners had told the man that they would pay for another tree and have it planted elsewhere in his yard, but away from the wall near the pool. He declined the offer. From his home I could hear the radio blaring out sambas or bossa novas almost the entire day—equally loud up ten stories high. As for the apartment building's occupants, they were never heard and few were ever seen on our coming or going. Young people played soccer in the street across from the building's entrance, but otherwise there was little activity in the neighborhood—only some noise coming from a bar around the corner and at times from a dead-end street near the bar where kids yelled while playing volleyball. A guard was stationed at the front of the apartment complex, in a small booth, from which he could see us leaving or returning and would open for us the electrified gate. The basement garage had an electric gate as well, opened by Newton's remote control.

In the late afternoon, Newton took us for a drive to Malota, an exclusive suburb. He asked permission of the armed guard for us to drive around and look at the homes and we were permitted to do so. Most of the homes could not be seen because of their high walls in front. One new wall was being constructed of pink granite and reminded María and me of the stone walls in England, built without the use of mortar; it was three or four blocks thick, and Newton said that he would love to have such a wall, polished smooth and shiny on the interior but left rough on the outside. The need for so much security everywhere was one feature of life in Brazil that bothered me. Its cause was apparent when one passed the poverty-stricken slums on the outskirts of São Paulo and even certain neighborhoods in Jundiaí. There was to me something depressing about having to live behind enclave walls. María grew up with that type of lifestyle and has always been disturbed by the lack of privacy in the U.S., where yards and homes are exposed to view from the street. Palm trees, thorny flowering shrubs against the walls, and a very richly pungent bush with bluish-purple flowers, which we stopped to smell, were some of the vegetation that we observed in the exclusive quarter. One home was guarded by five large dogs, with a sign reading *Cuidado com cão* (Beware of the dog), a common warning in the States as well. Even though the area was sweet-smelling with all the flowers and attractive from all the profuse ground cover, the idea of living in such an elite suburb did not appeal to me at all. However, now that I think of it, I did enjoy the gated compound in Cholula, Mexico, where we lived when I taught at the Universidad de las Américas, since María and the kids could freely and safely visit the families and children of other professors in the faculty housing.

On the way back to the apartment, we stopped at a supermarket that surprisingly was open on New Year's holiday. It too was protected by an armed guard, who issued a plasticized card that had to be shown on entering and returned on leaving. María and Elisa bought more fruits and vegetables, which were mostly for María's diet but also for the rest of us. Prices were, for us, quite high. The Brazilian *reai* was valued at about one and a quarter to a dollar, and most everything cost four or five *reais* (the "r" again pronounced like aspirated English "h"). Grapes were five *reais* per kilo, or about two and a quarter pounds. After supper, I washed the dishes, since Marinalva was off during the four-day New Year's vacation. María had for the most part been the cook, trying to give Elisa a break. It was so delightful to be with our daughter, to enjoy her sense of humor, and, especially, for me, to hear her Portuguese.

We had seen a bit of the local flora and fauna, including, on taking Isabella on a walk in the neighborhood, a large turtle at one house, moving on its turned-in or pigeon-toed front feet as if an early form of mobility that remains in the experimental stage. Constantly I felt that I was so ill-prepared to take advantage of the opportunity of visiting Brazil, with the language and the nomenclature of the country's botany and biology beyond me. I thought of how well Darwin was schooled in the subjects of biology and geology when he came on the voyage of the *Beagle*. In walking about the apartment grounds I had noticed that the earth was reddish and wondered if it was the basic color of the land around Jundiaí. Near Malota I had observed a lake that was the same reddish color and concluded that the drainage must be from earth like that in the apartment building's gardens. At a preserve in the distance we could see hills full of trees, vegetation, and apparently wildlife, all protected by the government. María thought of all the snakes that must have been lurking in the grass, and Newton noted that Brazil has some 32 varieties of poisonous species, while the U.S. has only four. Every paradise has its drawbacks. I was happy to return to my reading of *The Nature of the Book,* with its bookmakers, corsairs, and Stationers' Company during the English Restoration.

On January 2nd I awoke to find María calmly resigned to a disheartening loss. For months in advance of our trip she had knitted hour after hour a lightweight sweater for Isabella. The delicate design, which she worked out as she went along, consisted of a narrow band of warm blue, with a thin red border against the ivory of the rest of the garment, except for a row of what I thought of as printer's flowers. Unfortunately, she had brought no Woolite detergent with her, and the coconut soap, which Elisa had thought would be fine, allowed the colors to bleed into the ivory. To paraphrase Shakespeare, a lot of love's labor was lost in the wash. As usual, I selfishly related this to my own writing, thinking how much effort can come to nothing, not because the words run but because they hobble or go nowhere. Even so, my writing remains a delight to me, as does my piano playing, despite the fact that neither is so pleasant for others to read or hear. To me any trip means so much more when I try to capture in words what I have seen and heard and smelled and tasted. Had I to earn a living by my writing, as Dickens did, I suppose I would starve, or have to do journalism rather than write poetry or literary essays. My book on jazz has sold poorly, so not even music criticism would offer a remunerative source of income. I feel lucky to be able to teach and write on the side. My poetry, unlike María's sweater, serves no practical purpose, but it gives me great satisfaction, despite my never being completely pleased with the "finished" product. At times it can seem a waste of effort, but I cannot imagine my life without it. While others have their own modes of expression, mine is the poem, even though my descriptive word combinations will probably not prove colorfast.

In the afternoon, Newton drove us to a city some thirty minutes due north of Jundiaí, by the name of Itatiba (with the second "t" pronounced like "ch" as in choice). The highway curved up rather steep hills through towering eucalyptus trees on both sides. Here too the earth was reddish and could be seen especially in some bare, eroded cliffs and in the vegetable fields and grape vineyards on the rolling hills. Other trees along the highway included mimosa, pine, and palm. A plant that looked like the castor bean also lined the roadway. Newton confirmed that it was in fact castor bean, and said that the beans had supplied him and his friends with ammunition for play fights when he was a boy in Anapolis before he went off to school in Brasilia, the Brazilian capital. Cattle grazed on the sides or tops of hills and in open fields in between lush green areas thick with trees and shrubs. I learned that a favorite pastime for people was going to the stock ponds, which we observed along the way. Advertised as "Fish and Pay," the ponds were, like the earth, reddish in color and looked to me quite unappetizing. Obviously, those who had paid to fish were not bothered by the color of the water, since the ponds were ringed by people sitting with their rods and reels, their lines disappearing into what looked to me like reddish mud. It reminded me of the Red River in Oklahoma when I was a boy there; the river was the same reddish color as the pond water. My dad loved to go casting in the irrigation canals, where for some reason the water was not reddish like the soil. Usually, dad only caught ugly, inedible gar, instead of the catfish or bass he was hoping for. I had not thought before about the difference between the water in the river and that in the irrigation canal.

The eucalyptus trees that we passed also brought back

memories, but from Chile in 1966. In Santiago, before María and I were married, we would climb hand in hand up San Cristóbal, a hill covered with eucalyptus trees and topped by a statue of the Virgin Mary, just as Brazil's Corcovado Mountain in Rio de Janeiro is topped by a statue of Christ the Redeemer. Often lovers had cut their names or initials in the trees' trunks. Thinking of Rio always reminds me that in Melville's *White Jacket* he describes both the city and its Sugar Loaf Mountain; chapter L begins: "I have said that I must pass over Rio without a description; but just now such a flood of scented reminiscences steals over me, that I must needs yield and recant, as I inhale that musky air." The drive to Itatiba was pleasant both in itself and for all the recollections en route.

Itatiba itself was filled with furniture stores, one after another lining the city's main street. Elisa was looking for a table for the expected baby's room. With a forest near Jundiaí, Itatiba is also dotted with furniture factories. The stores display sample styles and the customers make their selection and place an order for the piece to be made locally. The woods used for the tables, chairs, beds, divans, armoires, desks, and shelves or bookcases included cherry, mahogany, cedar, and pine. Newton said that most of the trees—except for pine—were found in the north of Brazil. Although mahogany was still used, it was illegal to do so, but manufacturers circumvented the law by saying that before its passage they had stockpiled the wood, and like some mythical pile of logs it was self-replenishing. The pine forests east of Jundiaí were commercially planted in an area protected by the state of São Paulo, but while the pines could be cut and replanted, it was not permitted to hunt game or to build houses in the area. The prices for the furniture seemed too high to Newton, so we headed back to Jundiaí.

On the way out of Itatiba, Newton decided to stop at a small shopping center with a restaurant that featured a wood-burning stove. Inside on the walls of the restaurant were photos of early Brazilian farm implements, while outside of the establishment, there were exotic plants. A banana-type plant, with bright yellow and red flowers hanging from it, was called "beaks of parrots." I learned from Elisa that the same kind of red-blossomed plant that I had seen but could not identify in the apartment grounds was a type of hibiscus and was called "princess earrings" because, she thought, they were worn by the Indians in their pierced ears. While watching the traffic on the main street, I observed to Newton how many new cars there were. He said that Brazil would soon be the third or fourth largest market in the world for automobiles, which we both agreed was too bad, even though our trip to Itatiba had been made convenient by his own comfortable, four-door, wine-colored Fiat Tempra. Standing on the side of the highway I saw a woman who seemed to be waiting to be picked up. Newton said that such women plied the world's so-called "oldest profession" by being shuttled back and forth between Itatiba and Jundiaí. On this drive, we witnessed a little of the new and old Brazil, from fishing, furniture, early farm implements, and late-model cars to the timeless trade in sexual gratification.

In the evening, as María entertained Isabella while Elisa and Newton went out to a movie, I listened to a tape recording that I had brought for Elisa—an all-Bach program performed by André Segovia. In the tape insert, a quote from *Guitar Review* for 1947 commented on how, just as "a beautiful and graceful woman is able to wear, if she has taste, varied and different costumes," so Bach's originals are "not hurt nor diminish[ed]" by the guitarist's tonal dress but "bring forth new enchantment." This was entirely true of Segovia's touch on this recording of performances from 1954 and 1967 when the guitar master was in his sixties and seventies. One curious insert note that especially struck me was the statement that the Sarabande, which is included in Baroque suites, was "discovered during the occupation of the Americas." It was not clear if this meant that the dance form was native to the Americas, and if so, from which part or parts of the two continents. The insert notes also pointed out that in the 16th century the Sarabande was "brought back to Spain and performed in the courts. Eventually, it was considered too wild and lascivious a dance and was banned. It appeared again, in the 17th century, but in a much more dignified manner."

The Sarabandes in Bach have always been among my favorite movements in his works for various solo instruments, from piano to violin to cello. It was interesting to think of this form as having come from the Americas, which put me in mind of the fact that

Brazilian musicians have in turn been attracted to the compositions of Bach. Villa-Lobos' *Bachianas brasileiras*—including number five for soprano voice and eight cellos—is a marvelous tribute to the Baroque composer. The Brazilian composer has written that Bach's works are "a universal and rich folkloristic source deeply rooted in the folk music of every country in the world." I wondered if Villa-Lobos had in mind that the Sarabande had come from the Americas. The complete keyboard works of Bach recorded by Brazilian pianist João Carlos Martins are also a splendid example of homage being rendered to the German genius. I had first heard of Martins' versions from Newton's Uncle Ary, when he and his sister (Newton's mother), Maria do Carmo, visited Austin after Isabella had been born in the Capital in 1996.

Thinking of Segovia, Villa-Lobos, cellist Pablo Casals, and Martins (again the "t" pronounced as "ch"), it struck me as curious that musically speaking these Spanish and Portuguese descendants remain some of the greatest adherents of the German composer's compositions. As the insert notes observe, "in Japan alone [Segovia] influenced more than 2 million aspiring guitar students and amateurs," and the aspirations of the Japanese must have been owing largely to the Spaniard's playing of Bach. Every race and nation has acknowledged the German master as the greatest of all musical minds. It was gratifying to think that Bach himself was aided and abetted by the New World, both through the Sarabande and by means of Brazilians like composer Villa-Lobos and pianist Martins. All of these thoughts came to me through the fact that Segovia's forebears had brought back to Europe a "lascivious" folk dance that Bach developed into one of the loveliest and most moving forms of music.

María often muttered that while she was cooking, cleaning, and sewing, I occupied myself with "superior" things like reading, writing, and listening to music. Her common complaint was that instead of helping with Isabella—entertaining her or watching out for her—I was busy with my books. And it was true, but even when I did pay attention to our granddaughter I tended to antagonize her, on purpose when she was whining or not eating her meals. I would tell her that Alla—her version of *abuela*, grandmother in Spanish, which she herself had originated—had fixed the food especially for her, but this just made her more resistant if she was already unhappy with Alla because she had corrected or chastised her for some reason. When Miss Issa, as we sometimes called her, asked me to get her a yogurt on a plastic stick out of the refrigerator freezer, I did not know that it first needed to be thawed by placing the plastic cup in warm water and then gently twisting the plastic stick to remove it. As a result, when I twisted the stick in the frozen yogurt, it cracked and I could not get the popsicle out of the cup. Miss Issa threw a fit, which I took as simply typical of her tantrums, but later I learned that she had reacted so violently because she liked to save the sticks, intact, not broken. She went crying to her daddy with another yogurt so that he would get it out of its plastic cup, but then he had no warm water handy. I finally got the yogurt out of the first cup and took it to Issa, but she would have nothing to do with it. So I said that I would eat it myself, which enraged her even more. I then proceeded to eat it with a great show of doing so with relish, and this too irritated her to no end. Although she was highly incensed and unhappy with me, later she became more affectionate than she had previously been. There is no telling how our treatment of children will affect them. Despite my not having been the most attentive of fathers, Elisa and Darío would both turn out to be loving and very thoughtful adults. Of course, I credit their mother with more than 90 if not 100 percent of that outcome.

On January 3rd, after reading for most of the day in the Erenberg book on Swing music, I went with Newton, Elisa, and Isabella to a French supermarket, Carrefour. I was not impressed by the store but enjoyed discussing the merchandise and comestibles with Elisa. For María, who had stayed in the apartment to work on some curtains for the expected granddaughter, I bought a baby perfume that she liked, called "Julie," and some pepper sauce that she wanted to take back to the States for its flavor and mildness. As it turned out, the vegetables at Carrefour were all wilted and even gave off a fetid odor. The furniture for sale was more expensive than what we had seen in Itatiba and the quality much inferior, but according to Newton, since the store sold in bulk, the prices were generally much lower. In any case, María and I could never afford to live in Brazil on our salaries, or especially not on the amount that we will receive at retirement. A small package of oat bran cereal, for example, was the equivalent of two dollars for about four servings; soap could be almost a dollar a bar; and mozzarella cheese could be eight dollars for what we would pay half that amount. Food stuffs and other necessities for daily living were not nearly so expensive as gasoline, which could be forty dollars per tank when again we usually paid half the amount. The cost of such services as water, electricity, and telephone was also high, the latter requiring a payment of $150.00 per month just for the phone line, not counting the long distance and service charges. All of this, as they say, would be too rich for *our* blood.

In the evening we looked at Isabella's scrapbook from her classes at the Baby Center, which she attended during the regular semesters but at the time of our visit was closed for vacation. The instructions in the scrapbook seemed to me excellent, calling as they did for the children to identify shapes and colors, and to make comparisons and contrasts. They also were asked to discuss certain topics that required them to tell about themselves, their parents, their homes, and the locations of churches, stores, etc. The vocabulary they were expected to learn or recognize made me feel, again, like a baby, but then every language makes me feel that way.

Once in bed, I picked up my volume of William Langland's *The Vision of Piers Plowman* and continued in another difficult language: Middle English. I had left off in Passus XV, in which I now began reading about hermits and the lives of saints: "What penaunce and poverte and passion thei suffrede." Piers observes that "Both lettred and lewed beth alayed now with synne, / That no lif loveth oother, ne Oure Lord, as it semeth." I love the alliterative style and the poet's use of metallurgy and coinage in comparing and contrasting the pure lives of the earlier religious figures with the "alloyed" sinners who appear "lik a sterling" but whose "metal is feble." Although Middle English can be slow going, it is worth the effort to me, partly because it allows me to relate the language to modern English and even to words in French, Spanish, Latin, Portuguese, and Russian. One word that struck me was "payn" in the line "For hadde ye potage and payn ynough, and peny-ale to drynke"; that Middle English word for bread was close to Spanish "pan" and Portuguese "pão" but more directly seems to derive from the French "pain." Earlier in Passus XV, I had noticed the Latin word "mel" in two lines that develop a comparison between a person who eats too much honey and one who tries to scrutinize God's ways too closely: "non est ei bonum" (it's not good for him). Before coming to Brazil, I had made a marginal note beside the passage that honey in Spanish is "miel," and so it was with a "shock of recognition" that I saw the word "mel" on a jar of honey in the local fruit and vegetable stand, Frutaria e Quitanda, Santa Cruz, which also sold other food items. Even earlier in the poem, in Passus IX, I had noticed the word "mébles" in a passage that gives Jews credit for charity to those in need of "goods." In Spanish the word for furniture is "muebles" but in Russian it is closer to the Portuguese "mébles," though spelled with the Cyrillic alphabet: Мébель (mébel).

In the fall I had been sitting in on Russian classes for my third semester, and every day I wondered why I put myself through the misery of being so pathetic in my attempts to learn this for me impossible language. And yet I kept going back, never missing a class unless my editor's job made it necessary. Some twenty years before I had also sat in for almost two and a half years, but I had not learned so well then as I had on this second try, after having lost the little that I had learned earlier from never using it. After I had managed in the first attempt at the language to muddle through a bit of Gogol's "The Overcoat" and Pushkin's "The Bronze Horseman," I always regretted having had to stop sitting in on the classes, but my job had become too time-consuming to be able to get away. With more spare time as a lecturer and the coordinator of the Freshman Seminars Program, I went back for more torment. The connections that I have noted in reading Langland's poem, among Latin, Spanish, Portuguese, and Russian, with regard to the words for honey and goods/furniture, now make up for all the pain of being aware of how dense I was and for what at the time often seemed tedious, fruitless study. In this year that I am turning sixty, I could only wish that I had applied myself more diligently to all four of those languages. Only from having lived in Chile for a year was I able to develop more facility than I had ever achieved in high school Spanish classes. With German I was just catching on under a native speaker when I dropped out of the University in 1961 and never took courses in the language again. With a German dictionary I can still read a bit, but persistent study would have expanded my vocabulary and motivated me to read in the language and even to attempt to speak it. O how, as Shaw has said, "youth is wasted on the young."

On January 4th, the first workday after New Year's, Newton took us all with him to São Paulo. His company's office was on the main street of the city, Avenida Paulista, which he compared to New York's Fifth Avenue. María thinks all cities are pretty much the same: noisy and crowded and dirty; I find them stimulating but prefer to live in a place like Jundiaí, which seems more like a small town, even though the population in 1999 was over 400,000. In size Jundiaí is comparable to Austin, which at the time was a little over 600,000, but with much more traffic. The drive to São Paulo gave us a view of the landscape that we had not been able to see when we first arrived on the night of the 27th. The pine forests Newton had mentioned then were now visible along the highway, as was Klabin, a paper factory dependent on the nearby wood supply. In certain spots we could see where the trees had been felled, with some of the logs still lying on clear-cut slopes. On approaching the city we also passed a number of slums. Newton said that the government had arranged for housing for the poor but most people preferred to remain in their shacks. In São Paulo he pointed out new high-rise apartment buildings that had replaced a slum, but I failed to ask whether such apartments had been built specifically for the poor.

When we rode the subway in the city, we saw a group of Gypsy women in their traditional necklaces and brightly-colored pleated skirts. Newton and Elisa said that they found them annoying when they would insist that they let them tell their fortunes. María finds Gypsies fascinating, and she commented that today most of those in the U.S. are used-car salesmen—still associated with mobility even if no longer traveling in caravans. Newton said that in Brazil they are found living in circus tents, while María commented that in the U.S. they would remove walls of a house and build a fire in the middle of the space, as if they were in an Indian tepee. Habits or traditions are hard to break or change, and some people have no desire to do so—like smokers who are constantly appealed to for the good of their own health to give up tobacco. Some people would only live in cities, others only in the country. Wherever I am, I must have poetry, music, and María.

After we reached Newton's office building and he parked the car in its basement rental garage, María, Elisa, and I walked along Avenida Paulista. The city noise was already deafening at nine in the morning, even though many people remained on summer vacation through the entire month of January. We first stopped in a corner book-paper store, where I saw a collection of writings by the 19th-century Brazilian poet, João da Cruz e Sousa, a black born in 1861 in the city of Nossa Senhora do Desterro (now called Florianópolis), which is the same name as that of a church in Jundiaí that we had visited. I did not remember at the time that I had read this poet's work when I had taught one of the Freshman Seminars in the fall of 1996, for which I used the bilingual anthology *Twentieth-Century Latin American Poetry*, edited by Stephen Tapscott and published by the University of Texas Press. Called the "Black Swan," Cruz e Sousa interested me most for his late sonnets, three of which are included in the anthology in translations by Flavia Vidal: "Acrobat of Pain," "Good Friday," and "Sacred Hatred," with the translated title of the third concisely conveying the irony of the entire poem: "Wholesome hatred: good hatred! Be my shield / against the villains of Love, who defame everything, / from the seven towers of the mortal Sins!" (I have changed Vidal's "Sound hatred" to "Wholesome hatred" for both the sense and the alliterative sound of the latter, since the Portuguese *são* means both "sound" and "wholesome." The word *odio* for hatred is the same in Portuguese and Spanish.) The opening stanza and the last line of "Acrobat of Pain" contain similar ironies or paradoxes:

> Chortle, laugh, in a laughter of storm
> like a clown who, lanky and nervous,
> laughs, in an absurd laughter, inflated

with violent irony and pain.

. . .

laugh! Heart, saddest of clowns.

After María had bought a coloring book for Isabella and a few postcards to send to friends, we left the store to check out a nearby supermarket for some flavored water that Elisa could not find in Jundiaí, but we found the place closed until noon for inventory. This had also been the case with the Cambridge University Press Bookstore on the ground floor of Newton's office building. Returning to Avenida Paulista, we passed a stand selling jars of preserves and related items, and somehow a jar was knocked off and broken—perhaps by my notebook that I was carrying, even though it did not seem to me that I had come near the sales table. The salesgirl was enraged and, as Elisa indicated later, accused me of knocking the jar off the stand with my bag, despite the fact that I was only carrying my thin school composition book, which Elisa had bought in Chile with the picture of a pudu on the cover. (The pudu is a miniature type of deer that lives alone, not in herds, in the southern forests of Chile, and is now threatened by wild dogs that transmit parasites fatal to the species. How easy it is to be led away from a narrative by, to me, other interesting facts or associations.) The preserves in the broken jar had splattered the back of my khaki-colored pants, so maybe I was the culprit without realizing it and had received my just tongue-lashing. I should have paid for the preserves, but at the time I did not realize that I had probably caused the vendor to lose her merchandise.

On the Avenida we stopped at a newsstand that had a larger variety of postcards, both for mailing and for María's annual scrapbooks. While she was selecting a few cards, I spotted a special offer for two CDs with music performed by the Brazilian pianist Arthur Moreira Lima, one CD of Mozart and Haydn piano concertos and the other of pieces by the Brazilian composer Ernesto Nazareth. The price was only 12 *reais*—a little over ten dollars. I had been hoping to find a CD of Nazareth's music because María and I had discovered it through her fellow library worker at the Benson Latin American Collection. Russ had even played some of Nazareth's music at Elisa and Newton's wedding, as noted before, and I had memorized but never mastered a piece of his entitled "Victorioso." It seemed like one had to subscribe to the entire series of twenty CDs in order to buy the package of two CDs, which included a booklet on the two composers and a recording of Nazareth's composition entitled "Quebradinha." But after Elisa questioned the vendor I learned that I could buy each biweekly offering separately, and the next CDs, as I found when I opened the packet, would be of works by Bach and Chopin. I was delighted to find that the series was funded by the Brazilian government as a means of educating the public at a reasonable price. It reminded me of an RCA Victor series sold in a supermarket in Beaumont that helped introduce me to classic jazz performances and would lead decades later to the writing of my book, *Texan Jazz*. The stains on my trousers from the broken jar of preserves were all but forgotten in the joy of discovering this marvelous bargain in the realm of classical and Brazilian music as performed by a native pianist.

Since all the museums were closed on Mondays, we decided to take a subway to a shopping center fairly close by. Only after we bought the tickets and had passed through the turnstile did we see by the map that there did not seem to be a subway stop for the center. Asking an employee, Elisa found that the station we were in, Brigadeiro, was the nearest one to the center. Plop! as María would say. (She often quotes this comic conclusion to the Chilean cartoons that feature a character named Condorito, based on the country's Andean bird. The highly popular cartoons with drawings and dialogues are the work of René Rios, known as Pepo.) Realizing that we were too far from the center to walk, Elisa decided to go on to the hospital where she would be having her C-section performed. As we were trying to decide which line to take, two policemen approached and asked if we needed help. One was extremely friendly, and both gave directions for reaching our destination. We were to get off at Paradiso and walk two blocks to the hospital, down Rua Apeninos—both Italian evocations;

naturally, I was reminded of Dante's *The Divine Comedy.*

    The hospital, Santa Joana, was fifteen years old but looked quite fresh and new. We went to the reception desk where Elisa explained that she would be coming within the next three weeks for delivery and that her insurance was with AMIL. The receptionist wore a tag that gave her name as Elisabete. Wearing glasses and a black skirt and jacket, she spoke very professionally, and clearly enough that I could follow some of what she said. She took us to see one of the rooms for mothers-to-be and explained to Elisa many of the features of the hospital. The room was very inviting and the view out the window a pleasant panorama of that part of the city. Elisabete then conducted us to the nursery where babies were on display. She explained that five minutes after a birth, the baby could be seen on a wide-screen television in this same area, which also included a waiting room with couches and a coffee counter. Everything made us feel better about Elisa's upcoming procedure and the care she would receive, since we would not be able to be with her on her delivery date.

    Later in the day we went with Elisa and Newton to her scheduled appointment with her doctor, Toshio Arimoto, a Japanese-Brazilian; the Japanese community in Brazil is the largest outside Japan. We found the doctor reassuring and quite personable, but he chastised Elisa a bit for gaining three kilos when she was supposed to have put on only one kilo from the time of her last visit. Elisa confessed to eating chocolate, and when she asked if the baby would be very big, the doctor joked that it would be, if she kept eating so much chocolate.

    Before lunch we looked around in the Cambridge bookstore, which had reopened. There were paperback editions in the Penguin series, including Thomas Hardy's *The Mayor of Casterbridge,* which I would be teaching in the spring in my British literature survey course. I had included Hardy's *Far From the Madding Crowd* in my course in the spring of '97 and the students enjoyed it greatly, with one student even saying that it was the best novel he had ever read. In the Shakespeare section I spied G. Wilson Knight's *The Wheel of Fire,* but it proved too expensive: 38.50 *reais* for a paperback. I would, a decade or so later, acquire a Routledge edition and read with special interest the chapters on *Hamlet* and *Lear*, penciling stars in the latter beside the author's comments on Edgar as "the high-priest of this play's stoicism," on "endurance which forbids a facile exit in self-murder," and on his trumpet as a "symbol of natural judgement, that summons Edmund to account at the end."

I also came across Cruz e Sousa's *Missal/Broquéis* in an edition published in São Paulo in 1998, the price 13 *reais*. Scanning one of the book's sonnets, I only then remembered that we had read Cruz e Sousa's poetry in my Freshman Seminar class and that the students had considered his work among the best of the 19th century. That convinced me to buy the pocket-sized book with its paperback cover printed in a subtle maroon shade, with the back cover reproducing in blue part of the text of the poem "Tortura eterna" (Eternal Torture). The last poem in the book, "Eternal Torture" contains the line "O Dantesque circles of madness," and throughout the poet's poems in *Broquéis* there are references to pain, sorrow, grief, and death. The prose poems of Cruz e Sousa's *Missal* were all written under the influence of Baudelaire, and at the beginning of *Broquéis* there appears an epigraph from the French poet's "At the Hour of Matins." Looking back over the book, I find that a poem entitled "Tuberculosa" epitomizes the influence of Baudelaire on the Brazilian, who himself died of tuberculosis at age 37. Sousa speaks of that consumptive illness slowly taking over the body with its mystic preludes like psalms, the comparison typical of Baudelaire's equating of the beautiful with the ugly (e.g. the title of his book *Flowers of Evil*) and the sacred with sickness or sin. In one of the Brazilian's prose poems on the psychology of the ugly, he says openly that he enjoys ugliness because it denies the infallible, the absolute correctness of perfectly-consecrated forms, asserting that in its vileness the ugly has its own perfect forms, like a frog croaking beneath the muddy clay, like a star shining in the sky. Just scanning the prose poems I could see the names of the many writers, composers, artists, philosophers, and thinkers that Cruz e Sousa alludes to: among them Shakespeare, Heine, Büchner, Gautier, Bach, Beethoven, Mendelssohn, Schubert, Saint-Saens, Rembrandt, Schopenhauer, and Darwin. It was fortunate that I had first noticed the poet's name in the little book-paper store, or otherwise this fine-looking edition with an introduction by Ivan Teixeira might not have caught my eye. Always the high point of any trip for me is finding such books of poetry that represent the literary character of each particular country and culture; only then do I feel that I have experienced, through linguistic artistry, something of the profound life of the place, something of its rich imaginative reality.

For lunch we went to another vegetarian restaurant, whose fare was also quite delicious, including some palm heart "cakes" with pineapple slices, which had María in ecstasy. I myself ate a dessert with coconut and peaches. Afterwards we returned to Newton's office and waited for him to finish some business before we all headed back to Jundiaí. While waiting I looked through some catalogs of the software products from Newton's Austin company, National Instruments, but did not really understand anything much. Newton sells software for industries and had recently made a sale for over one-hundred thousand dollars. The past August Newton had completed his doctorate in biomedical engineering at UT and we had brought with us a bound copy of his dissertation, with color illustrations of circuits and graphs related to the causes of glaucoma as traced to the brain stem (as I understood it). I had served as one of his test cases, but I was not very helpful since I kept falling asleep! The sample circuits with computer chips, which were lying on tables in his office, were mysteriously impressive to me. My use of software is limited to word processing, whereas entire industries can be operated through the programs created by National Instruments. Newton's company began in Austin but has now established representatives not only in Brazil but in Japan and other locations internationally. Newton makes a good living but seems anxious to move into the biomedical field, perhaps with this same company, which plans to expand into that area as well. If he does transfer to another field, he would probably move back to the States, and of course we would welcome their being closer to us. On the other hand, it would be nice to have them here in Brazil so that we could have an excuse to visit again.

In fact, I would return alone in 2001, to help Elisa and her family move back to the States. They were then living across the bay from Rio de Janeiro in Niteroi. My travel notes from that trip include my visits with Sally Green Haddad, who was a member of the group of fifteen UT students with whom I first traveled to Chile. Sally lived in Rio and made it possible for me to meet the Brazilian poet Affonso Romano de Sant'Anna, whose 1999 collection of poems, *Textamentos*, I purchased at a book fair where he gave a talk on Brazilian poetry; afterwards he signed my copy of *Textamentos* and we chatted briefly. I later found and bought his 1993 collection, *O lado esquerdo do meu peito*. On the trip I would also purchase a copy of Lêdo Ivo's *O rumor da noite* from 2000 and a copy of the 4th edition of João Cabral de Melo Neto's *Morte e vida severina*, also from 2000. Professor Fred Ellison of the UT Spanish-Portuguese Department had given me the names of all three poets, whose work I found quite appealing and impressive. My mention of Sant'Anna's poems, "Cão poeta" (Dog Poet) and "Austin, 1976" (written when he was a visiting professor at UT), and Ivo's long poem "O rio," would appear in 2020 in an interview that Mary Anne Warken conducted with me for *Qorpus*, a literary journal at the Universidade Federal de Santa Catarina in Florianópolis, where she was a doctoral student writing her dissertation on Nicanor Parra.

Driving back to Jundiaí, we passed by São Paulo's own version of New York's Central Park. This turned the conversation, for some reason, to a serial killer—I was not following that closely what was being said, but it seemed that the killer picked up women in the park. The killer was charming, intelligent, and an excellent rollerblade skater. He murdered some forty women who were identified as his victims, even though he himself confessed to having killed one hundred. He was caught through one of his victim's partially-burned driver's license found by police in his apartment (or was it at his workplace?), and also through his teeth marks in the victims, since he was missing one tooth. That night when we returned to the apartment, Newton and Elisa watched a rented movie about a serial killer, featuring actor Dennis Quaid. María and I were too tired to stay up, but the next morning Elisa reported that the plot was not believable, that the killer, to her, did not have the profile of such a killer. She did not explain what she thought such a profile would involve, but in the case of the park killer, he had blamed an aunt for having raped him as a boy or a young man. The aunt denied the accusation. Who knows why people do what they do? Even when we learn the possible causes or motives, is any murder ever believable and does the murderer always fit a recognizable profile? The park killer also said that from watching cattle slaughtered when he was a boy that he had taken pleasure in seeing the creatures die. Even if true, it seems unbelievable. How many persons have witnessed such killings of animals for food and yet have never visited the same acts on humans? There seems no accounting for the desire to spill the blood of another being.

The night of January 5th, María and I did watch a rental movie, entitled *Karacter*. Newton had come in late from São Paulo and Elisa was tired and had already seen the film, as had Newton, who considered it too weird. A Dutch movie, *Karacter* is based on the best-selling novel by Ferdinand Bordewijk and was directed by Mike van Diem; it won the Academy Award for Best Foreign Language Film in 1997. We could read the subtitles in Portuguese well enough, but they were flashed so quickly that we could not finish a sentence before they changed and we were left wondering what the final words or phrases had said. Certain words were repeated frequently enough that we finally caught on to the plot. One word that I figured out from the context was *juros*, which means interest—on loans that the protagonist makes from his father, whom his mother will never marry. The main character learns English through an incomplete set of encyclopedias that his father, it seemed, had left surreptitiously for him. The son also listens to the BBC and speaks eloquently without having previously spoken a word of English, or that's the impression that I had. On passing the bar exam, the son repays the loan, but an argument ensues, the father is found dead, and the son is arrested. Eventually investigators discover that the father died six hours after the argument and not as a result of murder but of suicide.

What especially interested me in the movie was that it included a piece of music that I had long enjoyed. On the occasion of the son's having finished night classes that he had been attending, a party is thrown for him at an office where he works. He dances with an office mate, and the music played in the scene is by Jimmie Lunceford's Orchestra, a tune recorded in 1934 and entitled "Dream of You," by band member Sy Oliver. I had first heard the tune in the mid-1950s, as arranged by Pete Rugolo and recorded in California by his studio orchestra. Once again, here was a work of art, a film in this case, that combined my current and an ongoing interest: learning Portuguese and listening to jazz. Somehow, wherever I go I encounter these connections, at times without looking for or expecting them. I would say that in general I have something of a three-track mind, since I am always thinking about language, literature, and music (four and first if María included), and try never to lose an opportunity to be ready to learn more about all three. Even though I seem unable to gain fluency in a language, I never tire of expanding my vocabulary. The same goes for reading great literature and hearing great music, and relatedly, observing other cultures. Often I wish that I could start over and apply myself more rigorously to the study of those particular fields, but even so, I feel satisfied with and grateful for the life that I have been fortunate enough to live. Above all, I believe that I have been truly blessed in having found María, through whom we have Elisa, Darío, Isabella, and Newton and all the wonderful worlds that they have opened up.

Speaking of Isabella, she was left with me the morning of the fifth, while María and Elisa went shopping once again for a table for the expected baby. At first the two of us took a long, slow walk around the neighborhood, stopping to talk to her favorite dog, Madonna, who also lives on Rua Bela Vista. After returning to the apartment building, I took Miss Issa's plastic bicycle downstairs and she rode around the grounds for a while. Then she sat on the rim of a shallow circular pool and paddled her fingers in the water. Suddenly she decided that she wanted to put on her swimming suit and "swim." So upstairs we went on the elevator to the apartment so she could change into her pinkish bikini. Marinalva brought out her inflatable arm bands, I blew them up, and we returned to the pool.

Issa wanted to know why I did not put on my bikini, but I told her that I didn't have one. As usual, she asked Why, so I said that I didn't bring my swimming suit from Texas. Although my answer did not entirely satisfy her, she dropped the subject. I told her that I was afraid the water was too cold, but she insisted that it was hot. She lowered herself into the water slowly and walked around the rim, holding on, until she began to venture out into the middle of the pool, floating on her arm bands. She screamed with delight. The groundskeeper came by and told me that he was going to eat his lunch. Then Issa said she wanted to pee-pee. I had asked her repeatedly if she needed to go before she went to the pool, but she kept saying no. She got out of the pool and ran onto some grass and said she would pee on a cement slab. I said no, that we had to go back to the apartment. She began to cry but I grabbed her up in a towel and took her crying upstairs. Only later did I learn from Elisa that in fact she did allow her to pee on the cement slab, after which she would wash it off with a hose. Once again, Miss Issa knew what she was doing and I misunderstood. This was a continuing theme of my time with her.

When María and I were watching *Karacter*, we sat on the couch that had been my grandmother Keetch's. Elisa had had the happy idea to have the antique piece of furniture restored and reupholstered. Elisa's grandmother Oliphant had saved up and given to her $2000 for whatever she desired to use it. We were quite surprised when Elisa informed us that she wanted to spend the money on the couch. We did not think it wise and objected, but we would not oppose her decision. The company she contracted did a fabulous job, replacing the upholstery material with a beautiful, very pale, pink-champagne shade of satin cloth, with bouquets of roses, bands of lace, and sprigs of leaves and five-petal flowers worked into the satin. They had replaced the tacks along the bottom of the frame, refinished the wood there and on the carved feet, stitched perfectly the scalloping of the 8-foot seat back, and recovered the long seat cushion. They also replaced the springs, along with the support straps. A simple matching chair was also refurbished. After Newton and Elisa had brought the two pieces of furniture to Jundiaí from Austin, Newton had another chair and a foot rest reupholstered; those too were part of my grandmother Keetch's living room suite but were done in a pale green with lighter-colored flowers in pots and with chain-like designs on the material.

Seeing the pieces preserved and in Brazil brought back fond memories of my youth in Fort Worth when I would sit on the furniture before a winter fire in my grandmother's wood-burning fireplace. At Christmas time, Nan, as we called my grandmother Keetch, would hang silver dollars from sprigs of a type of lemon tree in her yard and on the sprig's thorns would stick gumdrops, which we grandchildren would pull off along with one coin for each of us. The one piece of furniture that I have long regretted that was not kept in the family was her wind-up Victrola, on which I loved to listen to my grandfather's records. Since grandfather Keetch had left my grandmother when I was a very young boy, I never had a chance to talk to him about the Gershwin and ragtime music that he had bought and that became so important to me in later years. Thanks to Elisa, something of our forebears and their lives has been preserved and now maintains a link with the past. The couch we sat on while watching the Dutch film with Portuguese subtitles seemed as at home in Brazil as in my grandmother's home on May Street in Cowtown. How far it had traveled! and yet how unchanged the memories it recalled. What would my contrary Nan have thought of her heirloom ending up in Jundiaí?

On January 6th I arose earlier than usual and was ready to go with Newton to São Paulo, but the weather did not cooperate, the rain continuing from the previous day. Newton decided that it would be too messy to go to the museums, which is what I had wanted to do, and that we should leave it for Friday. I settled back down with my book on the Swing era, reading about the relationship between the political Left and jazz during the 1930s. The conflict between John Hammond and Duke Ellington over the latter's failure to support black causes and to militate against black exploitation—all this according to Hammond, who, in the Duke's view, was born with a silver spoon in his mouth—was an episode that I had already encountered in my copy of *The Duke Ellington Reader*. In fact, not much in Erenberg's book was new to me, but the organization of his quoted material, from *The Daily Worker*, Otis Ferguson's reviews in *The New Republic*, articles in *New Masses*, *Down Beat*, *Metronome*, and various New York, Chicago, and Pittsburg newspapers, was an impressive marshalling of evidence for his case that the Left aided in integrating jazz, improving work opportunities for black musicians, and promoting opposition to Fascism. The idea that the world of music involved such political dimensions had recently become a popular subject for a number of studies, including but not limited to David Stowe's similar *Swing Changes*. While all of this interested me, it was the music itself that attracted me more and kept me listening, rather than its political ties or its economic considerations. It seemed to me that the art survived despite and even as a result of oppression, and although this does not justify the continuation of such treatment of African-Americans, better working conditions do not necessarily lead to greater artistry. Mostly the effect of more attention for jazz was the creation of a plethora of mediocre white big bands, while creative jazz remained largely a matter of individual development of the art outside Swing's big-band movement.

For lunch we returned to Vita Natural for another delicious, nutritious veggie meal. The beans and rice, a Brazilian staple, were once again quite tasty, as was the fried polenta, a corn-based type of hush-puppy or fritter. The okra (*kioba*) was as always one of my favorite dishes. Although I ate more than I usually do at lunchtime, I did not feel at all that I had overeaten, mainly because there was no meat. On this day we saw different faces at the tables, not the same ones that seemed always to frequent the restaurant. On the wall was the same sign encouraging an end to smoking, but only on reading it this time did I realize the meaning of the word *lute* in the phrase *Lute contra este inimigo*. In Spanish it would be *Luche contra este enemigo*. The sound of *lute* (with again "t" pronounced like "ch") and *luche* in Spanish is the same, meaning in both cases "fight" against this enemy (smoking). The ear slowly becomes more accustomed to the different sounds for very similar words—that is, for words that have in common many of the same letters but may exclude one letter or more or substitute another. With time I believe that even I could make the necessary aural adjustment.

In the afternoon I played with Isabella while María sewed on a skirt for the baby's bed. Elisa and Newton had gone to look for a birthday present for a friend of Newton's, Robson Freitas, whom we had known in Austin when both were finishing their PhDs at

UT, Robson in mechanical engineering. With Isabella I revisited childhood activities: matching figures with similar characteristics and coloring with crayons. The book we had brought from the States included stickers, which were to be licked and attached to the matching, outlined animals or objects. Unfortunately, the book had gotten wet when the airline personnel in Miami had left our baggage out in the rain while the plane's engine cover was being worked on. The stickers became soaked and the glue stuck them to the paper backing, so that the perforated edges could not be separated easily and the stickers, in pulling away the backing, could not then be stuck to the matching outlines. We gave up and began coloring in a Christmas book instead. Isabella colored with red, exclusively—faces, clothes, Santa's bag, toys, etc. While I tried to color within the lines, Isabella marked through the lines and into the white space around the objects and figures. My own lack of drawing talent perhaps stems from always staying inside the printed forms rather than venturing outside the prescribed margins. Hopefully Isabella will be more imaginative and less structured, less inhibited by preset patterns, models, or restrictions. On the other hand, there is something to be said for following instructions. A balance, in all things, is perhaps the ideal, even though those who can go beyond the bounds are our heroes and heroines, at least when they lead us to uncover better ways of living, relating, observing, hearing, making, being.

In the evening we attended Robson's birthday party, taking him a toy car for his collection of such. Grown-ups too must have their play. Robson's wife, Ana María, was studying law, but in her spare time she enjoyed sculpting. Her orangey-colored sculptures were found throughout the house: a horse's head lacking the ears that were broken off in their move from Texas; a man bent over a guitar; a woman's or, Elisa thought, a man's head on which the artist had placed a real hat. Among those in attendance, a family of three spoke only Portuguese, while the rest conversed in English. When the father of the family talked with Newton and Robson, all three spoke in Portuguese and I tried to catch a bit of their conversation, which at one point seemed entirely concerned with cars—how fast they went, how much they cost, if they had independent suspensions, etc. This was not a topic that would interest me in the least, but as ear training it was useful and entertaining.

When María and I spoke separately with Robson, he mentioned nearby towns that we should visit, like the cities of Campinas and Itu. Of the latter he said that an entertainer or TV personality had advertised the town as having in it everything bigger than anywhere else. As a result, Itu actually constructed larger traffic signs, telephone booths, etc., in order to match the image created by the entertainer. Ana María, he said, had grown up in Campinas, although she had been born elsewhere, and that they would like to live there, but that it was too far from his work in São Paulo. Robson was employed by a large U.S. corporation that constructed pipelines that had to do with energy plants. He traveled about 80% of the time, observing construction sites—for example, a pipeline from Bolivia across Brazil's Mato Grosso. He said that they had thought of living in São Paulo but decided on Jundiaí because the law school in the city was in a safer location. In São Paulo, the law school was in the old downtown area where, he said, people were constantly being attacked, that every five or six minutes someone was being assaulted and at times even killed. The population of São Paulo had been about 11 million until, with all the people coming in from surrounding towns like Jundiaí, it had swelled to over 20 million. These facts discouraged me somewhat from returning on Friday, to see the museums, but even so I still looked forward to knowing more of the big, bad, celebrated city.

The summer rains had set in and the visit to São Paulo looked unlikely for the 8th. Also, Elisa needed to have the baby's room painted with a pale yellow before two ladies, Valdereza and Helena, would come to sponge and stencil designs on two facing walls. And so on the 7th Elisa and Newton went to purchase the paint while I prepared the base boards with masking tape. When they returned and we moved the furniture, I began painting one of the walls. Elisa wanted only half the wall yellow, so I had to place masking tape in an even line 27 inches from the base board, using the handle of the paint roller to measure as I applied the tape across the wall. After roller painting close to the tape, I finished the rest with a small brush. All of this was like Isabella's coloring book—just staying inside the lines. In order to dry the paint as quickly as possible and to eliminate the paint odor, Newton set up a round ventilator, and by morning the one wall was ready and I could start on the next. However, everyone questioned Elisa's decision to do only one half of the walls in yellow, and once she talked with one of the women doing the design work, it was clear that I had to paint all of the two walls. This meant that the tape line showed when I continued with the other halves of the walls. But as it turned out, the women covered the line with a green line of their own, below which they sponged various pastel shades and stenciled above it animal characters from the books of Beatrix Potter.

The colors of the sponge work were reminiscent of Monet, but of course nothing of this project was creative in the true sense of original art. Elsewhere in Elisa's apartment she had hung framed prints of paintings by Monet—his scenes at Giverny—and by Renoir—his boating party and oarsmen at Chatou Giclee. She also had a Manet vase with flowers. During a semester of high school spent in Chile she had taken art classes, producing some fine pieces, including a leopard, some birds, and some glassware. At our home she had painted flowers and leaves on the folding doors of her closet. Darío is a good cartoonist, and María does drawings in her scrapbooks. At best, I do renderings with words, and probably stay too strictly within predictable forms.

We lunched once again at Vida Natural, and afterwards I asked Newton to see if by chance the newsstand across Rua Senador Fonseca had any of the series of classical CD recordings by Arthur Moreira Lima. At first the black man who ran the stand seemed not to know what Newton was talking about, but then from a shelf behind his register he pulled down three CDs. I already had one of the three, but one contained *Bachianas brasileiras* No. 4 of Villa-Lobos, as well as his *As 16 Cirandas*, both for piano; the other CD contained the three most famous sonatas of Beethoven (*Patética*, *Ao luar*, and the *Appassionata*) and a selection of classical favorites by composers from J.S. and C.P.E. Bach to Tchaikovsky, Debussy, and Prokofiev, among others. After buying and later listening to the two CDs, it was Villa-Lobos' *Bachianas* that interested me most, with its four sections: Preludio, Coral (Canto do sertão—song of the hinterlands), Ária (Cantiga), and Dança (Miudinho—a samba-like work). Dança appealed to me greatly for the composer's contrasts between upper right-hand and much lower bass register notes, often both at once, and for his somewhat dissonant melodies. The man at the kiosk had said that he was about to return the CDs to his distributor because they were not selling, and so I was happy to have gotten them before he sent them back. In looking more closely at the booklets that came with the CDs, I noticed again that they were produced under a governmental law designed to promote culture: *Lei de Incentivo a Cultura*. It seemed unfortunate in a way that as a foreigner I was the only person in Jundiaí interested in such a cultural program. Probably, however, not that many people, who would be interested in classical music, would be frequenting a newsstand selling mostly girlie magazines, chewing gum, and cigarettes. Also, the fact that such great music in a bargain offering was kept out of reach and plain view of the public would tend to defeat even those with the "incentive" to seek it out. Had I not seen the CD set lying on the table at the newsstand in São Paulo, I too would have missed out on this very worthy effort on the part of Brazil's Ministry of Culture.

In the evening I watched Elisa's rented movie, *Car Wash*, from about 1976, with Richard Pryor, the Pointer Sisters, and a cast of mostly black actors unknown to me. María started watching it with me, but gave up because she could not see much point to the film, and also because she has difficulty understanding black dialect. Elisa would have enjoyed the black sense of humor, but she felt that she should show Isabella *The Lion King*, which she had also rented. Many issues of the '60s and '70s were touched on in *Car Wash*, especially exploitation by the white owner of the business, black education, the appeal of Islam (one character who had changed his name to Abdullah insisting that he be called such and not by his given American name), and the questionable sincerity of the character played by Pryor: a minister who drives a Cadillac filled with sexy young girls (the Pointer Sisters), who basically preaches the power of the almighty dollar, and who believes that what he receives in the collection plate goes "where it belongs," into the pockets of his expensive trousers.

The film's main sentimental idea relates to the honesty of an ex-convict whose children love him. The daughter brings him a picture that she had drawn of him at school and that shows him working at the car wash. Such a pulling of the heart strings never fails to have its effect on me. Elisa always remembers how she saw tears coursing down my cheeks when I took her to see Walt Disney's *Song of the South*, with Uncle Remus's story of Brer Rabbit and the Tar Baby. Her decorating of the baby's room with stenciled images from Beatrix Potter's *The Tale of Benjamin Bunny* is another type of tear-jerking visual that gets me every time. Intellectual art certainly touches me in another way, but how can I say that it is deeper or even more authentic than popular art, when both speak to basic human desires for a greater feeling for others and a greater appreciation for the genuine in every aspect of life. That did not come out the way I wanted, for I never like the word "aspect" as a substitute for something specific. But as Fats Waller sang, "Skip it. It'll have to do, till the real thing comes along."

After lunch on the 7th we all went with Elisa to her appointment with the pediatrician. Dr. Mauri Senise had studied during his senior year in a high school in a small town of about 4,000 near Buffalo, New York. At first Elisa was not enthusiastic about the doctor because he would not talk with Isabella and had treated her roughly. Slowly, however, he became more patient and gentler. He seemed on his best behavior when we all crowded into his small patient room. He was dressed in a kind of long-sleeved winter undershirt with buttons at the rounded neck (something like the thermal top that I had worn in Chile when the cold was so penetrating in winter) and with white pants and white slip-on shoes. Elisa had said earlier that all-white was standard for Brazilian doctors.

At first Dr. Senise spoke in Portuguese, but then he began to ask us in good English where we were from. He grew more friendly as he recalled his year in the U.S., where he had gone through the American Field Service, had played U.S. football as the kicker of extra points and field goals, and had, Elisa said later, received a standing ovation when he graduated. He checked Isabella and found nothing wrong with her, even though Elisa had been concerned that she was developing a urinary tract infection. On the walls of the doctor's office were three paintings by his wife Leonora. One piece depicted what I took to be a couple eloping—the female nude but for a transparent nightgown. As the man spirits her away, their feet hurry and step perfectly together. The scene reminded me of the ending of John Keats' "The Eve of St. Agnes": "Let us away, my love, with happy speed; / There are no ears to hear, or eyes to see / …For o'er the southern moors I have a home for thee." The other two pieces were in an entirely different style—the elopement scene appearing like something out of the 19th century tradition of dark colors and narrative form, whereas the pair of paintings side by side on a different wall were devoted to scenes of Madonna and child, done in more modern primary tones—pale green the prominent shade. The child in one painting was nursing at the Virgin's breast, and just as in the elopement picture, here too the artist created a sense of transparency, having the nipple of the mother visible inside the infant's mouth. For a pediatrician's office, the pair of Madonna-and-child paintings seemed very fitting indeed.

Without planning it in any way, artwork had continued to enter my account of our Brazilian trip. In fact, I have given more attention to this topic and to my own reading, listening to music, watching rental films, and writing than to the place itself. This is largely due to the limitations imposed by not knowing Portuguese, by the weather not allowing me to travel to São Paulo, and by the lack of transportation, having to depend on Newton. Of course, even without such limitations, I am restricted, as María herself says, by my one- or three-track mind. This was true again on the 8th day of January, when we watched another rented movie and when, before that, I read in *The Nature of the Book* on the licensing restrictions of Stationers or publishers in Restoration England. When a publisher wished to print a text, he had to have approval from a licenser, and if the publisher feared disapproval for some reason, he or she would insist on the author making changes to the text. Thus: "All authors must be sure to work only within the limits of the licenser's understanding." Once publishers felt that they could print anything to which they and their authors appended their names, this made both of them responsible for a book's contents and brought about "authorship as a regulatory principle in place of licensing." The motif of remaining within bounds or limitations had also surfaced once again. And it would once more before the day was over.

At night we watched the rented movie, *The Rainmaker*, translated in the Portuguese subtitles as *O Homem que Fazia Chover* (The Man Who Made It Rain). The issue here was one of crossing the line of legal ethics. Matt Damon stars as a young lawyer, with Danny DeVito as his associate, Danny Glover as the judge, and Jon Voight as the corporate attorney defending a health insurance company's denial of a claim for medical treatment of a young man dying of leukemia. The character played by Damon accuses the corporate attorney of having been corrupted by taking money from his unethical clients. When the Damon character is questioned by a young abused wife if he would defend a wife beater, he at first says his job is to represent anyone, but he seems to become aware of his dilemma in wanting to do the right thing. John Grisham, the author of the novel on which the movie is based, was himself a lawyer. Unrealistic as the film's plot may be, it nevertheless raised the same question of where we draw the line, or whether we remain within it or go beyond it.

Even though our experience of Brazil had been limited almost exclusively to Jundiaí, and this city may not be representative of the rest of Brazil, we were constantly learning about other parts of the country. For instance, Dr. Senise's wife was originally from Ribeirão Preto, which is some four hours north of Jundiaí, and Newton's grandmother lived in Sertãzinho, which is only some twenty minutes from Ribeirão Preto, where Dr. Senise attended medical school and Newton and Robson went for their high school education. Newton attended a school named for Osvaldo Cruz, who was an important figure in the public health fight against mosquito-transmitted diseases, like dengue. Robson had gone to another private high school in Ribeirão Preto, but he and Newton both attended the same university in Brazilia, after having gone to Ribeirão Preto from their different states of Goias and Minas Gerais. Neither had ever known the other until they both ended up in Austin at UT where they studied in the School of Engineering. These intersections of places and people made me think of similar crossroads occurring in my own experience of Brazil.

The 9th brought another opportunity to "know" a different part of Brazil—the southern region bordering on Uruguay and Argentina. Robson and Ana María accompanied us on an outing to Viñhedo to eat at a popular barbecue "grill" called Espeto de Prata (*espeto*, something like a shish-kebab skewer or spit, and *prata*—or in Spanish *plata*—for that precious metal). María had stayed behind to work on her various homemaking projects, but mostly because she is a vegan for health reasons. At the eatery, the waiters—who were called gauchos and were mostly very Anglo-looking, several reminding me of Mormon boys— came from the South of Brazil, where jobs are scarce. Even though the young fellows earned very little at the grill, they were apparently better off in coming to the State of São Paulo, which accounts for 60% of Brazil's GNP—more than the rest of South America put together, according to Newton. Apparently, the wait boys lived rent-free in rooms in a building at the back of the grill, which must have been attractive to them in terms of the cost of living. All were attired in their native dress, which consisted of a white blouse-looking, long-sleeved shirt and black trousers, with a wide black belt under which was a sash woven of black, red, and silver-gray threads that hung down the left side of their pant legs. Circulating from table to table, each boy carried a skewer with pieces of just one cut of meat, the tip of the skewer inserted in a small type of frying pan with a base of wood. According to Newton, cattle are not frozen after being slaughtered, as in the U.S., and then cut up, which makes for smoothly sliced steaks, but rather the meat in Brazil is hand-carved while still fresh, with the butchers cutting along the natural curvature of the flesh, muscles, fat, and bone. Robson observed, however, that just the week before, the government had passed a law that forbid this practice because the fresh meat attracted flies—from now on, as I understood it, butchers would have to freeze the meat prior to carving it up, as in the States.

In addition to a variety of cuts of meat, the waiters also brought around fried bananas, baked pineapple (which they sliced off from the skewer the same way that they did the meat, by cutting off a piece with a large knife as the customer would spear it with a fork), fried cheese (melted circles hanging down from the skewer held horizontally), hearts and other parts of chicken, ham, lamb, and sausage, all of those meats on the same skewer. The meal actually began with a choice from an assortment of salads, pickles, olives, rice, asparagus, cod and crab, and "buffalo" balls of mozzarella cheese, all self-served at a type of smorgasbord buffet. Robson said the buffet was designed to fill you up so you would not eat as much meat. In any case, each person paid the same amount—about 10 to 12 dollars, regardless of how much he or she ate. Desserts were extra. I only sampled the meat since María had gotten me into the vegan habit. I did drink a Brazilian beer, a Kaiser brand, which was delicious but made me sleepy. The fried bananas appealed to me most and I ate three or four, and two pineapple slices. Unlike Vida Natural, Espeto de Prata left me feeling stuffed and with something of a headache. But as Newton said, it was an experience.

After the meal, we drove to Conviva (short for Condominium Viva Alegre) where friends of Ana María lived—the same couple that had been at Robson's birthday party. (The acronym reminded me that I had seen on TV a Brazilian official being interviewed, and as he spoke the station parodied his use of acronyms by having the letters fall from the top of the screen and pile up just below and to the left of his mouth.) When we approached Conviva's fenced enclosure, with its three armed guards and an automatic guard rail across the entrance, we were inspected and questioned before being permitted to pass through into a community of about 1,000 homes. All the houses that I saw were attractive, with small swimming pools and beautiful trees and flowers. The lot of Ana María's friends was huge—deep and fairly wide, with mango and lime trees, a garden, a guest house in back, and a house for the maid. I only saw the front area but was told about the backyard by Elisa, since I had not cared for the couple and begged off getting out and going in, with sleepiness as an excuse to remain in the car.

While I was resting, tremendous lightning bolts suddenly shot straight down to earth, accompanied by almost deafening thunderclaps, signaling the approach of a tropical storm. When the rain eventually began and we were driving back to Jundiaí, it was difficult to see the cars ahead of us. I rather regretted not going in and seeing the rest of the couple's grounds, but not so much from an interest in the landscaping as from remembering that the husband was a representative for a paper and ink company, whose products are of course related to printing and to my reading in *The Nature of the Book*. I realized that it might have been interesting to talk to him about his work. The night of the birthday party, he had bragged that he had 150 clients and knew each one by name. After ten years with the company he had bought their property, with the lot alone costing over 20 thousand dollars. It only shows that printing is still a lucrative business, thanks to Gutenberg and all the Restoration authors, Stationers, and private and royal patents. Publishing the Kenneth Starr report on the Clintons took 50 tons of recycled paper and I cannot recall how many gallons of vegetable-based ink (making the report easier to digest?). Will the computer chip ever wholly replace the printed page? I hope not—the handwritten either.

There is no denying the practical value of computers, of e-mail, of the time saved in retyping entire documents because of a few errors. But just to form words on a page in script is an irreplaceable pleasure to me. It is amazing how carefully and beautifully many pre-typewriter authors wrote their texts and correspondence. Too often I hurry my letters and leave them unclear and uneven. When I do write deliberately I find the results visually pleasing and enjoy the idea that the shapes that I make are uniquely my own, whereas all print is essentially impersonal, although type fonts have been distinctively designed by an artist like Eric Gill. My commercial artist friend Jim Jacobs always preferred Garamond above all other fonts. Galliard, Centaur, the latter the type face of my *Texan Jazz*, and Times Roman are all appealing to me for their readability and artful angles and contours. Reading in *The Nature of the Book* I discovered that the author cites an article by D.F. McKenzie, entitled "Speech-Manuscript-Print," which I had edited and published in *The Library Chronicle* in 1990. McKenzie quotes 17th-century writer Thomas Hobbes to the effect that speech is the most noble and profitable invention; however, as he then points out, speech is the most difficult to recover from the past as evidence of what was thought or said. This, of course, was prior to the invention of film, phonograph, tape, and so many other forms of media. As for the difference between writing and printing in terms of economics, the former has always been cheaper, affordable to most any person and especially to a poet like Louis Zukofsky, who would write minutely front and back on 3 x 5 cards or on sheets even smaller, at times in various colors so that he could follow his own lines of poetic thought. I recalled Gill and Zukofsky because the archives of both are at the Humanities Research Center at UT-Austin where, when I edited the *Chronicle*, I had seen Gill's artwork and Zukofsky's manuscripts.

 Before writing or printing must first come a story to tell; here is one that I shall call "In Search of Black Beans." It had begun on Thursday the 7th at the Russi grocery store on Rua Jorge Zolner in Jundiaí. María had wanted to cook black beans, and when we had all gone with Newton in his car, he had found them at Russi. On the 9th we had walked to Vida Natural to eat lunch while Newton was at work, and after the meal, María and I went on to Russi to buy more beans, while Elisa was at a lab picking up the results of a blood test. I approached a young worker stacking cans and asked if he could tell me where to find black beans. He could not understand me at all, and in turn I could not understand what he asked me. I went to another employee who was stocking pasta of various kinds and asked him the same question, and when he too seemed unsure what I wanted, I indicated for him to follow me. I showed him some clear plastic bags of what looked like yellowish beans, although they may have been hominy or a type of corn since next to them was popcorn, which I had learned from Isabella is *pipoca*. (Depending on the Latin American country, popcorn in Spanish can be *palomitas*, *rositas*, *cabritas*, etc.—that is, little doves, little roses, little goats.) I kept repeating to the worker the two ways I knew for saying black beans in Spanish—*porotos negros* (in María's Chile) and *frijoles negros* (in Mexico)—hoping the sounds of the words and/or the sight of the contents of the package would "ring a bell." But the worker remained uncertain about what it was I was looking for. He stopped a fellow worker and he too could make nothing of my words. Finally, Elisa arrived from the lab and could explain that I was seeking *feijoes pretos*. Not even *frijoles* had been close enough for me to communicate that I was searching for black beans. As basic as this food is, it could not be found except with the right words. And yes, even before the story come the words. Who invented them and how must be as rich and varied a history as that of any land or language.

After having viewed the Dutch film *Karacter* and then the American movie *The Rainmaker*, I had seen from the subtitles that *juros* and *juro* had two entirely different meanings; the latter in Portuguese and Spanish is the word for "I swear," as in a court of law. Having learned from *Karacter* that *juros* are interest on a loan, I had asked Ana María, since she was studying law, how it was that the two very similar words had such different meanings. She replied that she had never thought about it before and could not say. Jury in English or juror or jurisprudence would all seem to derive from Latin's *jurare,* meaning to swear or take an oath, but *juros* for loan interest seems far removed, unless it implies taking out a loan on one's word or oath. I am only guessing and would need to consult a Portuguese dictionary for the derivation. After I had retrieved my old paperback copy of *The Portuguese English Dictionary*, with only the Portuguese, which had fallen behind a bookshelf at home, I forgot to put it in my bag to bring with us. But then it was too limited to have provided the answer to my question, as I found on returning to Texas.

The whole mystery of how the sound *jurare* in Latin came to stand for swearing, and ultimately all the legal terms associated with it through similar words in romance languages, is just one instance of the interconnectedness among nations and the wonder and worth of learning other languages than one's own. The various words for popcorn all have in common an image that in one way or another describes that snack, once it has been popped. Rose and goat are to me closer than doves or pigeons to the look of popped popcorn, but each culture sees the world a bit differently and makes its own comparisons based on a shared habitation. Imagination goes into the creation of words, and this for me has always been fascinating to contemplate: that is, how over the millenia men and women came up with sounds and then letters for all the things that we see and use. Having names for things is not just a matter of metaphor-making but serves a very practical purpose, as in my search for black beans, for which I needed to know the words *feijoes pretos* in order to locate their whereabouts.

Beans, like so many other words, have taken on quite different symbolic meanings in different places and at different times. In Texas during the Mier Expedition, black beans meant the difference between life and death for the captured Texans who, blindfolded, dipped a hand into a jar and pulled out a white or a black bean, with the latter leading to execution by a firing squad. The name for the Mexican jumping bean is meant to describe the effect of the movement of the larva of a small moth, inside the legume, that causes the bean to jump. In Brazil black beans mean the essential meal, the timeless foodstuff whose name has been handed down from those who left behind sounds uniquely pronounced for objects observed or produced and for ideas conceived. Later, after the sounds naming things were created, letters were invented for longhand writing of the sounded words, and later still fonts were designed for printing of books, of brand labels on can wrappers or handy but biodegradable plastic sacks, and of recipes for beans, and other foodstuffs, published in so many languages to be read and followed in cooking of the protein so vital to life.

Years after the Brazil visit, our son Darío, a physician with the Veterans Administration, ordered a scan of a veteran with pain in the area of the gall bladder. In searching in a word-derivation book related to medicine he learned for the first time of the Phrygian cap, which is the lower back part of the bladder, named in 1916 by Bartel (full name unreported). The Phrygians, a people that migrated to northern and central Asia Minor between 1000 and 2000 B.C., wore a tight-fitting red cap that was folded at its apex; the Greeks knew of the cap and depicted it in their art; King Midas wore the Phrygian cap because Apollo cursed him with donkey ears; and Paris wears the cap in Homer's *The Iliad*. In the French and American revolutions, the cap, also called the Liberty cap, symbolized freedom, and in the U.S. it was also used on coinage, while throughout the world it has appeared on a variety of seals and flags. This is just one other example of words that originated from an object whose name, like black beans and *feijoes pretos*, took on meanings that encompass a wide-ranging cultural history.

On Sunday the 10th, Newton's grandmother, Juracy, his uncle Ary, and Ana, the uncle's girlfriend, arrived from Sertãozinho, where Juracy lives, and Ribeirão Preto, where Ary and Ana live. The grandmother's name has a native Indian origin, but she is called by the family Bi, which is the shortened form of Bisavó (in Spanish *bisabuela*), meaning great-grandmother. As noted before, we had known Uncle Ary in Austin when he came with Newton's mother, Maria do Carmo, to visit soon after Isabella's birth. Ary was generally unimpressed with the U.S. and ready to return to his beloved Brazil, craving above all his daily rice and beans, cooked just the way he likes them. We took him and Maria do Carmo on a drive in Austin's Lakeway area, where we saw deer wandering through an exclusive neighborhood on Lake Travis. This seemed only mildly interesting to Ary, but he was quite enthused by an article on the Brazilian pianist João Carlos Martins, which he found in a U.S. tabloid, published in New York by Brazilians. Through that article, Ary had introduced me to the project undertaken by Martins of recording Bach's complete works for keyboard. Ary also told me how the pianist had injured his fingers playing soccer, and that it was thought that he would never recover well enough to perform music again. After exercising conscientiously, he would make a remarkable come-back. As a result of the article Ary had read and told me about in Austin, I had purchased a two-CD set of half of Bach's *The Well-Tempered Klavier*, as recorded by Martins, and would become completely enamored of his playing. With Uncle Ary's arrival in Jundiaí, I reminded him of his having put me on to Martins; I also told him about the special series of 42 CDs by classical pianist Arthur Moreira Lima being offered by the Ministry of Culture at the very reasonable price of 12 *reais* for each set of two CDS. He seemed pleased to learn that I was "into" Brazilian artists.

    During their visit, I asked Ary if he knew about Villa-Lobos's composition, "The Little Train of the Caipira," and he explained that in Portuguese the title was simply "The Little Country Train," which made sense after I had learned earlier that *caipira* means country. He then went on with an extended explanation of how such trains traveled to the various coffee plantations in the interior of Brazil. He recalled that in Villa-Lobos's composition, the orchestra makes the sound of the train letting off steam. After I compared this to the puffing and whistling of Newton's rice cooker—which he had hurriedly set up to prepare the mandatory rice and beans for lunch—Ary then began to describe the country trains, especially their bronze pistons and the long bars attached to them for turning the wheels. He also talked about eucalyptus wood being burned in the firebox to heat the water and produce the steam power for the engine.

Only a few days before, Newton had bought me a booklet entitled *Império do Café: A grande lavoura no Brasil 1850 a 1890* (Coffee Empire: The Great Agricultural Business in Brazil 1850 to 1890) by another Martins, Ana Luiza, whose study (in its 7th edition) forms part of a series called *História em Documentos* (History in Documents). The booklet utilizes official texts, experiences of persons who wrote in different languages, song lyrics, literature, artwork, photographs, newspaper articles, and other materials from that particular historical period. As the title indicates, the booklet concerns the Brazilian production of coffee and includes a map showing the rail lines that served the industry, reaching from the east coast at Angra do Reis, near Rio de Janeiro, back west towards São Paulo and then north to Jundiaí, Campinas, Rio Claro, and almost to Ribeirão Preto. Among the documents is a poem written in 1877 by Antônio Carlos de Almeida on the impact of the locomotive on the "until then peaceful rural environment." The first stanza refers to the profusion of smoke discharged in the air from the eucalyptus wood and the steam from the boiler with its heated water that impelled the train into movement. The poem also refers to the noise of the engine that frightened the animals. The poet celebrates this emblem of human ingenuity, saluting it just as Walt Whitman had the year before in 1876 in his own "To a Locomotive in Winter": "Type of the modern…pulse of the continent…Law of thyself complete, thine own track firmly holding, / (No sweetness debonair of tearful harp or glib piano thine)…."

Newton's grandmother, Bi, speaks only Portuguese and assumes that everyone understands her. She reproached Elisa for speaking with Isabella in English, just as Newton's nephew, Aldo, had done when he was visiting for a few days. Aldo had asked Elisa why she did not speak with her in Portuguese since she was in Brazil, and Elisa replied that she wanted Isabella to know English as well as Portuguese. I can appreciate Bi and Aldo's attitude, but naturally I sided with Elisa. The grandmother was delighted that Isabella talked with her and even played with her, commenting to Elisa that her other grandchildren paid no attention to her anymore. She had just turned 85 but looked quite fit, even though she suffered from many ailments: high blood pressure, glaucoma, arthritis, incontinence. At 55 she had had a heart attack, but nothing seemed to slow her down. She devoured the beans and rice and beef stroganoff, as well as a good amount of Reese's chocolates, and, I was told, she consumes ice cream like it was going out of style. Her arms and legs appeared a little swollen, but she had endured a four-hour drive and would again on returning home on the same day.

It is typical of Latin Americans to go out of their way to greet friends or relatives, to see them off at the airport, no matter the hour, and to invite them for a meal or entertainment. In addition to paying us a visit, which was thoughtful in itself, Uncle Ary brought for María a collection of colorful butterflies mounted under glass in a pebble-edged frame. This reminded me of a similar "picture" made entirely of butterfly wings that my own Uncle Grigsby Keetch had brought back from his tour of duty during World War Two. It seems that he had purchased the composition in Brazil or Venezuela or perhaps Central America. Other than the frame and the wings under glass, what I recalled most from my Uncle's telling of his time in the Navy was how his ship had just left a harbor and was replaced in port by another U.S. Navy vessel when the latter was bombed or torpedoed. Had his own ship not weighed anchor and sailed off when it did, he would never have returned with the butterfly wings that hung in my grandmother Keetch's home. And of course, I would have had no memory to place beside Ary's butterflies and to make Maria's gift mean even more to me than it did by itself.

At last, on the 11th, I would be able to return to São Paulo. As we left Jundiaí in the morning, I remembered my thoughts on the day that we had driven to Viñhedo and had seen a building there under construction. Newton had commented on how ugly it looked in its incomplete state, with bare bricks and cement, rubbish on the ground, and unpainted vacant rooms without window panes or furnishings. The fact that there were no steel rods in the Brazilian construction recalled to me how in Chile buildings are designed to sway with the force of the earthquakes. This in turn reminded me of how Frank Lloyd Wright had created the architectural designs for the Imperial Hotel in Tokyo, which—like many of his creations, including perhaps his most famous home, built over a waterfall in North Carolina—was considered structurally impractical. And yet, when an earthquake rocked the Japanese city, only Wright's hotel survived intact. Here was a man who definitely ventured beyond the limits set by his profession. Not only this, but in his personal life, he, like his hotel, survived a catastrophe—the murder of his wife. Whether or not one can approve of his having abandoned his first wife and their children and his being so egocentric, the fact remains that as an artist he brought pleasure, comfort, safety, and tranquility to those who benefited from the homes, workplaces, and museums he envisioned and committed to paper. How many Brazilian architects, I wondered, must have been influenced in their own designs of buildings in Jundiaí and São Paulo by Wright's innovative, revolutionary art, with its functional yet aesthetic shapes and structural features. On our arrival in São Paulo, still thinking of that master of twentieth-century architecture, I looked at the metropolis with new eyes, even observing for the first time the way the poor made do, living in huge drain pipes that had not yet been used by city utilities, constructing shacks against the hillsides or stacking their ramshackle houses or huts one against another, in view of the city's aqua-colored, glass-sided corporate skyscrapers, a modern bank next to a nineteenth-century home, hospital, or convent, and the traffic jams from chemical spills and normal rush-hour congestion. What would Brazilian poet Mario de Andrade now say of his "Hallucinated City"?

    Unfortunately, since we were returning once again on a Monday, there was no chance to visit the many marvelous museums that were only open Tuesday through Friday. As a result, I was reduced to one possibility for viewing something of the art and literary heritage of São Paulo—the private home of Guilherme de Almeida. This writer's name and work were totally unknown to me, but a guidebook informed me that Almeida owned artwork by many of the principal figures involved in the famous Week of Modern Art of 1922. Even though I was not all that enthusiastic about this one literary sight, to which I was restricted by having come on a Monday when Newton regularly drives in to his office, it was awfully good of him to take the trouble to locate the Almeida house on Macapá Street, number 187, in the section of the city named Perdizes (meaning quails). The first good omen was that I spotted the name of the Brazilian writer Machado de Assis, whose work I did know, on a city bus a few blocks from Macapá, off Pacaembú. But the neighborhood did not at all look promising for a museum advertised as full of artwork, books, and manuscripts. We passed the place at first, but after turning around spotted the small, white house with an inconspicuous plaque that identified it as that of Almeida (1890-1969). At a table, at what seemed to be the side, private entrance, not the front of the house, a uniformed guard sat at the end of the driveway next to a poster with a photo of Almeida dressed in a jacket covered with ribboned medals. The guard politely and apologetically explained that the director was not there but should arrive momentarily, and welcomed us in. Only later did I learn that visitors were supposed to make prior arrangements to tour the house.

Accompanying us from room to room, the young guard provided us with information about the items on display, explaining that in fact everything was just as it had been when Almeida lived in the house with his wife Baby and their dog Ling-Ling. Labels identified some of the artwork and knickknacks, as well as a few poems by Almeida. My impression was that he wrote mostly on religious subjects, since one room contained a number of artifacts relating to the Catholic church. One item that caught my eye especially was a fragment of a carved figure of Christ; although no cross was visible, the description identified the piece as a crucifix from the state of Minas Gerais and dated it from circa the 18th century. The features of the figure's face—its aquiline nose and slender cheeks and chin—were finely rendered. Another piece depicted the holy family's flight to Egypt and was worked from a palm-sized piece of limestone. Friends of Almeida had given him various paintings, including among them poet Cecilia Meireles, whose poetry I knew; artists Anita Malfatti, Di Cavalcanti, and Lasar Segall; and others with whose work I was entirely unfamiliar.

Portraits of Almeida and his wife were among the paintings on the walls, as was a photograph of Baby that showed her to have been quite pretty, even though portraits of her did not seem to do her justice. Nothing of this interested me so much that I could not have gone perfectly well without having seen any of it.

In one alcove near the living room I spied a bookcase with rather old-looking bound volumes. Among those I found a copy of James Joyce's *Ulysses*, which was probably a first edition, although I did not open it or any of the other books, thinking it was not allowed. Also present were works by Rabelais, Mallarmé, Theophile Gautier, Oscar Wilde, Baudelaire, Flaubert, and Blake's *Songs of Innocence and Experience*. I asked the guard in my Spanish version of Portuguese if there were manuscripts of Almeida's poetry, but he did not understand until Elisa repeated what I had said. He confirmed that there were manuscripts and that the director could show them to me when he came. Later, when I was looking up at paintings on the walls of a staircase at the side entrance where we had entered the house, as I eased toward the door on my way out, the guard motioned to me to go on up to the next floor. A wooden stairs wound around to the second storey where there was another bookshelf on the landing, filled mostly with faded paperbacks. To the left of the landing we entered and found what the guard said was the poet's study, with a desk at which he worked as a lawyer. To the left of the desk was the couple's bedroom, with a bed ready to be slept in and beside it the armchair in which the poet had expired in 1969. Back to the right of the landing was a room with nothing but bookcases lining the walls. In looking at the shelves from top to bottom, I could discover some of Almeida's many interests.

Several books on Charlie Chaplin were not surprising, since just outside Almeida's study door I had seen a photograph that pictured the poet with the actor. Another photograph showed Almeida with D.W. Griffiths, as did another of an early movie figure whose name escapes me since I failed to jot it down. Copies of journals to which Almeida contributed and/or edited (such as *Jornal de São Paulo* and *Folha da Manhã*), books on Japanese literature, Thomas Mann's *Buddenbrooks*, memoirs of Tolstoy, Thoreau's *Walden*, Brazilian novelist João Guimarães Rosa's *Corpo de Baile*, *Sagarcana*, and

Vereda, and works by Brazilian novelist Jorge Amado, including his *Gabriela, Cravo e Canela*, which I knew of but had never read, as was the case with Rosa's most famous novel, translated as *The Devil to Pay in the Backlands*, though it was not among Almeida's books that I saw. Along with the complete works of Verlaine, I also noticed a number of volumes by Almeida, among them a book entitled *Natalika*. Downstairs I had also seen several volumes of the poet's works, including those with simple one-word titles like *Meu*, *Você*, and *Nós* (My, You, We or Us). He had written a critical work entitled *Do Sentimento Nacionalista da Poesia Brasileira* and a study on *Ritmo, Elemento de Expressão*. I was impressed with the range of his reading and writing but felt that he must have been a minor religious and sentimental author.

When I was about to descend the stairs, the guard indicated that there was a third storey to the house, and that it was there that Almeida did all his writing. We ascended another narrow staircase lined on the walls with artwork by the poet's friends. On this floor, which was probably a converted attic since it was one large room with a low ceiling, we found another writing desk, armchairs, bookshelves full of various volumes, more original artwork on the walls, and several pieces of bronze sculpture. The very first object that caught my eye was a telescope on a tripod. A wide, narrow window to the back of the house was opened by the guard to allow us a panoramic view of one part of São Paulo. He encouraged me to take a photograph, but I had already taken one from the second-storey window that was nearly as scenic. At that point I was more curious to investigate the rest of the room's contents.

Newton shut the window, whispering to me that the guard was letting in humidity that would be harmful to the books and artwork. He had earlier commented several times that it was a shame that the books and papers were not being better preserved, but it seemed that the poet himself had stipulated that everything in the house was to remain exactly as it was at his death. The guard opened a closet and showed us the poet's shoes and dress suits, which surprised Elisa when she saw how small Almeida had been—his clothes almost boy-sized. What attracted the attention of all three of us were two drawings of the dog, which were quite good. Also, I especially liked a view of São Paulo, done, I believe, in agua-forte by Di Cavalcanti. But it was a piece of sculpture by J. Brecheret that most intrigued me; entitled "Sóror Dolorosa," this work bore a label saying that it was inspired by an Almeida poem. The work consisted of two busts joined at an ell-shaped angle, with the face of a woman with shoulder-length braids looking down sorrowfully at the head of what must have been a representation of Christ. No one had been able to explain to me the word "Sóror," and since I had not seen the poem itself, I had been unable to read and perhaps understand the word in context. The title of the poem forms part of Almeida's book entitled *Livro de Horas de Sóror Dolorosa*, which would seem to refer to the medieval tradition of beautifully illustrated Books of Hours and to the sadness (Dolor) of the Virgin Mary. Years later, I discovered that although *soror*, with or without an accent, is sister in Portuguese, Brazilians use another word for sister, *irmã*, which must have been the reason no one could explain to me the meaning of *Sóror*. Without an accent, the word comes from Latin, while in Spanish *Sor* can refer to a Sister in an order of nuns, as in the name of the Mexican poet, Sor Juana Inés de la Cruz. Subsequently I will have more to say about *Sóror Dolorosa* in terms of Almeida's poetry.

Before leaving—and by then I could have stayed longer had Newton not needed to go on to his office—I asked the guard if it were permitted to take a photograph of the writing room. He seemed to understand my attempt at Portuguese, moved quickly out of the way, and motioned for me to go right in. I took two shots and then descended the set of staircases to the ground level, where the guard began talking to me spiritedly, indicating that I should enter what looked like the director's workroom, but first he wanted us all to see the backyard, where, he explained to Elisa, the dog was buried. We walked on some stepping stones in the grass beneath a shade tree—probably of some fruit—and came to a marble grave marker with Ling-Ling's name and dates, something like 1948-1960 or perhaps it was 1938-1950; whichever it was, the poet's pet had lived with him for twelve years. This very personal touch was but one of the many that made the Almeida house an unusual literary memorial. Still, I was not certain if I had had a choice between

Dave Oliphant

Trés Tragédias Gregas translated by Guilherme de Almeida.

visiting the Almeida house and one of São Paulo's impressive-sounding museums that I would have elected the former.

After we drove to Newton's office, Elisa and I set out for a university bookstore that I had noticed for the first time just two blocks from Newton's company offices. On crossing through a shopping area in a nearby building, we first stopped there at a post office branch to mail a letter and a few postcards. The line was extremely long, but Elisa explained that there was no one else in the line where she was standing. I had wondered why she had not fallen in behind the last person in the line where the rest of the people stood inside rope barriers. She told me that by law there was a special exception made for pregnant women. I then read the sign beside her and realized that indeed she was in a line all to herself. We were through in no time. From there we crossed to the corner bookstore, and almost immediately I could see a poetry section in bookcases along the walls on the second floor.

Before I had reached the poetry section, a name in the store's art section jumped out at me: Guilherme de Almeida. On the spine of a book entitled *Trés Tragédias Gregas* was the name of the author whom, as I had learned from some information sheets at Almeida's house, had been honored as "The Prince of Brazilian Poets." In a ceremony conducted in his native city of Campinas, where he was born on July 24th, 1890, Almeida had delivered a speech on the occasion of the homage rendered to him on December 19th, 1968, the year before his death. In the poetry section I again came across Almeida's name on the spines of two copies of his *Natalika*, which is actually a type of philosophical prose work that considers the nature of art, asserting that artifice is superior to the natural world. Comprised of eight assertions, the book alludes to Greek philosophy, Hindu thought, Persian religion, modern artists such as Cezanne and Picasso, and such writers as Blaise Cendrars, Anatole France, Oscar Wilde, Jonathan Swift, Lafcadio Hearn, and Goethe, as well as Beethoven, Einstein, and Debussy. My curiosity was piqued even more when I read that both books had been reissued recently, *Trés Tragédias Gregas* in 1997 and *Natalika* in 1993. I decided to buy them both, if only because I felt close to the man and his work from having visited his home on Rua Macapá.

Once I began to look through the book of *Three Greek Tragedies* and to read Trajano Vieira's introduction to Almeida's translation of Sophocles' *Antigone*, I was completely satisfied with having bought his, for me, rather expensive book—almost $30.00 in paperback. Not only does the work contain reproductions of three details of a painting of Almeida by Waldemar Cordeiro, dated 1947 and present in the poet-translator's home, but it also reproduces pages from the poet's working manuscript of his translation. The manuscript shows how Almeida had counted syllables and marked the rhythm patterns in Sophocles' *Antigone*, and also includes the title page of his translation of the play from 1952, when it first appeared in São Paulo, along with the original Greek text. Vieira, who had translated Aeschylus's *Prometheus Bound* and Sophocles' *Ajax*, writes that Almeida's deep interest in the sound of poetry derives from his affinity for French literature, in particular the work of Baudelaire and Verlaine, whose poems the Brazilian had also translated. What Vieira says further on this score I could confirm, thanks to our visit to Rua Macapá: even today it is possible to see, in the museum that bears Almeida's name, how he remained close to the French poets. Vieira goes on to quote from Sérgio Milliet on Almeida having inherited from French Parnassianism "a tendency toward difficult rhythms and intelligent assonances"; from Symbolism "a certain melodious obscurity"; and from Futurism "free verse." In a series of excerpts from Almeida's translation, Vieira demonstrates that the poet very consciously chose sounds in Portuguese that parallel Sophocles' Greek. For example, Almeida rendered a line concerning one of the two Argive captains, who arrests Antigone for covering her brother Polynices' body with dust, against the orders of King Creon, in such a way as to reproduce not only the alliterative "t" sounds in the Greek but to echo the sense of burial and the idea of Zeus's displeasure when men contradict the higher law of the gods. In some ways Almeida's method of translation emphasizes sound as a means of capturing the sense, which reminded me of American poet Louis Zukofsky's renderings of Catullus's Latin poems into an English that approximates the original, even when the effect is "difficult rhythms," "a certain melodious obscurity," and a "free verse" that does not follow normal English syntax. This comparative link between Almeida and Zukofsky made the minor Brazilian poet all the more appealing and impressive to me.

In reading the poem Almeida composed when he was named "Prince of Brazilian Poets," I discovered yet another similarity between his work and that of Zukofsky. Just as the American poet, in section 17 of his epic poem *A*, names the titles of and quotes from a number of his own previous books, so too Almeida works into his tribute to his native city, Campinas, the titles of all his collections of poetry. Again, like Zukofsky, Almeida was partial to one-word titles: *Meu*; *Você*; *Nós*; *Raça*; *Rosamor*. Zukofsky's own titles include *A*; *All*; *Little*; *Ferdinand*; and *Autobiography*. Both poets, who were contemporaries, although Almeida was born in 1890 and Zukofsky in 1904, had looked to some of the same French poets for their inspiration, especially in terms of their interest in sound. Zukofsky's early short poems have much in common with Almeida's haiku on the locust quoted on the inside cover of *Three Greek Tragedies*: "Diamante. Vidraça. / Arisca, áspera asa risca / o ar. E brilha. E passa." An approximate translation would be: "Diamond. Windowpane. / Elusive, rough wing scratches / on the air. And shines. And passes." I later learned that Almeida had introduced the Japanese haiku to Brazilian letters. The title of Almeida's book, *Livro de Horas de Sóror Dolorosa*, published in 1920, best exemplifies the poet's predilection for euphonic word clusters, with the "or" sound repeated in *horas*, *sóror*, and *dolorosa*, and even includes the "ro" of *dolorosa* in *livro*. However, without knowing more of Almeida's poetry, it would be impossible to say if he approaches Zukofsky in terms of a uniquely modernist style and conception. Yet even the conjunction of their work at certain superficial points prompts me to look further into the more than 25 volumes of verse published by Almeida between 1917 (the date of *Nós*) and 1954 (the date of *Acalanto de Bartira*—his *Toda a Poesia* having appeared in 1952).

The second visit to São Paulo was indeed a full one. After lunch at the same vegetarian restaurant where we had eaten on the previous visit, Elisa and Newton departed for her appointment with Dr. Arimoto. The baby had dropped a bit more, but not enough for the doctor to set a date for the caesarian. Meanwhile, I ventured out on my own to look for two music stores, one in a center filled with very small shops and the other a regular mall called Shopping Paulista. The first store had nothing of interest to me—I was seeking in particular some CDs of Ernesto Nazareth's swinging Chopin-inspired tangos and more recordings by Martins of Bach.

On the way to the mall it began to rain, so I ducked into a bank on Avenida Paulista called Bradesco and watched as others either took shelter in the same bank lobby or passed on by protected by their umbrellas. Many vendors along the main street offered umbrellas for sale to the passersby, but I hoped the shower would not last long. Once again, the mix of racial types and social classes was striking, the skin shades amazingly varied, predominated by a color neither black nor dark brown but like coffee with milk, along with what I took to be blonde-headed and very light-skinned Anglos among the crowd. Back on the street, I dodged the puddles, passed several vendors selling assembled dinosaurs, formed from round wooden pieces attached to a long spine, or tickets to theatre productions. Entering the nearby mall I discovered a whole other world of well-dressed salespeople, stores with elegant offerings, bossa-nova-type music piped in, and fashionable shoppers everywhere, in the corridors, on the escalators and elevators, and in the shops themselves. I first pored over the Brazilian section of a bookstore and found one book of poems by an 18th-century figure whose work sounded quite good, but I decided to pass on it, as well as several volumes by Carlos Drummond de Andrade, since they did not include his "An Ox Looks at Man," which I had read in English translation:

> They are more delicate even than shrubs and they run
> and run from one side to the other, always forgetting
> something. Surely they lack I don't know what
> basic ingredient, though they present themselves
> as noble or serious, at times. Oh, terribly serious,
> even tragic. Poor things, one would say that they hear
> neither the song of the air nor the secrets of hay….

Mostly I was looking for collections by younger poets like João

Cabral Melo Neto, whose work I had also read in English, like his "The Emptiness of Man": "the emptiness of man is more like fullness / in swollen things which keep on swelling, / the way a sack must feel / that is being filled, or any sack at all."

Continuing my search for record shops, I finally located one, but it had nothing of what I had hoped to find. Just as I was giving up, I came across another shop and there I found a CD of Ernesto Nazareth's piano music, coupled with Darius Milhaud's *Saudades do Brasil* (Longings for Brazil). Before our trip I had known that in composing his work, *Le Boeuf Sur le Toit,* Milhaud had made use in it of Nazareth's music, including his wonderful "Brejeiro" and "Escorregandos." Not buying this CD at the time, I returned later with Elisa and bought it, as well as a recording of early music from the period of Gregorian chant and Monteverdi, as a birthday gift for María.

January 12th was the day my devoted mate of 32 years, my Beauty, entered the world in Ovalle in the "little north" of Chile. Our being in Brazil took me back to that twelfth day of the month in which María's mother had given birth to her second girlchild, and how now we were here in Jundiaí shortly before the birth of our second grandchild. We had hoped to witness the arrival of Annabella, but the doctor had extended the due date only after we had purchased our plane tickets; even so, we would not have been able to delay our return trip because we both had to be back at work in the week to come. At least we had been with Elisa during the final days of her pregnancy and could celebrate her mother's birthday near the time of our daughter's delivery. Never knowing quite what to give María as a gift, I had been relieved to find the CD with the kind of early music that she loves so well. Also, in asking Elisa what she would suggest, I learned that Beauty had seen a blue and white plate at a shop in Jundiaí that she very much wanted but thought too expensive. This would be perfect and would add a Brazilian piece to her collection of blue and white china.

Included in María's blue-and-white collection is her own mother's set of china made in Japan and one piece made in England by Spoad, the latter bought on our first trip to Britain in 1996. I had also brought her a plate from my trip to Spain in 1989. This new addition features in the center of the plate a lake among hills, a sailboat, and above it in the foreground a tree branch. Around the edge of the plate are flowers and on the very edge a design of tiny white arches with blue inside of each. The firm on the back is given as FAIART, a registered brand. The delicate shades of blue—light to dark—and the variety of flower shapes are so soothing to the eye. More than for eating on, such plates—imitated by the English from the Chinese—are for contemplation, like Keats' Greek urn; their timeless scenes evoke tranquil reflections on the beauties of nature and the serenity of the person steering the boat in view of a towered house on the lake shore, where the routine of daily life goes on unseen but easily imagined as essentially the same in every age. The plate also called up the journey of Marco Polo who married east and west, if only through mercantile exchange, just as María and I have wedded Latin and Anglo lives through an exchange of vows, our love blending the blood lines of Chile, Texas, Brazil, and Mexico, the last from our son's marriage and offspring.

During her birthday, María went right on sewing on the baby's protective bed pad that would serve as a guard against her bumping her head on the wooden slats. She also finished a diaper bag that would hang on the wall, with a tasteful pink trim at the top. While sitting for most of the day at the Singer sewing machine, she also managed to entertain Isabella, asking her why her beloved Maine coon cat Tigger had not phoned from Texas to wish her a happy birthday. Isabella replied that he could not, and when María wanted to know why, she said because he was a cat. María insisted that surely he could dial the telephone with his paw, but Isabella would not buy it, repeating that he could not because he was a cat. Meanwhile, in the expected baby's room, the two women continued decorating the walls with a picket fence, blue birds in the branches of a tree with oak-looking leaves, and a penciled outline for the rabbit family to be painted under the tree limbs. I spoke with the older woman, Valderez, who revealed that she was originally from Recife in the far north, where it is hot year around. She thought it was a beautiful area, settled by the Portuguese and also the Dutch.

After a buffet lunch at our favorite spot, we all walked to the area of Jundiaí's Municipal theatre, Polytheatrum, a white building with no posters or signs anywhere on its bright front wall. We were looking for the city library so that I could check on a few facts relating to Brazilian poetry, but we found its pale-blue building closed, to be reopened on the 15th. People inside the front door stared at us and then a man came out and explained that they were installing computers and doing some renovation work. As we walked back to Newton's car, he observed that his own native city of Anapolis is much lusher than Jundiaí. He and everyone else recommended that we see other parts of Brazil, and of course we would have liked to, but time and money always impose their limitations. Nonetheless, in so few days, I felt that we had experienced much of this vast and varied country, its language, culture, and quotidian life.

In the evening we celebrated María's 55th birthday, but not with cake and ice cream, since her diet did not allow for eggs, dairy products, or sugar. Instead, we had fruit cocktail, after which she opened her gifts. Elisa and Newton gave her a lovely gold necklace with a mounted pearl hanging from the chain. Afterwards, Robson came by to show off his bound dissertation. He took great delight in explaining how he had come up with an equation to measure the volume and pressure of water and an icing and de-icing solution (as I understood it) for the preservation of islets in human cells in the treatment of diabetes. His graphs with curves for the time it takes for the solution to penetrate the interior of a cell and for it to return to a certain volume and size were printed on slick paper with vivid colors that made following the changes in the cell quite clear and fascinating. Although I could not understand the equations or the many concepts from physics, physiology, and chemistry, I found the project impressive and the stages of the experiments stimulating to observe. Nevertheless, I could not imagine dedicating so much of my time to such a field of study. As ever, I prefer to spend hours and days on the vocabulary of *Beowulf*, the figures of speech of every literature in every epoch, the soliloquies of Shakespeare, rather than on the mathematics, modeling, and Bond Graphs of utilitarian science and biomedical applications of engineering. I would rather have talked with Robson's wife about Campinas and Almeida, but she did not come along, having just learned that she too was expecting, which depressed her since she did not want to have a child before she finished her law degree. Robson, however, wanted to be a father before he was too old and set in his ways. This happy birthday ended, then, on something of a lower note, but I could still be more than thankful for my Beauty and my very patient daughter, who gives so much quality time and attention to Isabella, both of them so generous, considerate, and full of love. Even though I remain too selfish to deserve them, I yet take endless pride in their being "mine."

For several days, María had been saying that on our return to Texas she feared that she would suffer from withdrawal symptoms. I too would miss the carefree, idyllic life that we had been leading in Jundiaí. Mostly, she was referring to the washing, straightening up, and making of beds, and especially the ironing that here had all been done by Marinalva. María had even told Elisa that she thought that she would have to take the maid back home with us. Elisa and Newton both insisted that she had been on her best behavior with us, that normally she was nasty to visitors. But we had seen nothing of that side of poor Marinalva. With her blonde streaks of hair in the back, her strange blue-gray eyes, and her penetrating but rather pretty look of inquisitiveness when we attempted to speak to her in our version of Spanish-Portuguese, she had made our stay so very pleasant, both by her unfamiliar, almost exotic presence and her untiring labor that had relieved us of so many chores and worries. We had felt sorry for her, not only because she had to work so hard while we relaxed (although María had toiled away on many a sewing project for Elisa and her girls) but also because she had a sore left hand, for which Elisa bought her a special glove and had her go to the doctor for treatment. Each morning Marinalva had prepared fresh-squeezed and blended juice—my favorite the pineapple and carrot, so delicious to see and drink, so nutritious, and so good they say for the eyes. She was always sweet to Isabella, and when she said her name and talked with her it was a special treat to hear her tender, musical voice.

Already I could foresee that I would miss rising late to a rooster's insistent crow, opening the sliding doors to the refreshing outside air (to which María and I had no allergic reactions as we do have to Austin's molds and cedar spores), with the city spread out below, its sounds of traffic going to work, and the three-note phrase—mid-range, high, and low—played by the gas man announcing his coming with fuel for sale. More than anything I knew that I would miss the leisure to read and write, aside from being with our daughter, our granddaughter, and, in a way, the unknown grandchild to come, and would even long for the struggle to learn the language (*ter saudades da luta*). Also, the casual dress and seemingly unhurried manner of the people had become for me quite appealing.

On the 13th, Elisa took us out to a restaurant called Concerto, in the same block with the Municipal Theatre. It had been closed on María's birthday, and so Elisa had made reservations for the following evening. The owner, in a white t-shirt with "Universal Road Wear" printed in black, was a young fellow with something of a bulging gut, a day or two-day old unshaven face, baggy black pants, and a friendly, open look. The restaurant, on the other hand, was elegant, furnished with fine furniture and at the entrance black-and-white checkered marble walls, on one of which was a gold-metal lion's head with flame-like mane, whiskers, a large bulbous nose, and an open mouth from which water poured into a triangular basin. White marble columns between two dining areas, the larger with a small bar, and with windowpanes with frosted glass into which "Concert" and some floral designs had been etched, all gave the place a formal feel, while the owner and a heavy-set, white-bearded man at the bar lent the restaurant a very relaxed atmosphere. Our waiter, who we learned was in training and therefore unsure of himself, had on a green apron with "Concert" printed in white. His dress was more proper in form than the owner's and more in keeping with the bronze Greek busts on a mahogany-looking piano and the large white male bust of a Greek figure on a table behind the bartender. The delicious food was served on blue-and-white china made in England and described on the back as microwave safe. Hanging on one wall was the scene of an English gentleman pictured riding to hounds in his red hunting jacket and blowing a horn; the depiction had been printed in London on the Strand in 1879. A gray, cast-iron heater for keeping coffee or other beverages warm sat on the floor below the framed picture, with above it a wooden ceiling and chandelier, and to its side casement doors with stained-glass panes. At the back of the establishment, outside the door to the kitchen, shelves held tall boxes of various liquors above and cut-glass and pink-and-white china below. The second floor featured a fireplace and more fine wooden tables and chairs with ivory-colored, woven seat bottoms. On the wall up a curved staircase, prints of sailing ships also appeared to be of English origin. We learned from the young owner that the restaurant had been his family home, which he had converted into the restaurant. It appeared to me that he had kept the house much as it must have been when he lived in it as a boy.

Elisa had discovered Concert when she and Newton first attended a function at the Polytheatrum. On going to a local ballet school to see if she would like to start taking classes again, she heard that another school was having its year-end performance at the Polytheatrum, and so she phoned for information on the date and cost. Leaving Isabella with a babysitter, she and Newton went to watch the students' presentation and thought it quite well done. Afterwards they noticed Concert and went in for a late meal, which they both found delicious. The night that we all ate at the restaurant, María had her usual vegetable plate—prepared especially for her on Elisa's having ordered it beforehand—and I had a luscious ricotta with spinach pasta and mushrooms topped with a rich cheese sauce, while Elisa and Newton ordered a type of chicken-fried steak with broccoli and rice.

In my mind I kept comparing Concert with "our" Vida Natural. Although the atmosphere and décor were entirely different, the food in both was wonderful, and just as the owner of Concert was quite informal in dress, so too the proprietor of Vida Natural always wore blue jeans, a white jersey-type shirt, and a two- or three-day growth of his black facial hair. Instead of signs reading "Eat all you want but don't waste it" and "Get more for your money by buying ten meals at a time," as seen at Vida Natural, Concert displayed English nineteenth-century prints and Greek sculpture. The lighting in Concert for night-time dining was from soft, candle-like lamps and shades, whereas Vida Natural was only open until two in the afternoon and was therefore flooded with natural sunlight. In contrast to the frosted panes on the windows and the stained glass on the casements of Concert, Vida Natural had raised windows letting in the sounds of traffic and the fresh noonday air. The only touch of color or patterned design at Vida Natural was its beaded type of curtain hanging in the doorway to the kitchen, with its round brown beads and four- or five-inch lengths of unpainted cane, the beads forming diamond shapes among the canes hanging straight down on the strings that held both beads and cut-up poles. Which shall I remember more? I suspect that Vida Natural will take the memory cake, if only for the word *porém*, meaning "but," in the sign "Eat all you want but don't waste it." For while Concert appropriately piped in classical music, from Vivaldi to Tchaikovsky's *Romeo and Juliet* and his *Nutcracker* themes, only Vida Natural's buffet type of café furnished me, through that Portuguese conjunction, with a link to the longest and greatest early English poem, as I will explain in this next paragraph.

At the same time that I had bought the two books by Almeida, I had also picked up a copy of *Beowulf* in Portuguese. The first translation ever in the Brazilian language, the edition that I purchased was published in São Paulo in 1992. Ary Gonzalez Galvão, the translator with the same first name as Newton's uncle, declares in his introduction that the 8th-century *Beowulf* is "the oldest anonymous epic in a modern European language." In discussing the possible background of the poet and his likely use of poetic license to relate events from a time remote even to his own, the translator twice employs *porém*, meaning, as I can understand the word in context, either "but" or "yet" or "however" or "nonetheless." Any of those meanings works well for the sign at Vida Natural. Perhaps, I thought, I would soon forget the connection between the conjunction and the vegetarian buffet, but for the time being it had brought vividly to mind one of my favorite English works of literature with its alliterative tale of the eponymous hero grappling bare-handed with Grendel in Hrothgar's mead hall at Heorot.

Reading that marvelous work in Portuguese could not match the experience of going through the epic word-by-word in the original Old English, which I had done in about 1972. Although I had lost the ability to read the poem in the original, I had had

Beowulf in Portuguese translation.

an opportunity to teach it in a modern translation every semester that I had taught the English literature survey course. Buying the book in Portuguese seemed a whimsical thing to do, but already I had found my appreciation of the poem renewed and deepened by seeing it rendered in another language. When I will teach it on returning to Texas, I will mention the Portuguese text and its fairly recent appearance, along with a poem by the Irish poet, Seamus Heaney, which was published in October 1998 in *The New Yorker*. Heaney's poem contains his version of the digression in *Beowulf* concerning the murder of one brother by another and the great pain the father-king endures in condemning his remaining son to death, as required by the tribal law of blood retribution. In referring to Heaney's poem, which he wrote in response to Ted Hughes' last book, consisting of his letters to his wife Sylvia Plath, I will note how the retelling of the *Beowulf* digression is the most moving part of the Irish poet's poem and shows how alive this Old English epic is for the modern world. Likewise, I shall point out how Gonzalez Galvão believes that *Beowulf* is both a great literary work, deserving of a readership among Portuguese speakers, and a valuable social document. In this latter regard I will point out that the translator reveals that while the poem may be a work of the imagination, it is possible, *porém* (nonetheless), to trace historical parallels between characters in *Beowulf*, like lord Hygelac and even the hero himself, and actual, historical figures in the oral tradition of the Scandinavian and Anglo-Saxon worlds of the 6th century. All, in a way, brought to mind through a cafeteria-style eatery on the corner of Rua Senador Fonseca in Jundiaí.

The morning of the 14th I ran out of pages in the blank book that I had brought from Austin to record our trip, and so after breakfast I set out to buy a new one. María told me not to purchase something expensive with archival quality paper but just anything cheap to get by with, since our money was running out. My search took me up some of the same streets and retraced the same steps of our visit to the church of Our Lady of Exile and our evening at Concert, of which I snapped pictures as I went along. At the Americas *papelaria* (a combination paper products shop and bookstore), I found a spiral tablet for the unbelievably low price of

30 cents. Afterwards I stopped to ask the black vendor at the kiosk across from Vida Natural whether or not a new installment of the Moreira Lima recordings had arrived. In trying to understand when it might show up, I learned more clearly that the days of the work week—after Saturday and Sunday—are numbered as 2nd, 3rd, 4th, 5th, and 6th *féria* (weekdays). The fellow knew that the CDs came every fifteen days and suspected that the new installment would come the following week, but I told him that unfortunately we were leaving on Sunday.

Thoughts of our departure, as ever in such cases, brought mixed emotions. Even as I looked forward to getting back to the life we had left, I regretted leaving this other world with its distinct character and language. To take something of it back for friends, I continued on to the Russi grocery store, but it was out of the soap that I like so much—Phebo brand, a glycerine bar described on the wrapper of red, black, and yellow-gold as having the odor of roses. Walking on to Superbox, I found Phebo, but it was more expensive than at Russi, so I only bought five bars. I had already bought five of Savage, another brand, which was described as *Cravo de Índia*. The word *cravo*, meaning clove, is in the title of Brazilian writer Jorge Amado's novel, *Gabriela, Cravo e Canela*, but *cravo* can also mean "nail," just as in Spanish *clavo* means both "clove" and "nail" (of metal). For the first time I noticed that words with "r" in Portuguese would have "l" in Spanish, as in *praza* and *plaza* or *prazer* and *placer* (pleasure) or even *escravo* and *esclavo* (slave). Such similarity and difference in a single word can open up a whole world of "heretofore unrealized" meanings, as in that William Carlos Williams phrase in his poem "The Descent." I preferred the smell of Phebo, which is even "wilder" than that of Savage, but I thought that the name of the latter would evoke for friends the "barbaric" existence that we had experienced in "primitive" Jundiaí. In addition to their exotic aromas, both brands are colored a deep brown that, for some reason, recalled for me the famous carnival-time movie, *Black Orpheus*, which I had seen in Austin in about 1960 at the then Texas Theater. I don't recall, but perhaps I thought of Orpheus as I sniffed the bar of Phebo (Titaness mother of Leto and grandmother of Apollo and Artemis), since both names are part of Greek mythology, and anyone interested in literature cannot but think of such associations.

Back at the apartment it was clear that we were wearing out our welcome. Newton was growing edgy, worrying about his finances, since the Brazilian currency had been devalued by eight percent against the dollar. The cost of the paid vacation for the maid, who would be going to see her parents in Bahia, two days away by bus, and the expense of having the baby's room decorated with Mopsy and a naughty Peter Rabbit, were weighing on our son-in-law's mind and making him irritable. He exploded when he saw Marinalva climb on top of the washing machine in order to hang clothes from lines high overhead. Elisa tried to explain that she had permitted this as the only way to manage to dry the laundry, and that she did not think it would harm the heavy machine since the maid was small and light. María got into the discussion and asked Newton if he knew the folktale of "The Man Who Tied the Cow on the Roof." She told him how the man criticized the wife's way of running the house, so she proposed that he stay home and she would go to work in the fields. When the wife returns, there is no food ready or it's burned, their baby has not been fed or changed, and thinking it was too far to take the cow to the pasture the husband tied it to graze on the sod roof, but it had fallen off and he and the baby were pulled up the chimney because he had tied one end of a rope to the cow and the other to himself while he was holding the child in his arms.

Of course, whenever Newton misbehaved, I came in for criticism too, since it made María remember the many stupid things of the same nature that I had said about her running the house and how when I had been left in charge I had managed things so poorly. She also recalled how horrible it had been in Mexico when she had to deal with the laundry. We had no dryer, just as Newton and Elisa did not, because theirs could not be hooked up, since Newton—with his master's degree in electrical engineering—had not foreseen the problem with a difference in voltage between their dryer made in the U.S. and the current used in Brazil. Newton began to exaggerate and to make outrageous predictions of gloom and doom, just as I have always done, which has infuriated María and made her declare that all men are such babies, the weaker sex, and insensitive brutes. I plead guilty, but I know that doing so will not be enough unless I change. I reminded Newton of "marriage math" and the fact that such expenditures as the cost of home decoration for satisfying the wife cannot be calculated like regular finances, but he was in no mood for humor. I too find it virtually impossible to laugh at myself in the middle of what seems an economic crisis, while later on I can see how as usual I blew the whole matter completely out of proportion and made the family suffer from fear that, as María says, "the wolf is at the door."

At the time that María retold the Norwegian tale of the cow on the roof, I thought the story was the source of Milhaud's musical composition, *Le Boeuf sur la toit* (*The Ox on the Roof*), but I was wrong, since it is the name of an imaginary bar created by Jean Cocteau, who wrote a pantomime on which Milhaud based his score. The French composer had lived in Brazil from 1917 to 1919 as an aide to poet Paul Claudel, who was the French ambassador to the country. As mentioned earlier, Milhaud's *Saudades do Brasil* was influenced by Nazareth's music, with *saudades do* meaning "longings for" or "nostalgia for." To me, Milhaud's *La Créacion du monde*, his 1923 jazz-influenced work, had always been my favorite jazz-classical composition, along with Gershwin's jazz-infused classical works like his *Rhapsody in Blue*, *An American in Paris*, and *Concerto in F for Piano and Orchestra*. In high school I had learned that Pete Rugolo, the jazz composer-arranger mentioned earlier in connection with the music of the Jimmie Lunceford Orchestra, and Dave Brubeck, the popular jazz pianist of the mid to late 1950s, had both studied with Milhaud, but it was the connection between the composer and Brazil that came to mind while in Jundiaí and made me, even before we departed, long for and nostalgic about the country that had produced such evocative music, inspiring Milhaud to write two of his most memorable works, apart from his wonderful *La Créacion du monde*.

In the evening, when the husband of a Chilean came for supper, there was much discussion of the current Brazilian attempt to manage its monetary affairs. Carlos Ruotolo is married to Lucía D'Albuquerque, a friend of our Chilean friend Irene Rostagno, who had done her Ph.D. in American Studies at UT-Austin. I was immediately reminded that Irene had written her dissertation in part on the publication in English translation of such Brazilian authors as Jorge Amado, João Guimaraes Rosa, Clarice Lispector, and Gilberto Freyre. This, in turn, called to mind Freyre's *The Masters and the Slaves* of 1933, a revolutionary study in which he extolls black culture and identifies Brazil as a country receptive to racial differences. Freyre had been educated from age 18 at Baylor University in Waco, Texas, and took his master's degree at Columbia University. In my *Civilization and Barbarism: A Guide to the Teaching of Latin American Literature* of 1979, I quote from Freyre's essay "The Civilization of Man Sitting," which later influenced my poem "The Historian Has Lost His Chair" in my *Backtracking* collection. As part of Irene's dissertation, she wrote, at my suggestion, an essay on Freyre and the other three Brazilian authors for an issue of *The Library Chronicle* when I was editing the journal at UT's Harry Ransom Center. In developing the topic of her dissertation, Irene had worked in the HRC's archive of Alfred A. and Blanche Knopf, publishers of all four of those Brazilian writers.

Carlos had come alone for supper because his wife Lucía was in Chile at the time. A graduate of the University of Missouri's doctoral program in journalism, Carlos spoke excellent English, which he switched to from the Spanish that we were speaking at first. Short, with a beard and glasses, a hearty laugh, and an up-to-date knowledge of Brazilian commerce, he entertained us all and seemed very at ease with himself and us. He had met our son Darío in Chile and the two had hit if off famously, so he asked how Darío was and what he was doing and sent his best regards. At the meal Carlos told how he had missed Brazilian beans while in Missouri, and he recounted how he had met his wife through a student from England who came to the States to study British literature and who also longed for her country's beans. I found such bean *saudades* as strange as the English student studying her own literary tradition at a university in the States. In any case, Carlos and Penelope, the English student, had arranged to fix beans for some of their friends at her apartment and Lucía and Carlos met and married as a consequence. Needless to say, this was yet another twist in the saga of the Brazilian's staple food.

In addition to discussing his dissertation topic, which was newspaper readers in Brazil, Carlos mentioned a trip that he had made to Berlin where he could not communicate with East German taxi drivers because, aside from German, they only spoke Russian or Polish. Mostly he explained that although he had been the first professor of journalism at his Brazilian university, he had gotten out of full-time teaching and was now only an adjunct professor, working primarily as an analyst of buying patterns for shopping centers and related enterprises. He found the Brazilian system of teaching journalism wrongheaded, since, unlike in the U.S., students majoring in journalism began from the first year to study journalistic techniques instead of receiving in the first two years a broad education and only after that specializing in journalism the final two years. He also talked about an approach to journalism that a prominent figure in the field at UT-Austin had developed, which he called "agenda setting." This approach took the view that newspapers and other media do not change either readers' or viewers' points of view but only bring to their attention issues to which they apply their pre-set perspectives. This "approach" was to me only too familiar in the realm of politics.

Carlos's ideas stirred Newton to ask him what he thought about the current economic situation in Brazil and later why he thought that he, Newton, could not place articles on National Instruments, his Austin company, in Brazilian magazines devoted to engineering technology. According to Carlos, the State of Minas Gerais had defaulted on its loan payments to foreign banks and to the Brazilian central government, which had prompted a rather severe devaluation of the country's currency. Carlos felt that probably the adjustment in the value of the *reai* would eventually pay off for Brazil, since it had strong reserves and a commitment for support from the U.S. and Europe. As to the magazines, he recommended that Newton try different angles in an attempt to interest the editors in news about National Instruments. He encouraged him to keep trying, which Newton accepted as good advice. They then spoke for a time in Portuguese and I was able to follow their conversation fairly well, but just as it seemed that I was doing better with understanding the spoken language, our time to leave was soon arriving and my lessons would unfortunately be coming to an end.

At bedtime I continued where I had left off in the Portuguese version of *Beowulf*. Once again I came upon the motif of limits that had arisen from time to time throughout the writing of these travel notes. This occurred when I read the translator's comment that (in my own translation) "It is in these instances of great decisions and of great pride in the codes of honor that Beowulf is presented in all the splendor of a hero who transcends the limits of the common man." (I should note that it is easier for me to read Portuguese when it pertains to literature, since the language or terminology used in discussing it is so familiar to me; in addition, my Spanish is a significant aid in reading Portuguese.) Perhaps I have placed too much emphasis on the idea of limitations or have paid too much attention to it when it has occurred to me, but it has always been a topic of interest, and is, in fact, the theme of my essay entitled "Place," written in Chile in 1966 and included in my collection of essays and book reviews, *On a High Horse: Views Mostly of Latin American & Texan Poetry*.

María, meanwhile, dedicated herself to our everyday needs, the creature comforts that made the present more pleasant and would make the baby's arrival as well. She had recovered the car seat used by Isabella that she had outgrown and would be taken over by Annabella—we had brought with us a new, larger one for Miss Issa. For supper, María had prepared a meat loaf, even though she had eaten none of it herself, both because of her diet and because she is happy no longer to consume animal products. The butcher failed to grind the steaks and so I was asked to do them in a grinder that Newton had found thrown away by a neighbor. As María watched the ground meat drop into a bowl in worm-like strings, she revealed, for the first time, how much raw meat always sickened her. This made me all the more inclined to join her in sticking to fruits and vegetables and grains. Yes, we men can be insensitive to what women have to put up with, while we look away to "higher" aims, more "heroic" feats of skill, courage, and derring-do. Such thoughts also reminded me how little Marinalva earned for all her work: 185 *reais* per month, some $150 in U.S. dollars.

It was then that I was also put in mind of an article on folk poetry that I had read in a publication that Newton bought in the Americas *papelaria*, which I forgot to mention in writing about the day on which he discovered it—the 13th I think it was. A thin paperback, the publication contains the work of the Academia Jundiaiense de Letras, which appears to be something like writings by members of the Poetry Society in the U.S. The poems by Jundiaí residents proved, as I had suspected, that in fact there were writers in the city, and some of the poetry struck me as artful in construction, even though the themes seemed rather sentimental. One sonnet entitled "Certainty," by Domingos Pauliélo, demonstrated a skillful handling of the form, as did a piece in rhyming quatrains entitled "Friend" by Olga de Brito. A poem on the 1932 conflict between the State of São Paulo and the rest of Brazil and a piece on tedium were likewise quite competent, both by Aristides Prado, whose line "Oscila entre o ser ou não ser" alludes to Hamlet's famous "to be or not to be" speech and plays effectively with sounds in the phrase "um guru botocudo" (meaning perhaps a mixture of an oriental guru and a Brazilian medicine man), since the "o" at the end of the word "botocudo" is pronounced in Portuguese like the letter "u" in "guru." The conflict between São Paulo and the rest of Brazil was over the coup d'état of Getúlio Vargas and the country's Constitution. The State lost the war but many of its demands were later met by Vargas; it was the last major armed conflict occurring in the history of Brazil.

The article in the publication that I found most meaningful was on folk poetry related to the May 13th anniversary in Brazil of the 1888 abolition of slavery. Of special interest were the article's colorful passages taken from a sung dialogue between a white and a black prisoner in the penitentiary at Recife, the city, incidentally, where Gilberto Freyre was born in 1900. Improvising on the theme of racism, the black tells the white that although the singer is black, he smells good, while the white needs to take a bath before he sings with him. The white responds that he does not know what the black was before May 13th, 1888, but now the white is the color of silver and the black is vulture-colored. The rhymes are witty, the humor cutting, and the description rich in metaphor. The author of the article points out that even though blacks were illiterate, they could go directly to the heart of a problem in their songs, as when an ex-slave sang that he was a slave and yet (*porém* again) he had worth and a woman had guided him to an education, while his antagonist, he implies, was born free but has done nothing to lift himself up through study. Limitations overcome, *porém*, and poetry right here in Jundiaí, what more can I say? Well, now that I think of it, the folk poem reminds me of William Blake's "The Little Black Boy," who proves more loving than the little white boy since the black boy can take the rays of God's love, while the white needs to be shaded from them by the black.

    Rain during the night continued into the day of the 15th. In the morning I wrote, and at lunch time we were taken by car to Vida Natural for the final meal. A neighbor in the apartment building drove us, since Newton had gone to São Paulo to pick up his mother, who was flying from Anapolis to see us off and to stay with Elisa during her delivery. Maria do Carmo and Newton arrived at the vegetarian buffet just as we were beginning to eat. After lunch, I walked to the public library while the others returned to the apartment for a nap. Even though for days the reopening of the library had been announced at the gate, when I reached the front steps I was met by a lady who said the renovation work had not been completed and the library remained closed. I went back by way of Superbox and picked up some more bars of Phebo and a pound of Brazilian coffee for my mother. At the apartment everyone was taking a nap, so I sat in my grandmother's chair, propped my feet on the foot stool, and shut my eyes for a while. Then Elisa's friend Giovana rang the doorbell and that was the end of my rest. Soon everyone awoke from a nap and we went to see Isabella's nursery school, which had acquired a new plastic play set with a slide, tubes to crawl through, and various levels to climb on. One of the teachers gave us a tour of the facilities, showing us Isabella's classroom, the dining area, art room, and play store. For some reason I had gotten up in the morning in a somewhat foul mood, and the tour only added to my impatience with everything connected with my granddaughter.

    That morning Elisa had asked me to sit with Isabella while she painted with a brush on some sheets of paper spread out on the floor. I was in the middle of writing and was not wanting to be interrupted, but got up and went to Miss Issa's play area next to the kitchen. I tried to convince her to paint with more than one color, but she insisted on only using red. She then began to paint her hands, brushing her fingers one by one. I watched, then told her that she would have to wash her hands before she touched anything. When she finished, I carried her to the bathroom and washed her hands, after which she returned to paint some more and I went back to my writing. Elisa came to complain that I should spend more time with her since we were leaving the next day, so I joined Isabella again. She said that she was painting a picture for me to take to Texas, after she had not wanted to give me one the day before. I was angry at myself for being so uninterested and impatient, but this would go on for the rest of the day without my being able to control my childishness.

On our coming back from the Baby Center, Maria do Carmo showed me a book that she had brought for me from Anapolis. Knowing of my love of literature, she wanted to introduce me to the poetry of Cora Coralina, a poet from the State of Goiás whom she had known personally. Since Coralina had not gotten past the third grade in school, she was self-educated, yet (*porém*) her work was recognized widely. A letter from Carlos Drummond de Andrade was printed on the back of the volume of her poems, entitled *Dos Becos de Goiás e Estórias Mais* (Two Alleyways of Goiás and Other Stories). One of her poems was a "Prayer to Corn," which because of its subject matter reminded me immediately of Joel Barlow's "The Hasty Pudding," which, as I have said elsewhere, is, along with Pope's "The Rape of the Lock," my favorite mock epic. In Coralina's introduction to an even longer poem entitled "Poem of Corn," she has the humble plant speak, as Barlow does, of corn not being made into a type of universal bread, of its not belonging to a hierarchy of wheat, but rather of being the food of those who work the land, and if not noble like wheat, it feeds country people and beasts of burden. Also, in the longer work, Coralina writes that corn is the "calendar, the astronomy [astrology?] of the laborer." In addition to these pieces on corn, the Goiás poet wrote on compost, as did Whitman, in her poem entitled "For My

Visitor Eduardo Melcher Filho." She observes that the repulsive, rejected organic material will turn into (or provide) "the perfumed taste of a strawberry ice cream." Other poems concern creatures like the vulture and a bird called "Bem-te-vi" (I saw you well), while others speak of poetry and the poet. The corn poems meant more to me, partly because Maria do Carmo also brought with her a popular Brazilian food made from this native American plant, a dish called *pamonha*. Similar in appearance and consistency to the Mexican *tamal* (tamale), it is two-or-three times larger, cooked with vegetable oil rather than lard, has a bit of cheese at its center, and is wrapped like the tamale in corn shucks. We had seen *pamonha* advertised along the highways at small eating places, but Elisa and Newton had said that the *pamonha* in Jundiaí could not compare with the *pamonha* in Anapolis. It is certainly the most delicious form of corn-based food that I have ever eaten.

In the evening we were invited to a kind of farewell party at the apartment of Valdereza, her husband, and son. They lived on the nineteenth floor of a twenty-storey building overlooking the plaza where the bus station is located, only a half-dozen blocks from Elisa's apartment building. We already knew Valdereza and Helena, the two decorators of the baby's room, but we were to meet Helena's mother, Carmen, who played the piano, and a friend who accompanied her on violin, as well as their spouses. Carmen had set up her electric keyboard with every imaginable type of programmed sound: of guitar, flute, bandeon, Latin rhythms, etc. Edgar, the violinist, whose instrument was made in Cremona around 1910 (as I understood him to say), was quite enthusiastic about playing and never seemed to tire, even though he was perspiring through his shirt. First performing tunes from movies, like *Evita*, Charlie Chaplin's theme from *Limelight*, and *The Scent of a Woman* (the film in which a blind Al Pacino dances a tango with Gabrielle Anwar), the two musicians later played a variety of pieces from Brazil, Argentina, and Spain.

When the pair stopped for a wonderful meal, but before it was served, I asked Carmen if she would play something by Nazareth, and she obliged by giving us his "Odeon," which she performed beautifully in the composer's uniquely lilting style. Everyone enjoyed the performances by the two, but at times I was distracted by Isabella's flinging herself on a couch next to a low table with, on top of it, many fragile pieces of glassware. Although I only told her to calm down, Elisa knew that I was unhappy and put out. I suppose I am too uptight around small children; I was the same when Elisa and Darío were young. Now I enjoy so much their company, even though María criticizes me for ignoring them and going off to write or listen to music when they come to the house to visit. I can never excuse myself on this count or many others. In a way I spoiled the party with my selfishness; otherwise, the evening to me was most entertaining and the people could not have been more gracious and attentive. To paraphrase Nicanor Parra, "Poetry had acquitted itself well / I had conducted myself horribly."

Following a full plate of rice with a sauce made with cashews and shrimp, a turkey breast type of casserole, and a serving of a mix of eggplant, tomato, onion, and other cooked vegetables, we were treated to two desserts, one with cooked grapes and stringed egg yolks and the other a kind of pie of passion fruit. Afterwards, the two musicians played again, beginning with "Jalousie" and continuing with "La Cumparsita," "A Media luz," "Adiós, pampa mía," and other Argentine tangos that María's mother so loved to listen and dance to. Once the duo had stopped for the night, fearing the neighbors might start to resent their playing so late, I reminded Carmen that they had not done a piece by a Jundiaí composer whom she had mentioned to me earlier. She immediately plugged in her keyboard and played José Bovolento's "Valsa," which was a popular type of song with a nice progression from G minor to C minor, as I could see from Carmen's chord notations on the sheet music. She then asked if I would like to hear a piece of her own, and I replied "by all means." As it turned out, I found her piece, "Sonhar…," even more to my liking than Bovolento's waltz. One section featured staccatoed pairs of descending quarter notes, and the main melody was quite lovely.

In addition to being entertained by the music, I had been able to ask about some of the poets in the Jundiaí selection in Newton's publication, which I had brought along to the party. The violinist knew Olga de Brito, guessing that she was between 55 and 60 years of age. Carmen was a good friend of Mercedes Cruañes, whose work was not among the poems that had leaped out at me when I looked through the selection, and on reading her poetry later I would not find it of much interest. I did regret not having the time to meet the poets and see more of their work. Everyone hoped that we would return to Jundiaí and if we did they would invite some of the poets for another party. They had insisted all evening that I play the piano, and when we were waiting to leave, Carmen pressed me again. I finally agreed and tried the Bach piece that I had been working on but lost my way after a few bars and gave up, wishing that I had not gone along with Carmen's request. But all in all, it was a memorable farewell, though bittersweet, as is any such parting from those of whom we have grown fond.

Some of my impatience with Isabella stemmed from the little time remaining. Although I should have been enjoying her while I could, I was more concerned that I was not being left alone to write down my thoughts and impressions of the last few days. María was already pushing me to think about packing and straightening up the room where we had slept on the floor on Elisa's mattress (which had felt good to María's back) and making it ready for Marinalva to clean and prepare for Maria do Carmo. After I had finished some chores in preparation for driving to São Paulo in the evening, I sat down on the 16th hoping to finish Erenberg's book on Swing, but Isabella found me in the bedroom and climbed into my lap. I set the book aside and she got up in my face and stared deeply into my eyes and then began pulling my beard. She would pull softly and then as hard as she could, watching my reaction. It was difficult to fathom her thoughts. Was she letting me know that she knew that I had not paid enough attention to her? Or was this her way of showing affection? She began to jump from the chair that I was sitting in onto the mattress on the floor, and then to crawl back in my lap, singing each time part of a song in Spanish. The words of the song I have already forgotten but knew them from María having sung them to Elisa when she was a young girl. It was not the song that María had taught her on this trip, "No More Monkeys Jumping on the Bed," which would have been more fitting! Now that I think about it, the song may have been Isabella's favorite:

"*Por un pepino, por un tomate, por una taza de chocolate*" (For a cucumber, for a tomato, for a cup of chocolate).

At lunchtime, when Isabella wanted María to bring her some water, María asked her "What should you say?" but Issa refused to say "please," so María said that she would not give her any. She explained to our granddaughter that people will do anything for you if you say please. But Isabella persisted in not practicing the politeness that her grandmother had tried to instill in her. Elisa wanted us to have a good influence on Isabella and was sorry that we could not be with her more. Already she was speaking more English with us, although, as María noted, with an accent that she had not had when we had last seen her nine months before. Elisa and Newton blamed the English teacher at the Baby Center who, they said, mispronounced so many words. I was unsure if I had had any positive effect on Miss Issa. At lunch, she did finally say "please" to María and later said "thank you," so everyone applauded. When she was about a year and a half, I was the one who had gotten her to go to sleep when she would not do so for Newton or Elisa. I then called myself the Enforcer, but now at almost three Isabella was being enforced in terms of politeness by María. Also, her grandmother had helped her learn to whistle each time we rode down on the elevator. Her parents would whistle "Pop Goes the Weasel" and Isabella would try to whistle too. María kept encouraging her, and even tried to show her how to whistle with fingers in the sides of her mouth (which María can do so loudly that she can even stop a cab on a dime), and on our last day Isabella finally managed a soft but distinct whistle.

Just as this last day in Jundiaí saw Isabella learn to whistle, it also brought completion to another process. Valderez and Helena at last concluded their decoration of Annabella's room. After adding butterflies to the wall with the rabbit family and the wall with the picket fence, as well as the final flowers on the grass and along the fence, the two artists packed up their brushes while we were packing our bags. María was so pleased that we could see the finished product, which she photographed, as well as her own needlework for the baby bed. The two ladies signed their names in one corner and then photographed their artwork for future use in advertising their services. Witnessing the progress of their work had added much to our visit. Not only had both women grown on us, but Valderez had made it possible for me to know more of life in Jundiaí and had even made me aware in a small way of Recife's history. The night before, at her home, I had shown her the songs by prisoners at the city's penitentiary and she informed me that the institution had been converted into a fine cultural center. As I read in the Erenberg book, I remembered the Recife singer in the article on folk poetry who reversed "the racial expectations of who was in charge," just as Erenberg points out that Charlie Parker "used aggressive put-ons, publicly imitating whites with a variety of roles and accents," in order to counter the mockery of white minstrelsy and other forms of white prejudice and stereotyping. When I first heard Valderez speaking and saw her imitative artwork, I was not much interested in her, and because of my doing a "superior dance"—contrasting in my mind stencils of pop culture with the water lilies of Monet—I almost missed out on learning through her more about Brazil. The lessons that I had learned on the trip were many, and came from unlikely sources or from ones that I would not have suspected: among others, our granddaughter, a home decorator, a vegetarian café, a "minor" poet, a newsstand selling a collection of CDs produced by, of all things, a governmental agency.

Waiting for the hour when we would leave for the airport, I asked Maria do Carmo if she knew anything about Guilherme de Almeida. Earlier she had asked me if we had visited Campinas, and I had said no, that we only drove as near as Itatiba. Her question then reminded me of Almeida, and so I asked if she knew of him since he was from Campinas, but she had not heard of the "Prince of Brazilian Poets." However, she did know of a famous opera composer from Campinas, by the name of Carlos Gomes, whose best-known work is entitled *O Guaraní*. This made me wish that I could look more closely into the cultural life of the area near Jundiaí, including Campinas.

Some of my impatience with Isabella came from my feeling that there was so much to find out about this one small part of Brazil and that no time remained to do so. Even though I was looking forward to returning to my routine in Texas, I was sorry to think that I would be losing a chance to dig more deeply into a world that each day revealed new and fascinating dimensions. Always when I leave Latin America I suffer a bit of culture shock. I find somehow that English has grown foreign to my ear, that its speakers are unreal, even when I have so many difficulties understanding Spanish as well as I would like, or comprehending even a bit of Portuguese. Knowing how limited my experience had been also frustrated me, and yet I realized that each person brings to another country on visiting it his or her own peculiar perspective on or special interest in its particular culture. My own views, of course, are so heavily slanted toward and even biased by my obsession with poetry and music that my view of Brazil had necessarily been colored and narrowed by those two, as it were, aesthetic blinders.

On the way to the airport, Newton again worried out loud about the Brazilian economy. The *reai* had taken another devaluation dip, and his buying power would be seriously affected. He praised the U.S. for its management systems, but I said that it seemed to me that Brazil would soon be a superpower, once it overcame its problems with political corruption and began to protect its resources. I mentioned the destruction of the rain forest, to which he responded that the government had laws in place to preserve its resources but no money to enforce them. He said that Japan had huge paper mills in the middle of the Amazon jungles but that the government could not regulate or control them. I was unclear how this worked, but he insisted that no one wanted to go into the area and keep watch on such industries. I admitted that my view was obviously uninformed and overly simplistic and let it go at that. How could I hope to understand such vast issues when I could hardly follow a grocer's conversation, much less comprehend how Brazil had become what it was, how it had changed, or where it was going. For certain I could see after three weeks that, to paraphrase Gertrude Stein, there was more here *here* than I had ever expected, or to fall back on Hamlet, that there is more to Brazil than I had dreamed of in my limited philosophy.

At the airport we discovered that the departure tax was more than we thought. We had held back from spending quite a few dollars, based on what we had been told, but not enough to cover the required amount. Fortunately, we were allowed to pay the tax with a credit card. This extra expense was a bit distressing, but nothing compared with seeing Elisa so saddened by our leaving. We had so wanted to be with her at the birth of Annabella, but it had not worked out. Elisa wept and told her mother that she adored her and thanked her for all the sewing that she had done for the baby. I told her how proud I was of her and she hugged me, kissed my cheek, and said that she loved me. Any show of affection always leaves me a bit embarrassed and speechless, even though it means so much to me to hear expressions of such deep feeling. Afterwards I just wanted to get on the plane, for it was painful to leave her behind. Isabella was indifferent and Newton essentially a cool observer, partly because he would be coming to Austin in a little over two weeks for a business meeting. We waved goodbye and entered the restricted area for passengers only, knowing that we would never forget our stay or ever be the same.

During the direct flight from São Paulo to Dallas, we watched a documentary on the space program, building up to man's first landing on the moon. I did not put on the headphones but merely viewed the familiar scenes, remembering vaguely the famous line about a giant step for mankind. I could not help asking myself what our trip had done for the betterment of humanity. I hoped that we had not merely added to pollution and to poverty, recalling all our driving on sightseeing tours and the beggars we encountered on the streets—one man clapping at us angrily and another arguing with Newton and almost threatening him physically before we could get away. In the documentary I saw one of the astronauts in his huge space suit hopping off in his special shoes after having traced the letters TDC in the dust or sand, leaving behind what looked like a metal bar of some type brought from planet earth and used to draw the initials, cluttering up the landscape of another celestial body. I later read that astronaut Gene Cernan had used his finger to write his daughter Tracy's initials in the dust, whereas other versions say that he carved or etched the initials in lunar dirt, but no version mentioned a writing instrument being left behind.

Will all my letters, words, sentences, and paragraphs amount to no more than graffiti and wasted tree pulp? What had I accomplished with so much prose? Had I at least lived up to E.M. Forster's injunction: "Only Connect"? Once we arrived safely back home I found a copy of the *Beloit Poetry Journal*, sent by Karl Elder, a poet friend in Wisconsin. His poem in the issue was entitled "Alpha Images" and contained a stanza reading "The rim of the moon. / Peephole into an igloo. / Shadow of zero." Looked at from every place on earth, the moon appears the same, it seems, yet is seen in so many different ways—Yeats' "the silver apples of the moon," Debussy's "Clair de lune," the full one we had seen against the exploding fireworks of New Year's Eve that brought thoughts in Brazil of Handel and Ives. The moon changes and so do we, some of us through travel but some like Emily Dickinson while staying at home and writing her poems. I had needed this trip to grow smaller, humbled by Isabella and all that I heard and saw, but broadened through the people met, the poems read, the words written down to record the days and their thoughts and ideas, learned or guessed at and perhaps later even to be understood.

Chile (May-June 2006)

Forty-one years after I had first traveled to Chile in 1965, with an exchange program between the universities of Texas and Chile, I returned with María and seven members of a class that I would be teaching on Chilean poetry. My class was one of the University of Texas at Austin Maymester intensive courses conducted abroad between May and June. To me, it was like coming full circle from the life-changing experience of having gone to Chile myself as one of fifteen UT students selected for the exchange program. It was then that I discovered a new world of literature, and in the following year, on returning to Chile on my own, I would meet and marry my cherished María, when she and I both worked at the Instituto Chileno-norteamericano in downtown Santiago, she as a librarian and I as a teacher of English and of American literature.

Leaving Austin with some 95 degrees on May 19, 2006, at 5 p.m., María and I would join my students in Dallas for the flight to Chile, which was delayed by almost three hours. The students had learned of the delay, and two of the seven did not show up at the departure gate until about an hour before the plane would begin boarding at 11:30 instead of the original time of 8:35 p.m. I felt like a mother hen worrying about her missing chicks. One of the students, who had been in the waiting area, was not at the gate at 11:30 because, I learned, he had gone to watch on TV the NBA basketball playoff game between Dallas and San Antonio, and so I had to go looking for him at the very last moment. Finally, we all boarded the plane and were off for Santiago and a long night of difficult sleep, made more so in my case from a strained muscle in my left calf and the need constantly to move my leg. During the flight I was torn between the exhilaration of returning to Chile with María and the worry that the students would find the late fall weather in Chile far too cold after the customary Texas heat. One of the two male students in the group was wearing shorts and moccasins without socks. It concerned me that the group would not be dressed properly, and I also worried that they would be disappointed in the country to which I was deeply attached. All of that kept me from fully enjoying the flight back to Chile and its rich literary life.

Being anxious about keeping all the group together in Dallas had already lessened the pleasure that I would have taken in a very unexpected encounter. Just before we were preparing to board the plane, I suddenly saw, coming out of an arrival gate, a fellow whose face was definitely familiar but that I could not quite place. As I joined him and we walked in the same direction, I said to him, I know you, and he in turn asked me, Aren't you Dave? When I replied yes, he said, I'm Paul Quinton. Only then did I know who he was—a member of the group of UT students with which I had traveled to Chile in 1965. This coincidental meeting also brought the present trip full circle. Later, María and my students exchanged greetings with Paul and some of his relatives, who were flying with him to Argentina by way of Santiago. Paul was taking a sister and two nieces, and the fiancé of one of the latter, to his property in Argentina, near Córdoba. María asked him at one point how his 1965 trip to Chile had affected him, and he said that it had radicalized him, making him aware of the country's real poverty and turning him toward Communism, whereas our State Department-sponsored exchange had been intended to convert Chileans to capitalist democracy. María later wondered to me how Paul treated the workers who managed his absentee-landlord property. After graduating from UT, Paul had become a medical doctor in San Diego, specializing in physiological research. Despite my preoccupation with shepherding the students, it was symbolically a satisfying reunion with this member of the 1965 exchange program and seemed to bode well for the whole trip that meant so much to me as a means of introducing the students to *Chile lindo* (beautiful Chile).

Without incident, we landed in Santiago, on Saturday May 20th (our daughter Elisa's birthday), passed through customs, and were met by Héctor Cruz, a Puerto Rican who had taken a Ph.D. in Political Science from the University of Wisconsin-Milwaukee and now worked with the Council on International Educational Exchange. Héctor was there to welcome us on behalf of the CIEE and to settle the students in their accommodations. María had been met by her sister and brother-in-law and went on with them to their home in the Las Condes section of Santiago. Traveling in two separate vans, the students and I all headed for the Apart-Hotel in the Providencia section of the city, where the students would live during three of the five weeks of our stay. Once they had left their bags in their rooms, we were all taken out to eat at a restaurant which, I was later told by my brother-in-law, was past its prime but famous for Chilean food. A singer had been invited to serenade the group with Chilean songs, including one by Victor Jara and two by Violeta Parra. The former was infamously murdered during the military coup of 1973 and the latter was the sister of Nicanor Parra, one of the Chilean poets we would be studying and meeting in person during our course on Chilean poetry, entitled "Chile: Land of Epic Poets." The singer was quite good and a pleasant fellow, with an artist's almost de rigueur long, wavy hair and rather fashionable bohemian attire. The students seemed to enjoy the singer greatly and two of them even bought CDs that he offered for sale. As for the meal, the students did not seem to enjoy it as much as I did, even though five of them went along with me in ordering *pastel de choclo*, a kind of pot pie in a bowl with onions, ground meat, and olives, with a baked corn crust on top. The point was that they were having a taste of popular Chilean fare in a typical setting, even if the restaurant had seen better days.

On Sunday the 21st, Héctor conducted us on a tour of the facilities at FLACSO (Latin American Faculty of Social Sciences) where our classes would be held, in a building near the U.S. Embassy on Dag Hammarskjold Avenue. At a nearby Metro station, we purchased cards that we could simply flash at the turnstiles to pass through and board the trains arriving and departing constantly. The cards could be used over and over by paying for peso amounts to be added to them at teller booths. Getting off at the first stop, Tobalaba, we walked through what Héctor said was the Wall Street of Chile, where high-rise banks abounded and much new construction was going up. We passed the Embassy, the International Organization of Work, and CEPAL (Economic Commission for Latin America and the Caribbean), arriving at the very modern building of FLACSO, with classrooms the students found more elegant than any at UT. After being oriented in the building, we walked for lunch to the Piccola Italia, which served delicious pasta dishes and scrumptious desserts. I had fettuccini with spinach sauce and a raspberry mousse. On finishing our lunch, we were picked up by a tour guide and her driver in a van that was large enough to seat all of us comfortably. Our first stop was at the top of Cerro San Cristóbal, with its famous statue in white of the Virgin Mary, overlooking the city. Unfortunately, smog and a partly overcast sky prevented us from seeing Santiago in all its glory. Still, the students thoroughly enjoyed the visit to this hill in the center of the capital, beginning with photos they took of themselves with two policemen, or *carabineros*, and their uniformed dogs. The students chose to ride the *Teleférica* (or cable car) down to the bottom of the hill, while I rode in the van with the tour guide and driver.

The tour guide, whose name I fail to remember, was part German, having been born in the south of Chile, where many Germans had settled during the 19th century and after World War Two. Her accent in English suggested the influence of what had probably been her first language, German instead of Spanish. She was very pleasant and tried to furnish us with many facts about the sites we visited and about historical figures associated with them, even though her English was not perfect. For example, she used the word "embarrassed" in English when she meant "pregnant"—a common mistake, since in Spanish *embarazada* signifies expecting a child. English speakers also confuse the word *embarazada*, thinking that in English it means embarrassed; as a result, they end up saying they are pregnant, which in the case of men comes out sounding embarrassingly funny.

Our next stop was Cerro Santa Lucía, which I suggested because I wanted the students to see on the top of the hill (*cerro*) a statue of the aboriginal chieftain, Caupolicán, about whom we would be reading in our Chilean poetry class. Driving up the hill we passed many couples *pololeando*, the Chilean word for dating, and in most cases "necking" in public. The students got a kick out of the openness with which the couples showed their affection, or simply leaned against one another speaking so quietly that their words could not be heard. The Terraza de Caupolicán, as the area at the top of the hill is designated, was dotted with couples, and also with families and their children, as well as art students who were drawing the vistas of Santiago and its snow-topped surrounding Andes mountain range. One young fellow had drawn the side of the National Library that faced the hill. An attractive early building with towering palm trees growing beside it, the Library is in full view of the part of the hill that is crowned above the Terraza by a reddish stone castle, or a small version of such. Higher than the castle walls, on rock that it seems was worked from the hill, rises the statue of a figure representing Caupolicán. It is said that the sculptor modeled the chieftain after a North American Indian, complete with a feather headdress not worn by the native Araucanian peoples. What I had always taken for Caupolicán's bow was, according to the German-Chilean tour guide, a type of native golf club used in a game still played in Santiago.

From Santa Lucía hill, we drove to La Moneda, the Presidential Palace (originally the first Chilean mint), which faces the street of the same name, which means money. There we saw cannons from 1866, *carabineros* on guard, and orange trees inside the walls of the Palace in a type of courtyard. In the plaza in front of the Palace was a newly erected statue of President Salvador Allende, indignantly decorated with pigeon droppings. Some blocks away, we visited the Plaza de Armas (*armas* meaning military arms). It was in a shop fronting the plaza that María and I had had one another's names engraved inside our wedding rings. On climbing down from the van, I was struck by the aroma of peanuts (*maní*) roasted with a sugary coating, which brought back many memories of my first days in Santiago in 1965. On one corner of the Plaza, we could view a statue of a mounted Pedro de Valdivia, the founder in 1541 of the city of Santiago. Meanwhile, a group of girls and boys dressed in the attire of *huasos* (Chilean cowboys) were performing on a bandstand a *cueca*, the national dance, as music blared out from loudspeakers and a crowd gathered to enjoy the entertainment. At the same time, men seated at tables were intently playing chess and ladies sat on benches knitting—all very typical of Chilean plazas. We could see the front of the original Post Office, which is said to have been the home of Pedro de Valdivia before his death at the hands of the Araucanians, with whom he had fought in a futile attempt to subdue those fierce, proud, original Chileans. The history of the war between the Conquistadors and the Araucanians, including Caupolicán, is recounted in *La Araucana*, Chile's epic poem, written by Alonso de Ercilla (1533-1594). The following day we would begin to study Ercilla's 16th-century poem, so that our visit to the Terraza de Caupolicán and to the Plaza de Armas both provided an appropriate introduction to our Chilean poetry course.

That night on television, I watched Michelle Bachelet, Chile's newly elected president, giving her first speech as the first woman to be elected president of the nation. More dramatic were scenes from a protest in the port city of Valparaíso, showing hooded (*encapuchado*) protesters fighting with the *carabineros*, who used water cannons on armored cars to quell the crowd. The water-spouting vehicles are popularly referred to as *guanacos*, the name of a Chilean animal—a type of goat-deer—that spits at predators. Some of the hooded protestors were tossing Molotov cocktails that exploded in flames on impact. The protest was partly in opposition to a law that affected the Mapuche Indians, one of three aboriginal groups historically known as Araucanians. Four Mapuche men were in prison and had gone on a hunger strike. As I pointed out to the students, the Araucanians are still at war with the European invaders, and have yet to be fully "conquered" or "pacified" after over four hundred years. The hunger strike sent the local Senators scurrying to change the law after the four Mapuche men threatened to go on with the strike until they died. As we would learn in *La Araucana*, the Chilean Indians did not believe in surrender. It seemed that the protestors were also demonstrating against gas prices, changes in school regulations, and numerous other developments in recent days, as well as the new president and some of her policies.

The next day, May 22nd, we began our classes at the FLACSO facilities with a discussion of Ercilla's epic, published in three parts, in 1569, 1578, and 1589. We immediately observed the poet's use of epic simile:

> As the keen crocodile, who loves to lay
> His silent ambush for his finny prey . . .
> So, in their toils, without one warning thought,
> The murd'rous foe our little squadron caught(;)

and of personification of Fortune and Avarice:

> She, unconcern'd at what her victims feel,
> Turns with her wonted haste her fatal wheel(;)

> Insatiate Avarice!—'tis from thee we trace
> The various misery of our mortal race"(;)

and also of actual events in Chilean history, through which the poet celebrates both sides in the war, though more often presenting hyperbolically the Araucanians as having the bravest hearts ever to inhabit the human form:

> Equal ye are in courage and in worth;
> Heaven has assign'd to all an equal birth:
> In wealth, in power, and majesty of soul,
> Each Chief seems worthy of the world's control.

The equality theme in this stanza predated, of course, our own Declaration of Independence. Also, we found in the poem that women play a dominant role. Pedro de Valdivia's lover, Inés de Suárez (named Mencia in the poem), saves the Spanish settlement when it is attacked by the Araucanians. Other important female figures include Guacolda, wife of Lautaro; Tegualda, wife of Crepino; and Fresia, wife of Caupolicán. Through Ercilla's vivid descriptions in artfully rhymed stanzas, the male Araucanians show their bravery and skill in battle, but the warriors' women prove in many ways to be the most impressive characters in the poem

The fragments of the epic that we read were rendered into English by William Hayley in the early nineteenth century. Even though Hayley turned Ercilla's lines into heroic couplets instead of the poet's original eight-line rhyming stanzas, the translator faithfully and imaginatively conveys the poet's epic themes, illustrated by characters based on historical figures. The following day I had three students report on an article entitled, in translation, "The Lament of Tegualda: Mourning, Apparition, and Community in *La Araucana*," by Raúl Marrero-Fente. The essay discusses Canto XXI, in which Tegualda searches for her dead husband, who had died along with Lautaro when the Spaniards surprised the Araucanian camp in the early hours of the morning. The students' report was well done and furnished the class with a number of valuable insights into such themes as: Ercilla's views on women; the relationship between love and death; the universal theme of the need to bury the dead in order to preserve them in our memories and to keep them from evil spirits (or being separated from their ancestors); and the poet's condemnation of war, the very one in which he participated while recording his experiences on bark, leaves, or any material handy in the midst of battle. We could see the connection between Tegualda's need to bury Crepino and that of Antigone, the principal female character in Sophocles' Greek tragedy of the same title. The article on Canto XXI, published in the fine Chilean scholarly journal, *Atenea* (founded in 1924), reveals that the Mapuche tradition of burial lies behind Tegualda's search for Crepino's body but that Ercilla would not have known of this ritual. Even so, the poet must have recognized the universal urge to find the missing in action and to provide them with a proper interment.

The most dramatic section of *La Araucana* concerns Fresia, when she confronts her husband Caupolicán after he has been captured by the Spaniards. Since the Araucanians did not believe in surrender, the wife brings their fifteen-month-old infant son to the scene and repudiates the father-husband when she finds that

> The stronger arm in this shameful band
> Has tied thy weak effeminated hand.

She recalls their life together and regrets that her heart was deceived:

> In all the noble pride with which it heav'd,
> When through the world my boasted title ran,
> Fresia, the wife of great Caupolicán!
> Now, plung'd in misery from the heights of fame,
> My glories end in this detested shame,
> To see thee captive in a lonely spot,
> When death and honour might have been thy lot!

She goes on to ask,

> Where are the vaunted fruits of thy command,
> The laurels gather'd by this fetter'd hand?
> All sunk! All turn'd to this abhorr'd disgrace,
> To live the slave of this ignoble race!

She prefers that he would have died in battle ("a gallant exit gives immortal fame"), but seeing him a captive, she declares that he has dried up her mother's milk and that he himself must raise the son, who "was a tie most dear, / Which spotless love once made my heart revere." Of course, in Caupolicán's situation, there is no way that he will be able to take over the raising of their child, for he will soon die from having his innards punctured by a sharpened pole, on which he will seat himself without a grimace or any sound of pain. Throughout Fresia's harangue, Ercilla allows the wife to call him and his fellow Spaniards a "shameful band" and an "ignoble race," and after she has spoken,

> . . . with growing madness stung,
> The tender nursling from her arms she flung
> With savage fury.

In spite of the Spanish soldiers' attempts

> To make her breast, where cruel frenzy burn'd,
> Receive the little innocent she spurn'd,
> [She] hast[ened] from our sight,
> While anguish seem'd to aid her rapid flight.

At lunchtime I went alone to the Piccola Italiana to meet and have lunch with Francisco Véjar, a longtime Chilean friend and poet. We had a warm reunion after five years, and he looked very much the same, with piercing eyes full of enthusiasm and concentration. Francisco has always seemed so eager to hear my views, especially on the antipoetry of Nicanor Parra, the world-renowned "antipoet" who was born in 1914 and whom I had met for the first time in 1965. When I lamented that Parra had never received the Nobel Prize, and yet has deserved it more than so many other writers who have been honored as laureates, Francisco was thoroughly delighted, mostly, it seemed, because he knew that Parra would love to hear me say as much. He reported that the antipoet was quite fit at 92, seeming younger each year, as Francisco said that he had told him the last time that they had been together. His secret, according to Francisco, who had it directly from Don Nicanor, was mega doses of vitamin C. An anecdote that Francisco shared with me involved Parra's granddaughter Josefina, who asked him why he took so many pills, to which the antipoet replied, "Not to die." Josefina then began to chant, "Vas a morir lo mismo, vas a morir lo mismo" (You're going to die the same, you're going to die the same), which Parra thought was marvelous. Probably this will show up in a new antipoem, if it hasn't already. It was great to see Francisco again; he is such an unassuming, generous person, genuinely interested in others, and always ready to promote his mentor Don Nicanor and to involve me in any project related to the antipoet and Chilean poetry in general.

The next day in class we began to discuss the poetry of Vicente Huidobro (1893-1948), and this was a shocking leap for the students from Ercilla's 16th-century epic to Huidobro's Creationism, the movement through which he opened the way for Chile to become a central player in the Modernist period of 20th-century poetry. (I should note that although Chilean poets existed in the nineteenth century, there was none with an international reputation between Ercilla and Huidobro.) We first worked our way through Huidobro's various Manifestos, in which he declared the rules for writing a Creationist poem: 1) no copying nature or plagiarizing God but rather creating one's own world and language; 2) no use of modern technology for its own sake; 3) to humanize every object by passing it through the poet's body or soul; 4) no overly poetic writing—no gilding the lily or adding to what is already poetic; 5) to make the abstract concrete, and vice versa; 6) to consider the "Creative force" above all else; and 7) no anecdotes or description, but rather patterns of images that reveal a world other than the real one of nature, as when he recombines mountain and horizon to form *mountizon* or *horitain*. To the students, ideas or meaning seemed missing from Huidobro's poems, and they struggled to accept what one of the group, Andrew Lara, considered arrogance in the poet's claim that poetry had yet to be written. The other students by name were: Lucila Castellano, Álvaro Corral, Diana Meléndez, Gabriela Orta, Ashley Thomas, and Karen Villarreal. As should be evident, all the students, except for Ashley, were Hispanic, and all but Ashley spoke some Spanish.

In our textbook, *The Selected Poetry of Vicente Huidobro* (New Directions, 1981), a bilingual edition with translations by ten translators, we looked fairly closely at "Equatorial" (1918), a poem with images of war, wings, flight, sailing, world travel, borders, horizons, cigar and pipe, telephone and telegraph, and the Cross and the Eiffel Tower. We considered the negative implication of "Men with short wings" and the positive connotation of the "Lone plane / which will sing in the blue one day." But it was difficult for the students to find much significance in the shifting, though at times repeated, imagery. For this reason, I assigned four students to read an essay by Willie Van Peer, from the journal *New Literary History*, on how to read an e.e. cummings poem "top-down, bottom-up," and to apply this approach to Huidobro's poems. The main idea of the article is that "In order to construct an adequate interpretation a reader has to detect relations between sentences that may not be connected explicitly, and he must be able to see the meaning of such relationships." After reading through a poem, the reader may form an idea about its theme, but to corroborate his notion he or she must go back up through the poem to see if its various words and phrases and their comparisons and/or contrasts confirm his or her interpretation. In the next class meeting, the four students would report on the "top-down, bottom-up" approach for reading Huidobro's challenging poems.

Prior to each class on Chilean poetry, two young women, who worked for CIEE, came to the FLACSO building to instruct the students in Chilean culture. This was a very informative part of the educational Council's effort to supply the students with some of the history and traditions of their host country. The women furnished printed material and discussed in dialogue with the students a number of points of view and practices. One point of view had to do with the need for love, but not necessarily in terms of marriage or for social or religious reasons, as was the case with previous generations. With regard to having children, the preference in Chile was for two or three. Another point of view concerned the tendency in contemporary Chilean families to have close relationships between parents and children but ones that are democratic rather than rigid, intolerable, and overbearing or overly protective on the part of the father and mother. It was pointed out, however, that while modern Chilean parents allow their children greater freedom than in the past, they still do not want them to leave the home until they have married, even when they are in their twenties.

Other areas of Chilean culture discussed by the women included the popular form of speech used in confidence and called *el voseo*, an alternative to the second person singular intimate form, or *tu*. They also discussed the many slang forms of speech, a number of which were quite popular at the time and had been brought to Chile by vacationers from Argentina. Of particular interest to me was the discussion of all the colorful *modismos*, or expressions, used by Chileans that derive from references to animals. For example, a person who is considered a coward is called *achunchado*, a form of the word *chancho*, meaning pig. Many of the animal-related expressions find their equivalents in English; for instance, the Chilean *más vale pájaro en mano que cien volando* (a bird in the hand is worth more than one hundred flying) is fairly close to the English "a bird in the hand is worth two in the bush."

That evening I finally made contact with my friend and fellow jazz fan, Pepe Hosiasson. Born in Poland of Jewish parents, Pepe (or José) came to Chile as a young man and fell in love with jazz, learning English along the way, probably for a better understanding of the music and its musicians, since he collected a vast library on the subject. He had personally known such figures as Louis Armstrong, Count Basie, Duke Ellington, Erroll Garner, Paul Desmond, Chet Baker, John Lewis of the Modern Jazz Quartet, Wynton Marsalis, and so many others. At Pepe's home, a note by trumpeter Marsalis, written on a photograph of Pepe and himself, hoped that he, Marsalis, would be as tall as Pepe when he "grew up." When I phoned Pepe, he was on the point of leaving his house for the Hyatt Hotel, to hear a jazz group that he had gotten together for a group of Canadians who were in town for a mining conference. (One of Chile's principal commodities is copper.) Pepe invited me to come to the hotel, and so I took a bus and got off some eight or ten blocks from the Hyatt, not knowing exactly which direction to go from there. I stopped a couple of young girls and asked them the way to the hotel, and received a very cordial response. Attractive and speaking very clear Spanish, the two—who seemed to be twin sisters, though not identical—suggested that I take a taxi because it was about 20 or 25 minutes away. I have never cared for taxis, which have always seemed to me an excessive expense; María, however, thinks they are the only way to go. After the girls pointed me in the right direction, along Américo Vespuccio street, I joined other pedestrians heading the same way, and arrived at the domed, elegant Hyatt, where I asked for the location of the bar. I could already hear the jazz band playing and could have followed the sound, but the attendant courteously led the way and I quickly spotted Pepe, seated up close to a six-piece combo. A young girl on tenor saxophone was playing with obvious gusto. I was soon "blown away" by this 17-year-old named Melissa Aldana, who was still in high school but had earned a scholarship to study at the New England Conservatory (although she ultimately chose instead to attend the Berklee School in New York City).

Melissa had been taught by her father and grandfather, the former a noted saxophonist who had been one of the 25 finalists in the recent Thelonious Monk competition won by Joshua Redman. Pepe informed me that Melissa was better than her father, and he said that when an American saxophonist (whose name I did not catch) had come to Chile, she had "cut him"—jazz parlance for one musician outplaying another. Even before Pepe told me of her background, I could hear for myself that she was a phenomenon; yet seeing her standing there in old-fashioned, black-and-white high-topped tennis shoes, long pants, her face expressionless, and with a saxophone seemingly too large for her, I doubt that before hearing her play anyone would have thought Melissa capable of performing jazz in the tradition of Charlie Parker, but she certainly was. She had an incredible feeling for swing, and an unbelievable ear that enabled her to hear the chord changes in tunes that Pepe kept telling me that he was sure that she did not know.

In addition to Melissa on tenor, the group consisted of an altoist, a trumpeter (his horn with its main tube and bell bent upwards like Dizzy Gillespie's), a pianist, drummer, and bassist. All were excellent, and the altoist and trumpeter, as well as the pianist, were older men with many years of experience, and yet Melissa was clearly the most imaginative improviser, and she produced such a big, rich sound from her saxophone that it was truly thrilling to hear her perform. I had never heard such an amazing live performance, not even from Gillespie when he appeared in Austin toward the end of his life.

I asked Pepe if I could call a number—that is, suggest a tune for the group to play—and he said just tell the pianist the name of the piece. Pepe had told me earlier that the pianist could not read music, but from age 5, he had taught himself to play, which he did very well indeed. Pepe also told me that the altoist had mental problems from drugs and alcohol, talked in endless detail, but could play anything. Since he thought the pianist was brilliant, I assumed that he would recognize the title of the tune that I wanted to request— "The Way You Look Tonight"— even if he did not speak English, since Chilean jazz musicians (and I believe aficionados of the music the world over) know the titles of commonly improvised-on pop songs. The pianist, however, did not recognize "The Way You Look Tonight" by title, so Pepe told me to sing it for him. I said, You sing it, but he said he could not think of the melody. Fortunately, I had been listening to a version by Erroll Garner, and even though I cannot usually recall a tune on the spot, it slowly came to me and as soon as I hummed a few notes of the melody, the pianist picked it up and simultaneously Melissa took off playing the theme note perfect. After that the entire group joined in and they performed better than on any other tune. One of the Canadians pointed at me to render credit for my having called a tune that had evoked such a stirring performance. Naturally I was quite pleased with myself, but the real credit was due to the musicians, and especially to Melissa, who played at the highest level of jazz improvisation, with turns of phrase worthy of John Coltrane and the saxophonists of his generation and ingenuity. It was truly a memorable experience to hear at the beginning of her career such an amazingly talented musician. Six years later Melissa Aldana would win the coveted Thelonious Monk award.

The following day we concluded our discussion of Huidobro's poetry, with my friend Francisco Véjar in attendance. The four students gave reports on four different poems by the Chilean poet, using the "top-down, bottom-up" approach for their analysis. The first to report was Karen Villarreal, who discussed Huidobro's "Eiffel Tower," with its comparisons of the tower to a flower, to which the poet's words are attracted as bees to nectar. Next came Ashley Thomas, who discussed "Monument to the Sea," with its celebration of the sea and its "singing constellation of waters." In commenting on the first stanza's repetition of the word "Peace," I suggested that this was perhaps a kind of blessing, as in the Catholic Church's "peace be with you." Francisco agreed that this could be, and he remembered later, when we spoke during a break, that Nicanor Parra had lifted the same Huidobro stanza for a poem of his own about Huidobro, in the 84th section of Parra's "Also Sprach Altazor." In the Huidobro stanza Parra altered one word, changing "translator" to "transla(trai)tor," one of his typical witty puns. "Altazor" is the title of the longest and perhaps most famous poem by Huidobro, which we discussed but I failed to mention it in my notes. "Altazor" was written between 1919 and 1931, while the other famous poem by Huidobro is his "Arte poética," from 1916, which looks forward to his Manifestos in that it calls for the poet to "Invent new worlds" and asserts in its final line that "El Poeta es un pequeño Dios" (The Poet is a little God), in keeping with the injunction for the poet to create his or her own world and language.

The next student to discuss a poem was Diana Meléndez, who had chosen to analyze "Song of the Deathlife," even though I had assigned her "Song of the Laughing Life," which probably put her off because it was much longer. Even so, we could see many of Huidobro's typical stylistic features in the shorter piece, beginning with its title, "Canciòn de la muervida," which in Spanish combines the words for death and life: *muerte* and *vida,* to form a new word, which fulfills Huidobro's Manifesto requirement for creating a new language. Another neologism appears in a line about the dead being "encielados en el cielo" (inheavened in the sky—*cielo* being the word for sky but used by the poet as a verb like *encerrar*, meaning to enclose or shut in). The first stanza incorporates contrasting metaphors for parts of the speaker's own body: his right hand is a swallow; left hand a cypress; front of head, a living man; and back of head, a dead man. Later the poem contrasts the living and the dead in terms of various images, including again swallow and cypress. While the dead are "desterrados de la tierra" (exiled from the earth), the living "extend their cypress / To say good morning to the swallow." I wondered if cypress was a symbol of mourning in Spanish, as it is in English, and whether or not the living, in extending their cypress, were putting off or delaying death. Francisco did not think that the cypress represented mourning in Spanish, but later he changed his mind somewhat. He definitely changed his mind about Huidobro, for he told the class that he had never been very interested in his poetry, but as a result of our discussion he saw what a great poet he was.

The final poem to be discussed was one of Huidobro's late pieces, published posthumously in 1948, the year of his death. Entitled "El Paso del retorno" (The Return Passage), the poem concerns his return to Chile in 1933 after having lived abroad since 1916. In Andrew Lara's report, he found in "passage" an example of the poet's constant imagery of travel, but also an allusion to his idea that he was leaving behind all poetry that came before him, and even the idea that no poem had really been written until Huidobro invented "Creationism." Andrew could still not see this attitude toward his precursors as anything but arrogance, but Francisco assured him that other poets had also spoken as representatives of a new vision, and he mentioned both Walt Whitman and Pablo Neruda, for which I was grateful and with which I was in total agreement. Andrew recognized that this late poem was more direct and less "surrealistic," and both Francisco and I agreed with him in this regard. Also, Andrew found a number of lines that supported his thesis that the poem was about Huidobro's new kind of poetry. Even though I did not entirely accept Andrew's interpretation, since the poem is more about the poet's life than it is about a new poetry, I applauded his otherwise excellent report and his use of the top-down, bottom-up method of analysis.

Later, when we would read and discuss Pablo Neruda's poem entitled "Poesía" (Poetry), it occurred to me that Huidobro's "The Return Passage" had in common with Neruda's poem the idea of being grateful to poetry. In Huidobro's case, he credits poetry with never having abandoned him, with having "cleared the way" for him, and, as Andrew had pointed out, with beginning his and poetry's "reign." Andrew had also correctly noted that the poem sums up the poet's life, and this too applies to Neruda's "Poetry," in which he reaches back in memory to "that age" when "Poetry arrived" to summon him:

> something started in my soul,
> fever or forgotten wings,
> and I made my own way,
> deciphering
> that fire,
> and I wrote the first faint line,
> faint, without substance, pure
> nonsense,
> pure wisdom
> of someone who knows nothing.

Like Huidobro, Neruda relates poetry or poets to "wings," and as he says, when he awoke to "planets" and "the great starry / void," he felt himself a "pure part / of the abyss," and as he "wheeled with the stars," his "heart broke loose on the wind." It came to me through our discussion of Huidobro and Neruda's poetry that in a sense my own "return passage" to Chile had been made possible by my awakening to poetry as a freshman in college and of my having discovered first the antipoetry of Nicanor Parra and then of Neruda, Huidobro, and the younger generations of Chilean poets that I had subsequently translated. Being selected to travel to Chile in the first place in 1965 had come about from my having written and published poetry in magazines and having been chosen to become the editor of *Riata*, the student literary magazine at UT-Austin. And now in 2006, I too felt grateful, for my attempts at poems and my interest in Chilean poetry, which had brought me back to Chile to teach this Maymester course, approved by the University Provost and the faculty committee for the travel-abroad program.

On Thursday the 25th, I was to dine after class with my longtime friend Irene Rostagno, a professor at the Universidad Metropolitana, who, after receiving her Ph.D. in American Studies from UT-Austin, had returned to her native Chile with her husband David Madison. After some seventeen years of marriage, Irene and David had divorced and she had married a former professor at UT, William Stott. We were to meet in Providencia, a very popular area in Santiago with its upscale shops, bookstores, and a café called Tavelli, known by most everyone and frequented especially by writers. When I arrived, Irene was in the café alone, marking her students' English papers—Bill would arrive a bit later. In her animated manner, Irene made it clear that she was quite upset because an exam for her university class had been canceled as a result of the previously noted student protests over various issues related to education in Chile. The protestors were mostly high school students, but the protests had also affected classes at the public university, which in Chile is often closed by political protests of one sort or another. Irene had invited me to speak to her class of graduate students who were themselves teachers of English and were taking courses to earn credit that would advance them in the profession or would secure for them a higher pay.

Irene's graduate course in English was on culture, and I had planned to speak on jazz in literature. I had struggled to locate excerpts from short stories on jazz by Eudora Welty and Julio Cortázar and to print them out, which had been difficult because my brother-in-law's server was not working properly and my niece's printer was out of ink. I had finally carried a "jump" plug to FLACSO where they could, after overcoming some technical problems, print out the pages. Irene had made copies for me of three poems by Langston Hughes, and I had gone to a bookstore where I was able to find a poem by Chilean poet Gonzalo Rojas entitled "Latin & Jazz," which I planned to discuss, along with the Welty and Cortázar short stories, and the poems by Hughes. I would also comment on the session that I had heard with Melissa Aldana and the "illiterate" pianist performing without the aid of any sheet music, which I would illustrate in literature by a poem by William Carlos Williams that says in part "that sheet music's a lotta cheese," and by a play by George C. Wolfe on the life and music of Jelly Roll Morton, which also concerns the idea that jazz played without sheet music is superior to that dependent on written notes. But in the end, all our efforts went for naught, since after we had dined and were on the way to the campus of the Metropolitana, Irene received a cell-phone call from a colleague saying that the University had been "taken over," meaning that the protestors had closed it down. The next day Irene had phone calls from students so disappointed that the class had been canceled. I too regretted the closure, after all my plans and preparations for sharing with the class my enthusiasm for both jazz and literature. Even so, it was gratifying just to have put together a presentation on Cortázar's story based on the life of Charlie Parker, Welty's story inspired by her having heard Fats Waller live, and on both U.S. and Chilean poets who had incorporated jazz into their writings. (In 2007, my *Jazz Mavericks of the Lone Star State*, published by the University of Texas Press, would include my essay entitled "Jazz in Literature," which discusses all the authors and works that I had planned to talk about in Dr. Rostagno's class. So it was hardly a total loss after all.)

During the night following my meeting with Irene, I felt queasy from the meal that she, Bill Stott, and I had eaten together, and later I learned that Bill had even experienced chills. But after taking Pepto-Bismol, I recovered and was ready for the next day's class, which would be held at the State Department's binational Instituto Chileno-norteamericano. In advance of our traveling to Chile with the students, I had contacted Jaime Quezada, a poet whose work I had included in my anthology of poetry by 22 Chilean poets, published in *Road Apple Review* in 1972. Jaime is an expert on Gabriela Mistral, who in 1945 was Chile's first Nobel-Prize-winning poet and whose poetry we would now begin to study. Jaime's edition of Mistral's complete poetry, published in Chile in 2001 by Editorial Andrés Bello, is a 788-page volume, and as a Mistral enthusiast, he was delighted to have an opportunity to speak to the students on Mistral's life and literature. On arriving in Santiago I had phoned him to say that I had arranged for the class to meet at the Institute, which pleased him greatly since, as he informed me, he was on the Institute's cultural committee—too modest to say that he was in fact its president, which I would learn later on.

Jaime arrived with a satchel crammed full of Mistral's books, including first editions. He informed the students that he owned manuscripts and letters of Mistral's, in addition to all five of her collections of poetry published during her lifetime, with her *Poema de Chile* (1967) having appeared a decade after her death. Unfortunately, of all the texts by the Chilean poets that we were using for the course, only *Gabriela Mistral: A Reader* was not a bilingual edition; however, Jaime had brought with him copies of three Mistral poems in Spanish, and it turned out that our text contained translations of all three poems that he distributed to the class for discussion: "The Parrot," "Ballad," and "Refreshment." For about an hour and a half, Jaime spoke to the class in Spanish without pausing, except to have the students read the poems aloud in Spanish and in English.

Jaime's analysis of "The Parrot" interested me most because it seemed to correct my impression that the poem is told from the point of view of a child, whereas Jaime informed us that Mistral had visited a zoo where she was told that a parrot with its "twangy voice / and satanic beak" had called her "ugly," to which the poet reacted by denying that this could be true. As Jaime pointed out,

Mistral was ridiculed during her lifetime for being less attractive than a certain woman poet of her day, who was celebrated for her beauty but whose poetry today is no longer read. In "The Parrot," Mistral offers various reasons why she cannot be ugly: her mother could not be ugly because she "looks like the sun" and light cannot be ugly; the wind that "carries her voice" cannot be ugly; the water she falls into is not ugly; and the world created and nurtured by God is not ugly. In other words, since the poet is related through her mother to all of those "beautiful" forces, she cannot herself be ugly.

In his analysis of the poem, Jaime explained that the parrot called Mistral ugly because, as the poem says, the bird had not eaten, so the poet brings it "bread with wine." In the end, the poet tires of looking at the parrot, its green and yellow "always a sunflower." Later, when the class would present their own reports on Mistral prose-poems descriptive of things and creatures, Álvaro Corral would relate Mistral's visits to zoos to her piece on the giraffe, in which the animal tells the poet that she, the giraffe, is ugly only because she resembles the poet's own "fractured passion." Jaime's lecture in Spanish proved quite helpful in our reading of Mistral's poetry and taught us some important lessons about her life as it applied to her literature. Although his talk may have been a bit too much for some of the students, I hoped that with time they would appreciate the opportunity that they had had to hear from an authority on one of Chile's more important writers.

For the final class on Mistral, I used a poem by Ralph Waldo Emerson, entitled "Days," and Shakespeare's sonnet 29, to compare them with the Chilean's poems entitled "Morning" (one of four poems on the time of day) and "The Lark," a prose-poem that speaks of the bird's "vertical flight." Such a comparative approach allowed me to bring out similar themes, at the same time that I could discuss the sonnet form. Mistral's famous "Sonnets of Death" had first brought her critical acclaim, but more useful for my purposes were "Morning" and "The Lark," since I wanted the students to see the value of a comparative approach through observing similarities and differences in the work of writers from cultures with their own traditions and concerns, including formal, stylistic, and thematic considerations.

Both "Days" and "Morning" employ phrases that suggest

that we need to take advantage of the time that we are given on earth: "empty-handed morning"—"forgot my morning wishes"; "hypocritic days"—"promised and cheated"; "to each they offer gifts after his will"—"rich with work"; "make yourself worthy"—"I, too late, / under her solemn fillet saw the scorn." Mistral's "Morning" opens with the paradox of the day being "the same yet new," and stresses the idea that one needs to raise her head from her "chest / and receive" every day. Emerson refers to the "daughters of time" as being "muffled and dumb," and emphasizes how little we take from the days that bring "diadems and fagots in their hands." Both poets seem to see that the days or mornings are deceptive, that in Mistral's words they "promise and cheat," yet both poets would appear to blame us for, in Emerson's words, forgetting our "morning wishes" and being satisfied with so little when each day offers so much more than we settle for. To Mistral, the morning is "empty-handed," which I take to mean that it is up to ourselves to make of a new day the most that we can. Each morning it holds out to us the possibility of so much, even though, as Emerson says, we tend to take from the day just "a few herbs and apples."

The Shakespeare connection that I suggested came from Mistral's use of the image of a kingfisher that "leaps skyward" and then swoops "down to us with song. / Hallelujah, Hallelujah, Hallelujah!" In the Bard's sonnet the bird is a lark that "at break of day arising / From sullen earth, sings hymns at heaven's gate." We also read the Chilean's prose-poem entitled "The Lark," and even though in this piece the bird's "straight flight toward the sun" parallels Shakespeare's, the point of Mistral's poem has more to do with achieving the "vertical flight" of Saint Francis, by which we overcome the "lukewarm rut: our habits." Whereas Emerson finds that our days scorn us for having made so little out of them, the speaker in Shakespeare's sonnet accepts his Fortune, and even his "outcast state," but "scorn[s] to change [his] state with kings" because of his friend's "sweet love." All three poets recognize that we have much to celebrate and appreciate in our mornings and days, and all three would have us remember the "wealth" that each can offer.

Most of our time was spent analyzing Mistral's "Mother Pomegranate," "California Poppy," "The Escape" (one of several poems about her own mother), and "The Other," an intriguing, enigmatic poem in which the speaker says that she "killed someone, / inside of me. / I didn't love her. . . . You must kill her, too!" Our textbook, the Mistral *Reader*, did not include one of my favorite poems by the Chilean poet, a prose-poem entitled "La Tortuga" (The Turtle) from 1926. Included in the bilingual edition of Mistral's *Selected Prose and Prose-Poems* (University of Texas Press, 2002), edited and translated by Stephen Tapscott, this prose-poem opens with the statement that "Fools allude to her in every conversation about progress, critiquing that lovely slowness." The poet enters the creature's life and presents her point of view through her contact with her environment: a square patio where she has lived for forty years, not knowing more of the world "than the distance a salmon can swim in eight days." The turtle touches the polished sand on the patio with her breast and it touches her, as if the sand has a sense of feeling. The creature's "two sweet gods" are grass and water. Leaves fallen on her back from the jasmine tree in the patio are yellow, and as if they contained autumn, she feels coolness enter her shell. A foolish child throws pebbles at the turtle, but an "intelligent hand" takes the child away. Without the turtle being aware of it, her shell thickens and she dies. "For a whole day no one noticed anything; she only seemed slower. . . . Her head entered her little casket. . . . The sand realized she had shrunk a little more. // They let her dry out in the air. Later they emptied her. Now on the table there is a spacious shell, an urn of old iron, filled with silence." One of the most empathetic works that I know, this prose-poem makes one aware of nature in terms of simple but quite profound relationships between a sentient creature and the imagined feelings of her surroundings.

In later years, Chile's other Noble-Prize winning poet, Pablo Neruda, would write numerous odes, and many of those exhibit an empathy similar to Mistral's, both for the natural world and for man-made objects. At the time I was unaware of Neruda's own poem on a turtle, or I would certainly have included it in our discussion. Here are a few lines from his own "La Tortuga" that are somewhat reminiscent of Mistral's poetic prose:

the turtle
armored
against
the heat
and cold,
against
the lightning and waves…
the turtle
remained
here
asleep,
and doesn't know it.
From being so old
she began
to grow hard,
ceased
loving the waves
and became rigid
as an ironing iron….

While still in Santiago during the last week of May and the first couple of days in June, we discussed Neruda's poetry, using his *Selected Poems*, edited by Nathaniel Tarn. Although I did not write any notes about our class discussions, I would take notes on our visits to Neruda's three homes, those in Santiago, Valparaíso, and Isla Negra. We covered a number of Neruda odes, but since the Tarn edition does not include one of my favorites, the ode to the "prodigious" scissors, I brought along for the students a Xerox copy of this wonderful poem, with its concluding lines:

And here with the scissors
of reason
I cut my ode,
so that it won't be long and wrinkled,
so that
it can
fit in your pocket

folded and ready
like a
pair of scissors.

As I recall, the students seemed to respond most enthusiastically to the odes, especially those on clothes and laziness. Probably the poem that impacted them the most was "I'm Explaining a Few Things," on the Spanish Civil War, with its image of "the blood of children [that] ran through the streets / as simply as children's blood."

At some point during our stay in Santiago, we would meet with poet-professor Armando Roa Vial and some of his students from the Universidad del Desarrollo (University of Development). The meeting took place in a large, three-story house called El Observatorio de Lastarria, built in 1912 and located in the historic neighborhood known as Barrio Santa Lucía-Mulato Gil de Castro. The area is also referred to as the Barrio Lastarria, named for José Victorino Lastarria (1817-1888), a Senator, Minister of Finance, and a literary figure who wrote a series of memoirs that he designated "notes for the literary history of Spanish America and the intellectual progress of Chile." The area is also known as Barrio Bellas Artes, since nearby is the city's main art museum, which we would visit on another occasion. The Lastarria house was painted red, its first floor was a cafe, in the basement were rooms for classes, an area on the second floor was for meetings, and on the third floor an observatory presented a view of the surrounding neighborhood. We gathered on the second floor where the students listened to Armando and myself carry on a dialogue regarding my work as a translator. Probably because I was the one doing most of the talking, I did not bother to make any notes on my responses to Armando's questions. In an e-mail that I sent to our Chilean friend Irene, I did mention that the students "were impressed that Armando and a graduate student raved about my translations of Enrique Lihn and kept saying how important my work was to Chilean literature. They said afterwards that they did not know that I was so famous!" It had been gratifying to have the students learn of my very limited "fame" on their own and directly from the Chileans themselves. Mostly I was happy for the students to hear from Armando and his students of Enrique Lihn's importance as a poet, since we would be studying his poetry in my own translations.

On June 3rd, we traveled to the coastal town of Reñaca, where the students took up residence, while María and I stayed in her sister's and brother-in-law's beach apartment in a high-rise building overlooking the Pacific. Our stay in Reñaca brought an entirely different scenery and also a very different CIEE personnel. The students were met on their first day at their beachside hotel by views from their windows of waves rising and crashing against the shoreline rocks. Unfortunately, the scene was somewhat spoiled by the sight of a Burger King and McDonald's; even so, the accommodations were pleasant in every other way. The CIEE staff welcomed us warmly and expressed both their delight in having us in Chile and their clearly heartfelt concern for our welfare during our two weeks in Reñaca.

Professor German Vogel welcomed us warmly on behalf of the Universidad Marítima (the Maritime University), where our classes would be held, as did the two women most responsible for seeing to the needs of the students and myself. A young, recently graduated elementary school teacher named Paula Olguín proved a tender, conscientious, and wholly attentive host to all of us. As I would learn during our stay, Paula's parents had been concerned to cultivate in her an appreciation for cultural history, and so they always spent their vacations visiting such sights as Teotihuacan and Macchu Picchu. Paula's mother was a teacher at the Catholic University and specialized in the Spanish exiles from the Civil War. In our text of Neruda's *Selected Poems*, we had already read and discussed his poem "The Heights of Macchu Picchu," and during our time in Reñaca, we would learn about Neruda's part in rescuing Spanish exiles through our visit to his home in Valparaíso. Professor Vogel, who taught in the law school at the Universidad Marítima, was also especially attentive and took a special interest in sharing with me literary publications that meant much to him, in particular the work of an Argentine scholar named Héctor Delfor Mandrioni, who had written in 1973 a work entitled *Sobre el amor y el poder* (On Love and Power). The professor had come to Reñaca twenty years before from Buenos Aires, and his reason for taking a special interest in Madrioni's book on power and love was that as a student of the law and its relation to power he came to realize that love should not be left out of his students' academic experience. At the end of our stay, Professor Vogel gave me a copy of *Sobre el amor y el poder* with a touching inscription.

Paula and Professor Vogel really made our stay in Reñaca the very pleasurable experience that it proved to be. Although the weather eventually turned uncomfortably cold and rainy, we enjoyed several days of almost ideal temperatures, even if the skies were mostly overcast. Our tour of nearby Valparaíso, Chile's major seaport, was the highlight of our first week. With Paula along with us, in addition to two tour guides from an excursion company, we were driven on the winding beach highway to one of Valparaíso's outdoor flower clocks, where a rescue ship was preserved in homage to its having saved thousands of troops trapped by the Panzer forces at Dunkirk, and from later having served to rescue Chileans during a tidal wave. The main tour guide, named Ingeborg, spoke excellent English, but I found her presentation a bit irritating, which was probably just my own problem, perhaps from my jealousy of her bilingual fluency. But I wanted the students to hear of the places we visited in Spanish rather than English, to have more of a flavor of the city and to learn more of the language. Of course, this made it hard on Ashley Thomas, but I still thought it better that the tour be conducted in Spanish.

Inge, as her name tag read, was eager and well-informed, but I mentioned to Paula my objections to the tour being in English. Inge then switched to Spanish, but spoke to us as if we were natives rather than visitors knowing little or nothing of the history or local names of the scenes passing quickly outside windows that only revealed a limited view. Once we had gotten out of the van and had begun to walk in the streets, we could see the city up close and take in Inge's commentary more easily. The students found the port city fascinating. We soon took one of the over one-hundred-year-old elevators, or funiculars, that rise straight up the cliffs of the city's some 42 hills. At the top of the cliffs were business buildings, homes, and once abandoned or deteriorated houses converted into museums and cultural centers. One museum, a beautiful example of the architectural styles that included nouveau and Italian futurism, had been the home of an eccentric figure whose name I failed to catch. The most famous museum above the seaport is dedicated to the work of the Italian-born cartoonist, Renzo Pecchenino, who signed his work Lukas and captured the peculiar appearance and life of Valparaíso. Our primary destination was La Sebastiana, one of the three homes of Neruda, which I will subsequently describe, together with our visit to the poet's home in Santiago, known as La Chascona.

After having toured La Sebastiana, we lunched in a restaurant named O'Higgins, after the first president of Chile. Back in the van again, we would ascend by curving streets the same hill that we had gone up in the funicular, but just before we began our climb, one of the students declared that she had a fever. Stopping the van, Paula and Inge took her to a pharmacy for some medication, and afterwards, fortunately, the student seemed fine. As for myself, I found the twisting streets made me a bit nauseous and suggested that we stop and get out for a walk. The tour guides assured me that we were almost to a *mirador*, or a place where one could look out over the port. The view was indeed worth the discomfort of the ride, for it took in the port, ships, colorful buildings, and the winding streets that we had just driven up. In walking in this area, we came across an entertainer who wore a red artificial nose and a long-tailed frockcoat, carrying in his hand a copy of Neruda's autobiography, *Para nacer he nacido* (To Be Born I Have Been Born). The fellow insisted that we squat down behind him as he took a steering wheel in his hands, sat down, and stretched out his legs to drive us around the port, making nonsense sounds in a high-pitched voice pinched by his false red nose. Apparently he believed he was Pablo Neruda, which the students found entertaining, even though Andrew joked that he was not going to squat down behind him because he was afraid of clowns.

We then passed through narrow, winding tunnels with graffiti on both sides of the walls—clever if vulgar sayings that unfortunately I cannot recall and did not have the presence of mind to jot down at the time. Later, Álvaro supplied me with two: *turistas/terroristas* (tourists/terrorists); *me cago en Dior* (I crap on [Christian] Dior). As Álvaro observed, the first was equating tourists like ourselves with terrorism, and the second was an attack on the jeweler-perfumer as a promoter of consumerism. Not long after our trip, I would encounter in Nicanor Parra's *Discursos de sobremesa* (After-Dinner Speeches) the line *me cago en Huidobro* (I crap on Huidobro). This was a typical example of Parra's satire of anything and anyone, including even his predecessor—without whom, he says in the same book of antipoetic speeches, Chilean poetry would have been reduced to Neruda's odes and the moans of another Chilean poet, Pablo de Rokha. Eventually we descended again to the main streets and visited a small bookstore called Crisis, full of volumes by Chilean authors and recommended to us by Alejandro Cerda, a young poet who had joined us at La Sebastiana and would accompany us on other of our excursions.

In Santiago, we had toured La Chascona, Neruda's home-turned-museum across the Mapocho River from the center of the city, in the Bella Vista district that has become an area of restaurants and shops that attract both citizens and tourists alike. On our way to the museum, waiters at the many restaurants offered us menus to entice us to dine in their establishments or at outdoor tables. The home-museum's name, La Chascona, came from the full head of hair of Neruda's third wife, Matilde Urrutia. Our tour guide at the museum was a young, very enthusiastic fellow who spoke excellent English, had a sense of humor, and did not take himself so seriously. He provided us with many insights into Neruda's poetic approach to planning and decorating his home.

Fashioned in the shape of a ship, the house was missing its porthole windows, along with many of the objects that Neruda had collected over the years. As the guide explained, the house had been ransacked during the coup of 1973 by those who resented the poet's politics. Smashing his china collections and destroying his paintings, books, manuscripts, and apparently anything in the house, the military and/or looters ravaged the rooms while the poet was being taken from his home on the coast at Isla Negra to a hospital in Santiago. He was then suffering from the deterioration of a condition that had weakened him for some time and had forced him to return to Chile from France, where he had been the Chilean ambassador. Upon his death shortly thereafter, the Neruda Foundation took over his properties that he had willed to the people of Chile—a reference to which we had read in his poem "Autumn Testament," where he writes "I left my landed goods / to my Party and my people." The Foundation attempted to restore the home, at least to a semblance of its original beauty and its representation of the poet's personal tastes, his almost child-like pleasure in every item he collected and so often wrote about in his endless outpouring of poems. Among the artworks that we saw were paintings by Picasso.

    The students were quite taken with the tour of La Chascona, with all its nooks in various parts of the house, often separated from one another by bridges or paths among the landscaped grounds. One set of rooms—a bar and a dining room with colored drinking glasses that the poet claimed made any beverage taste better—was connected to a guest apartment by a secret door through which we stepped after the guide had pointed out how the wall opened into the adjoining room. The guide also revealed that there were more bars in the house than bedrooms: two of the latter but three of the former. One bar contained photographs of Neruda's poet friends, as well as a large photo of Walt Whitman, which was in addition to many smaller ones in a number of the rooms. The story repeated by both tour guides—in La Chascona and La Sebastiana—concerned the well-known anecdote of a carpenter who on one of the walls had hung for Neruda a large picture of Whitman. When asked by the workman if the photo was his father, the Chilean poet responded that he could say he was, in the sense that the U.S. poet had inspired Neruda's own poetry. Another anecdote recounted by the guide was that when Diego Rivera painted Matilde, he wanted to include Pablo in the picture, but because the poet was still married to Delia del Carril, he asked the artist not to do so; nevertheless, Rivera did work Neruda's profile into Matilde's hair—that is, in the hair of one of two views of her head that Rivera painted on the same canvas.

    In one room I noticed a copy of Neruda's *The Book of Questions*, with which I was unfamiliar. I read a few of the questions to the students, including one that asked what could be more ridiculous than to be called Pablo Neruda. The guide then left us to fetch another book with some of the poet's questions and with answers given to them by school-age children. Some of the responses were highly inventive, in the style of Neruda himself, but unfortunately, once again, I did not jot down any examples.

While the view of Santiago and the Andes from the balconies of La Chascona was spectacular, the panorama of the seaport at Valparaíso from La Sebastiana was almost breathtaking. Here the house's seaport windows were preserved and the four floors we were able to visit offered one delight after another. As at La Chascona, there was a bar at La Sebastiana, behind which Neruda in costume would serve his friends. One room was full of memorabilia and photographs from many periods of the poet's life, including his boyhood years with his family in Temuco and his later reception of the Nobel Prize in Sweden in 1971. One copy of his autobiography in Russian and a number of his collections of poems in Spanish covered a table in this same room, which also contained photographs of several Spanish poets from just before the Civil War, including Federico García Lorca.

The item in the house that meant the most to me was a memorial written by a Spanish exile who paid tribute to Neruda's having arranged for Republican sympathizers to emigrate to Chile on the ship "Winnipeg." The writer, Modesto Parera, contrasted his fellow Spaniards' hatred—motivated by politics that had filled the streets with their own nation's blood—with the loving act of the Chilean poet and the warm reception the exiles received in Valparaíso (the Valley of Paradise). Parera concluded that Neruda's having saved hundreds of Spaniards would prove his most beautiful poem. All of this reminded me of our reading of Neruda's "I'm Explaining a Few Things," where he names García Lorca, calling to him in his grave "where the light of June drowned flowers in your mouth"—a reference to his assassination by followers of Franco. This poem marked a change in Neruda's poetry, from being almost purely nature-oriented to one of greater social consciousness, just as the poem itself contrasts his peacetime house in Spain—"called / the house of flowers, because in every cranny / geraniums burst"— with the wartime bombings, when "from every house burning metal flows / instead of flowers" and "bandits with black friars spatter blessings," the latter an allusion to the Catholic Church's collusion with Franco.

There were a number of excursions that I failed to keep any or much of an account of in my travel notes. One was of a visit to a pottery business in the town of Pomaire, about 60 kilometers from Santiago. We ate lunch there at a local home and toured the family's small pottery operation. The owners allowed the students to help make "empanadas" (a meat-, fish- or cheese-filled baked pie), and also to make their own pottery, or "to throw" pots, as the process is termed. We all tried our hand at creating a pot, and my clearest memory is of cutting a place in one of my fingers that took several weeks to heal, apparently from the clay that I was working with. In her albums, María preserved a page of notes in my handwriting that indicates that there was no lead in the clay and that impurities had been removed. My words and phrases, in English and Spanish (with bracketed translations in English not in the original notes), refer cryptically to the whole pottery process, and were perhaps intended as words and phrases toward a poem that I never wrote:

>   la caverna de los ladrones [the cave of the thieves]
>   el pueblo de los brujos [the town of wizards]
>   la greda sin plomo [the clay without lead]
>   [shapes of the pots] chancho [pig] tortuga [turtle] macetas [flowerpots]
>   licked earth from agates
>   unpainted pressed wood
>   grapes on vines w/ last leaves yellow
>   celos [jealousies] ignorancia [ignorance] desprecio [contempt]
>   empanadas & greda amasadas [empanadas & clay (both are) kneaded]
>   wheelbarrow of greda w/out impurities
>   horno [oven]
>   carbon [charcoal] fallas—no cocidas bien [flaws—not well baked]
>   humo de bostas—polvo en piezas [smoke from manure—dust on fragments]

wheel played with feet like an organ
ceramic music—shaped with wet hands, thumbs, polished w/ ágatas [agates]

The night before we were to visit the grand antipoet Nicanor Parra in his beach home in Las Cruces, Alejandro Cerda wanted me to go with him to meet another poet, Juan Cameron, at a café in Valparaíso. I was not that keen on going out that night but Alejandro insisted, so I reluctantly went with him on a bus. By the time that we reached the downtown area, where we were to meet Juan, it was pouring, with water running in the streets ankle high. We had to dash across several streets, splashing through the rainwater, dodging pedestrians, and trying to keep our heads dry without umbrellas. It was a mess and I was angry with myself for having agreed to go out the night before our visit with Parra. At the café, Alejandro and Juan talked endlessly while I paced about trying to keep warm from being so wet. I could not get Alejandro to leave and was certain that I would come down with a cold and be unable to visit Parra. Outside the rain continued and I could not imagine having to go out and wait for a bus. Finally, two women who joined Alejandro and Juan in their conversation said that they would be driving in the direction of Reñaca and invited us to come with them. I was so relieved and grateful. I finally made it back to the apartment and luckily the next morning was none the worse for wear.

On June 9th, the students, Paula, Alejandro, a driver, and I would travel from Reñaca to Las Cruces for what would be my fifth time to visit Nicanor Parra, the first having come in 1965 and the other three occasions having been in 1991, 1998, and 2001. For me the visit to Parra was to be the high point of the trip. I had built him up to the students and they had heard repeatedly from Chileans what a rare opportunity they were being given, since he did not receive just anyone. The two women at FLACSO, who had taught the students about Chilean culture, had told them that they were envious, that they wished they could come along with them to meet the famous antipoet. Once we were with Parra at his home, I asked if he still walked on the nearby hills every day and he said not any more, only around his house, because when people saw him, they gathered about and begged for his autograph. The front page of *Revista de Libros* (*Book Review Magazine*), the Friday Supplement to Chile's main newspaper, *El Mercurio*, even bruited that very day that the antipoet was a "Superstar." Also announced in the Supplement was the forthcoming edition of his *Obras completas y algo +* (Complete Works and a Bit More), to be published by the prestigious Spanish publisher, Galaxia Gutenberg.

    The drive to Las Cruces took us over the eucalyptus- and palm tree-covered hills, through a tunnel in one mountain, and up and down the coastal cordillera. Near El Tabo we passed a sign pointing to the home-museum at Isla Negra of Pablo Neruda. Some twenty minutes later, we arrived in Parra's small seaside town where first a taxi driver and then a man on the street directed us toward his address, Lincoln 113. There I hoped that we would find the antipoet and that the students would be able to experience him in person in all his glorious wittiness and wisdom. From my previous visit with Parra in Las Cruces in 1998, I recognized his house with its huge palm tree and with its first floor below street level, but I did not remember his VW Bug, which was parked in front. We never saw a number on the house, perhaps because the antipoet did not wish to encourage uninvited guests or autograph seekers. Leaving the group behind, I descended to the front door, which was open, and called out "Don Nicanor," to which a maid from a back room responded for me to come in. Entering the front part of the house—really a hallway filled with old manual typewriters—one of which I may have seen in a 2002 exhibit of Parra's "artefactos," labeled "La máquina del tiempo" (The Time Machine). Along with other artifacts, there was an ancient telephone, which in the same 2002 exhibit was labeled "El teléfono de Hitler / Colección de Huidobro" (Hitler's Telephone / Huidobro Collection), a joke on Huidobro's claim that in World War II he had captured the Nazi's telephone. The white statue of a life-sized Greek-styled nude held a sign in the antipoet's distinctive handwriting and read: "Soy frígida / Sólo me muevo con fines de lucro" (I'm frigid / I'm only moved by profit-making).

    Suddenly I saw Don Nicanor coming from the breakfast area, his face not wearing a look that said "Welcome, I've been expecting you." Since I had made arrangements ahead of time for the students and myself to visit Parra, I was quite surprised and disappointed. I embraced him, but there was no real response. He then saw Paula, and behind her in a line in the hallway the students and Alejandro. Parra asked Paula who she was, and she gave him her name, and then he asked her "Who invited you?" to which she replied that she was there with the student group. Parra then went down the line greeting each student, and afterwards asked "Where shall we go?" answering himself by saying "Follow me." He led us out to the left side of the house, through branches of a leafless tree full of light-green, apple-looking fruit. We climbed some cement stairs onto a piece of ground with unfinished brick columns at the four corners of a foundation, a few bunches of grass, some white plastic chairs, and several clotheslines. We all stood there, facing him, he in his usual khaki fisherman's hat, baggy pants, a homemade sweater hanging down below his backside, and canvas-topped, synthetic-soled, lace-up boots, all, as he later revealed, secondhand, even though he had won nearly a million dollars in literary prizes. His 92-year-old skin exhibited not a single wrinkle.

Without our asking a question or prompting him in any way, he began to speak to us, saying that he had never read *The Taming of the Shrew* before, but this was his present interest. He quoted some lines from the play and was especially taken by the word "baggage," with its meaning close to hussy or even whore. He said that the 13th- to 14th-century Spanish writer Juan Manuel had written a piece with the same plot, and that he was particularly eager to discover connections between the Spanish and the English versions. He mentioned Shakespeare's use of the word "basta" and wondered how that Spanish word for "that's enough" had come to the Bard. I ventured to suggest that it came through the Italians, whose plots he often usurped, as in the case of *Romeo and Juliet*. He ignored me and went on quoting some lines that it seemed to me were about a lion, but I was not for certain, unable at times to understand his pronunciation of the English. (The reference may have been to Petruchio's wooing Kate the wild-cat and his not being daunted by lions that roar.) At what I took to be an appropriate opening, I tried to turn the conversation to his own poetry and mentioned our having read his poem "The Nobel Prize," in which he asks that he be given the Prize for reading. This was a dig at the Swedish Academy for not having conferred on him the lucrative and prestigious award for his antipoetry, the same Prize that his fellow poets Gabriela Mistral and Pablo Neruda had received. I told him that only after Ashley—to whom I pointed—had read the poem out loud in our class did I realize that I had missed the fact that the last line asks not that the prize be given to you "as soon as possible" but "as soon as impossible." But again he ignored all this and said that he did not want to discuss his own work, only *The Taming of the Shrew*.

So far our visit had not gone at all as I had hoped or expected. My friend Francisco had assured me that Parra was anxious to see me, that he had said that Dave has a green light, that he wondered what he could do to repay me for all the support that I had given to him by translating his long poem, "Aunque no vengo preparrado" (Although I Haven't Come Preparraed—the extra "r" an instance of Parra's frequent wordplay on his own name). It now occurred to me that Francisco might not have gotten through to Parra by phone, and then remembered that when I had heard from Francisco the day before that he had said that he had tried all day to contact Parra but that his cell phone was turned off. Francisco had arranged for the visit more than a month before and had been in touch with Parra right along, but after Francisco had gone to Bolivia the week before, he apparently had not spoken to Parra by phone for some time. By now I was feeling totally dispirited.

When an occasion arose that seemed right for me to present the antipoet with two gifts that I had brought from Texas, I told him that I had a magazine for him, which he accepted and then for a bit looked at its cover. He was obviously puzzled by the picture of a movie actress and by several lines of type that included the phrase "Feel Good and Look Great." Suddenly he got it, and pointing with an index finger showed the lines to the students. I said, they stole it from you, alluding to the subtitle of his 2004 New Directions volume, *Antipoems: How to look better & feel great*, which I had reviewed for *The Texas Observer*. He quickly lit up with delight. I then gave him a copy of Helen Vendler's *The Art of Shakespeare's Sonnets,* in the 1992 hardback edition, which I had inscribed, although he did not open the book to the flyleaf but just thumbed through it and then laid it down on one of the chairs, along with the magazine. At this point I took out of my briefcase a copy of the brochure for our Maymester course and stuck it in the Vendler volume. He immediately removed the brochure from the book and started looking at it. A poster with Neruda's name was reproduced on the cover, but I showed him right away that his own name and comments on his work were on the inside flap. He looked more closely at the information printed in the brochure, and then said "Dave Oliphant," seeing my name as instructor for the course on Chilean poetry. "Then you're Dave," he said, and I replied "Yes," never having thought to say who I was when we first entered his home, thinking he knew who we all were, and that we had arrived exactly at 11:30 a.m. as instructed by him through Francisco. With this he came around the chair and grabbed me, hugged me warmly, and told the students, "We're old friends."

The ice having been broken, as it were, Parra began to ask the students about themselves: were they all from Texas, were they Mexican. In fact, three of the seven students were born in Mexico and the others were of Mexican descent, except for Ashley, a light-complected African-American. Learning that most of the students were from the border area, Parra launched into the recitation of a Mexican *corrido*, a long tale of border tragedy (apparently a song entitled "La tragedia de un mojado" [The Tragedy of a Wetback]). On finishing to recite the lyrics, Parra asked if the students knew this great song. Álvaro said that he thought that he had heard it, and Karen declared that she knew it well because it was her father's favorite *corrido*.

From there Parra began talking about the new generation of Internet users, telling the students that they belonged to the age of Google searches, and related them to the Penguins, the name for the secondary school students who, as mentioned earlier, had paralyzed Chile for almost three weeks by taking over schools, protesting in the streets, and participating in high-level discussions with the Minister of Education and other administrators representing newly-elected President Bachelet's government. I asked Parra why the students were called Penguins: was it because of their school uniforms of white and dark-blue that somewhat matched the arctic bird's colors and tuxedo-like appearance? He said that he himself had asked the same question, and he believed that they were called such by journalists because they have short arms or wings (as in Huidobro's poem "Equatorial"), but rather than flying they clutch and grasp at the snow and ice to get around. The attitude of the government had been that the students were too young to make decisions about the improvement in their educational situation, so they had taken to clawing their way into public consciousness in order to protest the unacceptable conditions of a system that did not guarantee them a quality education. His thoughts recalled to me Neruda's poem on the penguin, in his book *The Art of Birds*, in which he refers to the penguin not needing to fly nor to sing in order to gain the poet's admiration as a religious bird, a slow priest of cold, dressed in night and snow.

Parra has always been socially aware, even though he never seems to take any one side. At some point he told us that the world may be better off because of the United States, it *may* be, he emphasized, leaving the question open as so often in his antipoems that present both sides of any issue. Parra can always appreciate opposing positions, as he does in his "Also Sprach Altazor," a tribute to his predecessor, Vicente Huidobro, as mentioned before, from whom he declares, in that section of his *After-Dinner Declarations,* that he has learned practically everything. The antipoet can repeat Huidobro's famous claim that the poet is a little God, but in the next line assert that the poet is a little demon. Or he can sympathize with those who study the world and cannot help but become Communists, whereas those who study the Communist Party, he says, must turn into anarchists. Not stopping with the latter assertion, the antipoet goes on to state bluntly that anyone not idealistic at 20 is heartless but then adds that to be so at 40 is to be headless. Parra is surely the greatest wordplay poet of the 20th century and the beginning of the 21st. In fact, it would be difficult to think of another poet, other than Shakespeare, who has so thoroughly employed double entendres. For any and every occasion, Parra has been able to reveal insights into words, popular sayings, or ready-made phrases that add new meanings to their original usage. For example, his most famous *artefacto* is "USA, donde la libertad es una estatua" (United States: the country where liberty is a statue).

Having earlier in his "discourse" to the students called the Swedish Academy the bastion of ultraconservatism, which he also claimed was true of the Chilean Society of Writers, he later came back to the word "bastion," observing that we were standing in the ruins of his one-time citadel, which had burned down. To indicate what his former house had looked like, he pointed toward the other side of his present home where he said there was a house in the same style. Realizing that we could not see the building, he directed us to follow him. He led us down several embankments, under tree branches, and out onto a dirt road at the bottom of his property. We followed him on this road that turned into a concrete paving with pebbles washed onto it from the previous days' rain. We could see the bay with beautiful waves rolling in, crashing against rocks, and running up the inclined beach. I reminded him that on my last visit that he, Francisco, his girlfriend Kuki, and I had had lunch at the restaurant across the bay. He walked briskly on, headed in that direction, speaking of Shakespeare's use of iambic pentameter that was both blank verse and the most normal of speech patterns. When he reached the restaurant, he arranged chairs outside on a terrace of sorts with a gorgeous view of the ocean "endlessly rocking in its cradle," as Whitman wrote. The students gathered about him as he continued to speak of various topics that came to his mind, answering questions from Alejandro about his views on other Chilean writers like Roberto Bolaño. He was delighted when Alejandro showed him a copy of a magazine with a photograph of his youngest granddaughter, Cristalina. He noted that all his girls' names ended in "ina": Cristalina; her mother Catalina; his daughter Columbina; and his granddaughter Josefina. Alejandro praised his poem "Mi nieta juega en el jardín" (My granddaughter plays in the garden), which Parra revealed was written by María Monvel, which I had learned on visiting him at his home in La Reina in 2001. Parra had "lifted" other poems and made them his own, simply by changing a few phrases or a single word. In the case of Monvel's poem, he substituted *nieta* (granddaughter) for the original's *hija* (daughter), just as Shakespeare modified and added to works like *Romeo and Juliet*, *Hamlet*, and *King Lear*.

At some point, Álvaro asked Parra if he could take a

photo of him with me, to which the antipoet replied that it might be more objectionable to Dave than to him. Normally Parra does not like having his picture taken, even though innumerable photos of the antipoet have graced many publications, including one on the front cover of that day's *Revista de Libros* and five others in the various pages of a spread on him and his antipoems. After giving permission for Álvaro to take another photo with Alejandro included, Parra said to take one of him and Karen, toward whom he leaned over in his chair. Soon after these "photo ops," Parra turned to me and said "The English go away but do not disappear," rose from his seat, and walked back the way that we had come. Even though we had invited him for lunch at the restaurant, he had responded that it was too early, that he had just eaten breakfast. I saw him at a distance turn and wave his arms back and forth across one another, which I thought might mean that I should follow him, but when I started toward him he went on and never looked back again. I could see that our meeting with the antipoet had come to an end and so I rejoined the students. If Parra on leaving us was quoting from a poem, a song, or some other source, I cannot say, but he often quotes popular expressions and from other writers, and perhaps most frequently from the works of Shakespeare. Later I found a song with the same title as the phrase that Parra had used, apparently by pop singer Justin Bieber, but I could never find the lyrics of the song to confirm that it was the antipoet's source for the English going away but not disappearing.

After we lunched on fresh fish—I had a delicious, inexpensive *merluza* (hake)—we trekked back to Parra's home to say our farewells. I was curious to see if he had taken into his house the Vendler book and the magazine that he had left on the chair. They were gone. The front door was shut, and on it we could see in black spray paint the word *anti-poesía*, which either he had written or was graffiti. A dog at the door we denominated an *anti-perro*. We knocked several times and could hear him inside on the telephone. Finally, he opened a small, grated door within the front door and looked out at us. We thanked him for receiving us, and he thanked us for our visit, repeating what he had said on leaving us at the restaurant: "The English go away but they do not disappear." He waved, we waved back, and he watched us until we had gone down the street out of sight. Getting back in the van, we would continue our day dedicated to three of the greatest poets of Chile: Parra, Huidobro, and Neruda.

Surprisingly I did not record anything regarding our visit to Huidobro's tomb in nearby Cartagena. However, María did make a few notes, based partly on what I had told her, since she did not go with us on this occasion because she had what she called a phenomenal cold. Here then is my translation of the note in her annual album of our life together:

> From time to time I had read something about the lack of initiative of the city of Cartagena in publicizing the fact that the fantastic and original poet Vicente Huidobro had died there and that in the hills above was his tomb, on the land of the *fundo* owned by his family. There was no signage to indicate how to get there. I don't understand why his descendants had not taken care of the sandy and inhospitable place. Perhaps it was because they still have not recovered from having had in the family this black sheep who, by his bohemian and rebellious conduct, had caused scandals, and had been a Communist, etc., etc. Being a Communist I see as the intellectual's typical pose and a sure way, in his case, to horrify society and his family. And how was he going to be a Communist when he did not want to be ruled by anybody or anything, except for poetry.
>
> After a while, things began to look up, as the driver and tour guide figured out how to reach the tomb. But with the tremendous rain of a few days before, the dirt road, or rather of sand, was full of water and the vehicle got stuck. All working together the students managed to pull the van out of the mud, while Dave walked ahead and found the tombstone, which was located among sand and weeds and a ferocious wind. On the stone they could read a phrase from Canto V from Huidobro's poem, "Altazor":

*Abrid la tumba,
al fondo
de esta tumba
se ve el mar.*

[Open the tomb,
at the bottom
of this tomb
the sea is seen.]

Not long afterwards work must have begun to put up signage and to make the sandy and desolate place more attractive.

When María, Francisco Véjar, and I would visit the grave in 2013, it had been completely transformed into an inviting and much deserved monument to the poet. Even more impressive was a museum constructed to showcase manuscripts, books, and photographs, with background information on the various materials, all displayed in very professional exhibit cases.

After leaving Cartagena, we were driven to Neruda's home at Isla Negra, and once again I failed to make any notes on our visit. In part, the reason for my not writing anything was that Maria and I had visited the site in 1991; twenty years later we would visit it again in 2011. But mainly the reason for not recording anything about the visit with the students in 2006 was that we found the home was closed for repairs. After parking the van in a lot on the main street of Isla Negra, we walked to an unpaved intersecting street that led to the beach where Neruda's house is located. On turning the corner onto the dirt street, we passed by the side of a gray, stone building—a store or business of some sort—on which there was a mural that I had not seen in 1991. A photo of the students and myself preserved in María's album shows the details of the mural just as I remembered them from 2006: on the left, a bald Neruda with his chin in his right hand looks askance at wine bottles on a plank table, overlooked from above in the left corner of the painting by a ship's female figurehead, part of the poet's collection of such artifacts in his home; on the right is a painted boat on which Neruda and his friends would sit and talk, the real one beached in 1991 next to the house; and at the top of the mural, rocks along the beach, the blue Pacific, and the sky above. After walking down the unpaved road and turning to the left, we arrived at the Neruda home and could look over the fence at a metal fish within a globe, made of two overlapping metal strips, perched on top of the home's principal building with its peaked roof, and in the yard below it a massive black-and-red steam engine. To give more of an idea of the exterior and interior features of Neruda's home, I reproduce here my notes from María's and my August 8th, 1991, visit, when Irene Rostagno and her mother Lucy drove us from Santiago to Isla Negra.

> Passing along a damp, brownish, sandy path with wooden, staked fences and pine trees, with views of the Pacific through them, we approached Neruda's house on the beach, with its stone tower on the right—reminding me of Robinson Jeffers' Tor House on the California coast at Carmel—and several wooden buildings painted a cerulean blue, with the main house connected to other buildings by a stone archway. A seahorse fashioned from a kind of pumice stone sat atop the archway, and the two-story section where the poet had his bedroom was decorated with colored stones that formed fish of various shapes. From an inverted V of metal, a bell was hanging, and beyond the V and the beach we could see white waves crashing against huge boulders. Visible through the windows of the main house were Neruda's collections of figureheads from the prows of ships—men, women, etc.—and ships in bottles. We would return later for a tour, but in the meantime we drove for lunch to Quisco, a town continuing from Isla Negra. There in a cove of the ocean, seagulls and pelicans floated on the water or drifted and glided in the sky above. At a cafe I ordered *congrio* (conger eel), a seafood to which Neruda wrote an ode that I had translated over twenty years before. For

an appetizer we had tasty, slightly picante scallops. The sun was shining beautifully for our visit, with huge white clouds against a blue background. Two fishing boats rocked in the cove as the waves washed in and out. María ordered *caldillo de congrio*, the recipe for which Neruda describes in his ode on the same dish, with the *congrio* cooked straight from the sea.

On returning to the poet's home we could smell the eucalyptus trees and the ocean breeze's delicious aroma. I took photos of the house from the outside, including the black-and-red steam engine in his backyard. I wondered if Neruda had written a poem on the gigantic, heavy train engine that students had somehow managed to transport to Isla Negra from many miles away. If Neruda had written a poem about his gift, I would compare it with Whitman's "To a Locomotive in Winter." The ocean below goes on ceaselessly beating against the rocks that protrude from the beach, also making me think of Whitman and his "Out of the Cradle Endlessly Rocking." Several of the rocks bore various drawings, one with Neruda's face—washed when the tide is up by his beloved Pacific. The view of the Pacific was spectacular and had inspired other poets, including Jeffers. The changing skies, the altering shades of the water, and the constant movement of the sea brought new objects and perspectives hour by hour, and kept Neruda's pen repeatedly recording the scene to the ocean's rhythmic beat. I thought of another poem of his that I had translated, which compares an approaching storm to a menagerie of animals loosed upon the unsuspecting land. Peaceful and tempestuous by turns, Neruda's scene below his house is a perpetual drama that he captured over and over. In his poems on the ocean, he recreates nature's wildness, as he whipped it into performance on the page, like an animal trainer but with a pen in his hand to elicit his linguistic tricks. In the ocean's foam, its lighting, and its algae, he could watch designs appear, disappear, and others take their place and those in turn to be replaced. In a line he wrote in 1958, he says "Navegué construyendo la alegría" (I sailed constructing happiness).

He had bought the house in 1938, and inside it there is a vast array of items:

at the entrance, seashells embedded in the floor
picture of a ship with sails / whale spouting water
figurehead with braids, a rose in her hand, a hat on her head, in a blue & white sailor uniform
medusa—his first figurehead (people thought she was a saint & lit candles on her)
one figurehead as a scarecrow
Siren & Sir Francis Drake
(magnifying?) glass for looking at maps, steering wheel or helm (*timón*), ships & bottles everywhere
negro de popa (black on poop or stern?),
angels flying & playing trumpets
rigging hanging from wooden ceilings, rock walls, plates, glasses
key lost to a jug (of crystal) holding drink
Jenny Lind
place mats w/ ships, astrolabe, glass jugs
problem of getting steam engine here
bedroom [built in] '58[?]
[Neruda] left from here for Santiago in ambulance [1973]
black-faced lamb overlooking the bed
PyM—initials on wall [for Pablo and Matilde]
little cabin below where he wrote poems
low cane table with shelf for house shoes
painting by Henri Rousseau on wall—family in horse carriage
print of sinking ship
scenes of ships at sea, shipwreck
closet w/ hats of every sort—English, helmet, Indian, graduate, of elegant '20s, shoes, suits
bar Alberto Rojas Jiménez—[named] after subject of [one

of his] poems [entitled "Alberto Rojas Jiménez viene
volando" (Alberto Rojas Jiménez Comes Flying)]
wrote names of friends on beams as they died (see his
poem on this [in his book *Memorial de Isla Negra*:
"Los nombres"—"No los escribí en la techumbre por
grandiosos sino por compañeros" (I did not write them on
the roof-beams for being great but for being companions);
in addition to Jiménez, there are Joaquín Cifuentes,
Federico García Lorca, Paul Eluard, Miguel Hernández,
and Nazim] ship chandler / Pablo Neruda
captain chairs
bottles hanging in ropes
collection of glass flasks
ships in bottles
landscapes in sand in bottles
Christ on cross in bottles
wooden masks
foot warmers
butterflies, figurines of devils, insects
brass telescope
Mallarmé—same photo as at the H[umanities] R[esearch]
C[enter, University of Texas at Austin]
[photos of] Lenin, Keats, Mayakovsky, Baudelaire, Whitman,
Poe, Lorca, Miguel Hernández, and poems by Joachim du
Bellay, Dante, Leopardi, Petrarch
musical instruments (strings), gramophone, anchors
shells & globes—sailing ships—candle holders, compasses,
maps
Polynesian figure in wood
room of the horse—brought from Temuco (store burned
down but the wooden horse survived)
bordados [tapestries] made by children?
bird room
men's room with pictures of women, decaled commode—on
special occasions they prepared punch in the bidet
shell collections reminded me that WCW wrote a poem in
Pictures from Brueghel to Pablo Neruda the shell collector

This house and its contents reflect not only Neruda's taste for objects but his delight in the good life, Communist though he professed to be.

O mar o camarada...
tu regalo de oro
[O sea o comrade...
you gift of gold]

    The day after María and I had visited Neruda's home in Isla Negra in 1991, we had also gone to La Chascona, on Marqués de la Plata street, on a very cold day, one degree below zero, celsius. There we were shown a film on the house at Isla Negra, in which Neruda reads from his poetry, beginning with the lines quoted above. The sound of strained rigging is played as background to the video's panning from one ship-related object to another—the figureheads, the ships, the spy glasses, the compasses. From time to time Neruda is seen walking by the seaside, the first time wearing a red poncho and with a wooden cane. At one point the sound of helicopters is heard, which became a symbol of the military takeover in Chile in 1973, with appropriately sad music following. A sign says the house at Isla Negra is closed by order of the government:

the threat of the United States
against which each of his poems
was destined to be a useful tool
(he reading to this effect)

so great the absence (of Neruda)
(read apparently by his wife Matilde)

    A math teacher of María's was with us on this occasion—she had just lost her husband—and at this point in the video she breathed a deep sigh. The film then showed a hummingbird outside Neruda's house—like one that we had seen there the day before—hanging in the air beside a flower blossom like a helicopter hovering above the poet's lovely Isla Negra home. This was followed by views of Pablo and Matilde walking out of the house, past figureheads and a huge anchor on the beach. Neruda said of himself that he was "an amateur of the sea."

One of the most delightful excursions that the students and I enjoyed was to the community of Rabuco, near the famous "El Cerro Campana" (Bell Mountain, a National Park with scenic views of the Andes and the Pacific). Thanks to Paula, whose father had relatives in the area, we were able to spend much of Tuesday, June 13th, with a working family known by Paula since her childhood. That morning, however, I awoke not feeling so well, but decided that all the same I should go on the outing with the class. Looking out of the apartment windows, I could see thick fog, with almost zero visibility. Once in the street I almost regretted that I had not stayed in bed and just lounged around the apartment instead of going out in the damp, penetrating soup. At the students' hotel I waited for the group and Paula, their "babysitter," to come down to the reception desk. Álvaro was the only one already there, chatting with the chauffeur about the previous day's World Soccer Cup matchups and winners. I had watched a bit of the re-runs of the games the night before, with Spain defeating Ukraine by four goals to none and Germany sneaking past Poland one to zero. I asked the chauffeur the difference between *un gol* and *un balón*. I understood him to say that *balón* was when the ball entered the net, but when a goal is scored, the crowd always yells *gol*, not *balón*. I did understand that Spain had won a previous match because the other team had scored an auto-goal, meaning one of its players accidentally headed the ball into his own side's net. Finally, the students arrived, but Paula informed me that Diana was ill and that Andrew was going to stay with her, although she assured me that everything was under control.

Driving up the steep hills in the fog, we could barely see two car-lengths ahead, and the air was so frigid that I had to keep a muffler tightly around my neck. We were behind a gasoline truck that slowed us even more than the heavy fog. As we crossed over the Aconcagua River, the sun tried to peep through, but the fog still blanketed the landscape all along the way. But by the time that we reached the town of Quillota, visibility began to improve. After entering a four-lane highway going in the direction of Santiago, we could pass the gas truck, and once we reached Rabuco and were away from the coast, the day turned clear and not cold at all. The family's home that we were visiting was on the single, unpaved street that ran the length of the town of Rabuco. At a blue metal fence, the driver stopped the van and we were immediately greeted by the mother of the household, who had come out of the house and had passed beneath a grape arbor and avocado trees bearing green and maroon fruit. Also named María, the mother would accompany us for the rest of the day.

Just as María had greeted us warmly on our arrival, so did her mother, who was preparing breakfast for all the group. The fare consisted of freshly baked *sopaipillas* (a type of fritter) with butter and honey, along with fruits of various kinds, including pomegranate and one type of Chilean fruit that I did not know, whose name I now forget, but do recall that it was especially delicious. The grandmother invited the students to help her make the *sopaipillas*, just as in Pomaire they had rolled the dough for and filled the *empanadas*.

The walls of the house were hung with photographs of earlier generations and a TV was showing a World Cup game. Everything was modest but clean and homey. Paula was treated affectionately by the family members, which included the grandfather, two teenagers, a boy and girl, and a little girl of five. I spoke to the child and asked her her name and her age, and though she seemed a bit shy, she told me both, which I have not remembered. The grandfather was not talkative and remained on the outside of the house where there were ducks, chickens, another grape arbor, a variety of plants, and a bare patch, next to some tin or wooden sheds, where later the teenagers would entertain us.

After breakfast, we piled back in the van and were driven to the end of the street, where it intersected with a paved road onto which we made a left-hand turn and headed for a vineyard, whose name I failed to record. Parking the van at the entrance to the vineyard, the driver opened the side door and we all piled out and followed María into the nearest field where workers were pruning the vines. We were soon met by the owner, who began to explain to us the operation of the vineyard. He was apparently of Spanish extraction, whereas the workers were all mestizos or pure-blooded Chilean natives. The owner's pride in and enthusiasm for his occupation was fully evident in his explanations of the manner in which each grape vine was attended to, including the recording of its care and condition at every step of the process of pruning, feeding, and watering. He noted that because Rabuco is a stony area, the heat of the day is retained in the rocks during the cold nights, and as a result the grapes from Rabuco are among the best in the country. The owner also explained that each plant is distinctive and its characteristics are faithfully documented in order to know how well it produces, if the pruning by a specific worker was done properly, if the plant received too much or too little water, etc. He wished that we could see the vineyard when the leaves would be green, rather than brown and mostly on the ground. He encouraged us to come back and see the grapes hanging in their beautiful clusters from row on row of vines forming arbors like green archways.

It was wonderful to see how completely, after 25 years, the owner still enjoyed his work, with its cycle of observing and caring for the vines and their annual produce. As he himself informed us, he had gone to college to study for a career—perhaps it was pharmacy—but had realized that his heart remained in the fields. He said that he was thoroughly happy with his decision to return to the family vineyard, where he never tired of every stage in the growing of and the tending to his family's Chilean grapes.

Our next stop was at a nursery where flowers were grown from seeding through every step up to the time of blooming, when they would be sold in towns and cities. The work was labor intensive, from handling each individual shoot, and keeping it warm through wood-burning stoves in greenhouses, to the process of crosspollination (as I understood it). I could kick myself for not at the time having jotted down more of the information gleaned, since I can no longer recall the answers to several questions that I asked. The students were not very inquisitive, but I was fascinated by the system and asked about certain plants that the person at the nursery who was conducting the tour could not answer and so he had to ask a young woman who explained perfectly what and how and why—none of which I can now recall. This is the penalty imposed for not recording information as soon as possible, ideally at the very moment it is obtained. Rereading my journals I find so much that I had totally forgotten from trips taken years before or even more recently. There is no substitute for writing down facts, impressions, place names, people's names, and descriptions, which within a short time will be lost and gone forever. If one wants to relive the past, he must record it, and no one else will remember it exactly the same way. Although no one else may find anything one writes worth reading, the recorded experience endures should anyone at a later time care to share it, and especially the writer him- or herself. For me, the main reason for writing anything down is the sheer delight in doing so.

  Returning to María's home, we were treated to a lunch of *cazuela*—a traditional chicken soup of potato and carrot chunks and of other vegetables like acorn squash. Karen, who was always hungry for meat, pronounced this the kind of meal that she really missed, and she even ate the chicken of some of the other students who were not such big eaters. While we were finishing our food, the teenagers were dressing themselves in the traditional *cueca* attire for a performance of this native dance, with music from a CD player. The young man put on boots with spurs, a wide-brimmed hat with short, flat crown, a vest, striped pants, and a sash around his waist typical of the outfit worn by the *huaso* or Chilean cowboy. Meanwhile, the young lady adorned herself in a full petticoat that lifted her skirt up and spread it out around her. She then put on medium-heeled shoes, an embroidered blouse, and other accoutrements. Each of them held a handkerchief, which they would twirl during the traditional steps of the dance that imitates a rooster courting a hen. In the vacant patch of ground beside the house, they executed beautifully the movements of the *cueca*, even though the young man almost slipped on a muddy spot when he performed the dance's stomping pattern. The pair invited the students to try, and some did, but found it quite demanding, more difficult than it appeared when the couple moved about one another with ease and grace. The students all laughed at their own mistakes, enjoying a taste of this national pastime depicted in every Chilean travel brochure.

Our last days in Reñaca were spent in discussions of the poetry of Nicanor Parra and Enrique Lihn. Regrettably I did not write anything about the students' responses to the work of these two poets, since I just did not have the time. With the course ending, the many papers to be marked had started piling up on me. The students were stressed from what at least some of them thought an overload of assignments, which one student mentioned in the required student evaluations of the course: "I wouldn't change anything from this class, except maybe not have 2 papers due our last week here." Their final papers I was only able to grade after they had all departed for Texas, and when I did I found that three students chose to write on Parra's antipoetry and the other four wrote on Lihn, although Gabriela Orta, in addition to writing on Parra's poem "The Teachers," also wrote an original poem in Spanish on Lihn, entitled "Leer sobre Enrique Lihn" (To Read About Enrique Lihn) and Lucila Castellano, in addition to writing on Parra's "The Vices of the Modern World," also wrote a poem on Lihn, entitled "Para leer un buen poema se necesita paciencia" (To Read a Good Poem Requires Patience). I was especially pleased that Diana Meléndez wrote on Lihn's "Europeans" and Karen Villarreal wrote on Lihn's "For Rigas Kappatos," the latter written in memory of a cat named Athinulis "belonging" to Lihn's Greek friend of the poem's title. All the papers contained insights into the poetry of Parra and Lihn, but Álvaro Corral's paper on Parra was an especially fine, wide-ranging overview of the "Lessons of Antipoetry," including the antipoet's assertion that "In antipoetry, it is poetry that is sought, not eloquence."

On our final class day, the students surprised me with a framed photograph that had been taken of all seven at a beach area near Reñaca. At the top of the photo they had quoted from Parra's "Manifesto":

Señoras y señores
Ésta es nuestra última palabra
Nuestra primera y última palabra
Los poetas bajaron del Olimpo.

Para nuestros mayores
La poesía fue un objeto de lujo
Pero para nosotros
Es un artículo de primera necesidad:
No podemos vivir sin poesía . . .

[Ladies and gentlemen
This is our final word
Our first and final word
The poets came down from Olympus.

To our elders
Poetry was an object of luxury
But for us
It is an article of highest necessity:
We cannot live without poetry . . .]

On one side of the photo it reads: Reñaca—Chile—Junio 2006, and on the other side it reads: Maymester Program. Each student's face is perfectly clear, with every one of them smiling with obvious pleasure in being in Chile and having shared the experience together. The framed photo now hangs on the wall of my book-lined study, a treasured memento.

In addition to teaching the class on Chilean poetry and going on excursions with the students, I had been working with Alejandro Cerda on translations of the poetry of a group of Chilean poets, including a number from Valparaíso and Viña del Mar, whose poems would be published subsequently in the bilingual Austin magazine, *The Dirty Goat*. The two of us were also translating the poetry of a group of Texas poets whose poems would later appear in the Chilean journal, *El Navegante*, published by the Universidad

Dave Oliphant

University of Texas students in Chile, on beach near Reñaca. From left to right: Andrew, Lucila, Gabriela, Diana, Ashley, Álvaro, and Karen.

del Desarrollo. The students would meet several of the local poets, from the Valparaíso 5th Region, at a special banquet held in their honor, in the dining area of their hotel. The following are the poets whose poetry Alejandro and I had been translating and who read some of their work at the banquet: Pablo Arraya, Sergio Ojeda Barías, Alejandro Cerda, Karen Devia, Camila Escobar Escalona, Bernardo Chandía Fica, Guillermo Rivera, Marcia Saavedra, Karen Tovo, and Alexis Zamora. The other poets later included in *The Dirty Goat* issue were: Nicanor Parra, Armando Roa Vial, Sergio Rodríguez Saavedra, Boris Durandeau Stegmann, and Francisco Véjar. The Texas poets whose work we translated were: Stan Rice, Richard Sale, Charles Behlen, myself, Naomi Shihab Nye, Harryette Mullen, Robert Burlingame, Rebecca Gonzales, Beverly Caldwell, Walt McDonald, Susan Bright, and Ray González. For me, our translation project during the stay in Reñaca added so much to the overall experience of the Maymester sojourn, since it furnished an opportunity for the students and me to know some of the local poets.

    The students had regularly eaten at their beachside hotel, while María and I had prepared our meals at her sister and brother-in-law's apartment. For our final meal together as a group, we were treated to lunch at a restaurant started by one of the refugees from the Spanish Civil War, who was rescued by Neruda and came to Chile on the "Winnipeg," both the ship and the passage having been arranged for by the poet. Through the picture windows of the restaurant we looked out on the rough waters of the Pacific, while inside we dined on delicious Chilean fish, served with Chilean wine. I myself rarely drink wine, especially in winter, since it tends to make me congested—from the yeast of the fermenting process, I'm told. For all of us, it was a warm farewell to those who had made our stay so pleasant, especially Paula Olguín and Professor German Vogel. The next day we would be driven back to Santiago, and the students would depart soon afterwards, except for some who stayed a few days longer on their own. While María and I would return to Austin, most of the students would fly to their homes for summer vacation. My report to the Maymester Program included the following assessment: So far as I am concerned, the trip was—and I believe that the students would agree with me on this—a complete success. They were an ideal group and came together as friends who were affectionate toward and looked out for one another. They worked well together and helped make the trip pleasant for everyone. Everything that I personally wanted the students to experience they were able to see and do, thanks to the arrangements made by CIEE. The personnel of this organization were always helpful, even though I would note that the native Chilean members of the CIEE team were far and away the most caring and well organized.

On June 21st I received an e-mail from Francisco Véjar, who wrote to report on our visit with Nicanor Parra. Francisco had been with the antipoet in Las Cruces and Parra told him that at first he did not recognize me, but that he "intuited" who I was. He said that everything had been "muy ameno" (very pleasant), and that he had appreciated our gesture of coming by his house to say goodbye after he had left us in the restaurant. Francisco knew that Parra had asked to be reminded of our visit two days in advance, but because his cell phone had been turned off, by a battery failure according to Parra, Francisco had been unable reach him. Parra repeated to Francisco that I had a green light, whenever I wanted to return, and María and I would in the following year of 2007.

Chile / Chiloé (March 2007)

The first day in Santiago I slept two long naps, from not having been able to sleep much at all during the flight, which was terribly rough. The couple in front of us kept their reading light on most of the night, with their seats shoved back so far that their overhead lights shone down on us and their seats cramped our little space, which was reduced because we did not push our own seats back so that we would not inconvenience the two young women behind us. The rude couple in front were reading the entire trip, she a movie stars gossip rag and he a Crichton novel. At first, the two "girls" behind us talked considerably, one a gringa on her way to a job teaching businessmen English classes and the other a Chilean who could speak English, whereas the gringa could hardly say a word in Spanish; eventually, they quieted down.

En route, the morning sky was beautiful, revealing the mountains in tiers like wrinkles of some brown animal, with touches of snow on the highest peaks. After passing near Lima, the bumpiness subsided and we enjoyed the view of streams like silver ribbons running down valleys to the sea, among green patches and in some places fields laid out in perfect squares with clearly visible rows. Once we landed, we picked up our luggage, passed through customs, and met María's sister Coneja and her husband Checho, who were waiting for us. Since I had not been in Chile in fall or winter for some thirty years, the end of summer in Chile looked different to me, with so much more foliage and the light of day so warm and pleasant. María and I had married in the summer, and the memory of those months came back vividly on feeling and seeing the city now on the 1st of March, a month over forty years since we had departed for our honeymoon in Mexico City at the end of January of 1967.

The next day my longtime friend Pepe Hosiasson invited me to come to his home at 4 p.m., when he said that the leftist literary critic Hernán Loyola would be there. The new bus system had been heavily criticized, but the bus that I took went directly and quickly to my stop at Colon and Tobalaba, from which I walked to Pepe's home on Unamuno Street, 696. I rang at the outside fence and Pepe pushed the button that opened the electric gate. He looked pretty much the same at 76, though with a slightly noticeable shuffle. We had met for the first time in 1966 at the jazz club at the Instituto Chileno-norteamericano, where at the time I was teaching English conversation and American literature classes. He still smoked almost incessantly as he played his jazz recordings full blast. We chatted a bit and then Hernán arrived.

Having left Chile with the military coup in 1973, Hernán had obtained a professorship in Italy, where, after the return of democracy, he now lives half the year and the other half in Chile. He is still a fully committed Marxist and spoke at length of his ideas about Modernism as a movement that reached the highest point in man's search for a humane society. I had read his views in a piece on his current work on Pablo Neruda, which appeared in a leftist magazine entitled *Pluma y pincel* (Pen and Pencil). I had come across the article because an interview that had been conducted with me was printed in the same issue of December 2006. One of Hernán's main points was that Marxism was the grounds on which all discourse was conducted, so that even President Reagan had had to address the concerns that Marxism raised with respect to the welfare of the masses. Hernán and Pepe argued a bit over the definition of democracy and whether there could be a democracy even if a government was not Marxist. Pepe had told me that normally he did not discuss politics with Hernán, his old friend of many years, who knows that Pepe does not share his political faith in Marx. Pepe had said that they would mostly discuss jazz, which Hernán knows well, which he demonstrated to me when he asked Pepe if he had a recording of "Shoe Shine Boy" with Lester Young, from the Jones-Smith session of 1936. The Smith of the group was Carl "Tatti" Smith, a trumpet player born in Marshall, Texas, in about 1908. Hernán apparently thought of the recording on learning of my *Texan Jazz*, a copy of which Pepe had shown him from his vast jazz library. (Later, in 2012, Pepe would donate his 1,400 books on jazz to the Cultural Center Gabriela Mistral [GAM].)

During our discussion of jazz, I asked Pepe if he had any recordings of the Dave Pell Octet, a West Coast group with trumpeter Don Fagerquist, whose non-Pell recordings I had recently been enjoying. Hernán suddenly became ecstatic and began to rhapsodize about an album of Pell's with themes from the American West. I was unfamiliar with the album to which he referred with such enthusiasm, but I had always liked a Pell vinyl album of mine, entitled *Love Story*, from 1956. Surprising to me, Pepe did not have anything by Pell, which he knew after checking his computerized discography of his recordings. After we listened to "Shoe Shine Boy," Pepe put on the Jones-Smith recording of "Lady Be Good" from the same 1936 session. Hernán and I were both totally delighted to hear once again that Gershwin tune and the historical solo by Lester Young on tenor, as well as a fine solo by Carl Smith on trumpet.

Knowing how much Hernán appreciated the Smith-Jones recording, I was all the more anxious to read an essay of his on jazz in the writings of Julio Cortázar, published in March 1994 in the Cuban magazine, *Revista Casa de las Américas*. Before Hernán had arrived, Pepe had made for me a copy of the article, entitled "El jazz en Cortázar: La discada del Club de la Serpiente." On seeing the article, I immediately wished that I had known of it when I wrote my "Jazz in Literature," an essay that would appear the following month in my new book, *Jazz Mavericks of the Lone Star State*. I had known that Cortázar was an avid and very knowledgeable fan of jazz, and my essay includes discussion of his great short story, "El persiguidor," based in part on the life of Charlie Parker. (Later, I would incorporate Hernán's article into my "Jazz en Chile y en su poesía," an article published in 2008 in the Chilean on-line magazine *Extramuros* and included in my *Hallazgo y traducción de poesía chilena* of 2019.)

On taking his departure, Hernán invited me to submit something to the publication he edited, entitled *Nerudiana*, published by the Fundación Pablo Neruda. Hernán was also editing the complete works of Neruda for a Spanish publisher—perhaps Galaxie Gutenberg, which had issued Nicanor Parra's "complete" poetry. I offered to send him my elegy on Neruda that my Chilean friend Oliver Welden had just translated into Spanish, and he made me promise to do so. I did follow through, but in the end he did not think the translation was good enough and said that he was going to see about getting someone else to translate it, but afterwards I never heard anything further.

Reading Hernán's essay on jazz in Cortázar, I found that, as expected, he saw in the history of the music, and in its "extreme paradigm" of modern art, the incarnation of its "apparently contradictory tendencies": "democratic sympathies toward the lower social classes" and "aristocratic demands of authenticity and of high cultural values." Not surprisingly, then, he saw Cortázar as having considered jazz a means of accessing "the unrepresentable utopia." In the article he speaks of the need to correct the deficiencies and deformations of Modernism, and as he told me at Pepe's home, he had been pondering for years the history of Modernism, from 1450 to the present, and had come to equate jazz with the pathway to "a zone of utopia, but that zone is unimaginable," especially by postmodernists like Cortázar and Parra. Nonetheless, Hernán concludes in his article, through Cortázar's 17th chapter of his novel *Rayuela* (*Hopscotch*), that jazz represents a universal hope for reconciling opposites, through ridicule of national rituals and customs or long-entrenched conservative ideas. In order to bring together Mexicans and Norwegians, Russians and Spaniards, Hernán has advocated the teaching of a definition of freedom untaught in any school where ragtime or blues is never heard. It is certainly true that jazz is loved throughout the world, and that its improvisations and varied rhythms have been associated in the mind of many with freedom, even though as an art form it necessarily depends on historical music traditions, working within them and breaking from them to discover innovative approaches that yet owe much to the basic patterns and practices of the past.

Hernán's name had been familiar to me mostly from having read his review of Oliver Welden's *Perro del amor*, from 1970. I had only discovered Hernan's review from writing my introduction to a reprint of Oliver's book. Before we left for Chile, I had written to Pepe to let him know that we were coming to Chile, and had mentioned in the e-mail that I recalled his having spoken of Hernán's writings on jazz. In his reply, Pepe said that Hernán wanted to meet me but was leaving for Italy on March 15th. In order for us to get together I should contact him as soon as we arrived in Santiago, which I did. During our meeting at Pepe's, Hernán repeated much of what he had written in *Pluma y pincel*, but mostly he ranted and raved against a critic named Victor Farías, who had once been a Marxist but after the military coup had changed his position and had written of Salvador Allende as an elitist. Essentially Hernán was incensed by his view that Farías had taken up and discussed literary works without knowing them deeply enough, beginning with the complete writings of Neruda. Farías, as editor of the forthcoming Neruda edition, had asked Hernán to write something for the publication, but when the Spanish publisher saw Hernán's contribution, he decided that, in light of how poorly Farías had handled the editing of the volume, the publisher would invite Hernán to assume the position of editor. Hernán also criticized a new book by Farías on Gabriel García Márquez's *Cien años de soledad* (*One Hundred Years of Solitude*), which Farías interpreted as the dead-end of Marxist thought and the disillusionment of an entire generation of leftists. Hernán mentioned that an article by Farías had just appeared in *El Mercurio*, and that a critic from North Carolina, Greg Dawes, had repudiated Farías' interpretation of the García Márquez novel. Hernán totally approved of Dawes, who was/is also a Marxist critic. On Sunday March 4th I read an article by Farías in *El Mercurio*, his response to Dawes' article and to another piece by Ignacio Echeverría, the fine Chilean critic who had long championed the antipoetry of Parra and who also attacked Farías. (In a then unexpected future development, it was Greg Dawes who would publish, through A Contracorriente, his press at North Carolina State University in Raleigh, my *Hallazgo y traducción de poesía chilena* [2019].)

Only after typing up my notes on the trip did I remember Hernán's enthusiasm for the Dave Pell Octet's album with its tunes from the American West, and so I ordered a copy through Amazon. Entitled *Swingin' in the Ol' Corral*, the CD version of the 1956 Pell recording opens with "I'm an Old Cowhand"; the Shorty Rogers arrangement of that Johnny Mercer tune is typical of the West Coast style of the period, though perhaps more humorous than usual and even a bit corny. The music cannot compare with the jazz version by Sonny Rollins from 1957, nor with the version by Kenny Dorham from 1960, and not even with Jack Teagarden's rendition from 1936. The Pell Octet's performances of arrangements by West Coast arrangers like Rogers, Jack Montrose, and Marty Paich, the latter the Octet's pianist, are more novelty than serious jazz, with few solos that offer much in the way of real musical thought. Even trumpeter Don Fagerquist is not at his best, though his playing on "I'm an Old Cowhand" is technically impressive. I could see why Pepe did not have any of Pell's recordings in his massive archive. Despite my disappointment with *Swingin' in the Ol' Corral*, I still enjoy *Love Story*, whose many classic tunes, like "Can't We Be Friends," "If I Could Be With You One Hour Tonight," "Let's Do It," Ellington's "Solitude," and "I've Found a New Baby," tell a clever musical tale and inspire more and better solos by Pell and Fagerquist, as well as some sparkling piano by André Previn.

On Monday the 5th I met my friend Irene Rostagno at Tavelli, the popular café in the Providencia district. She, as a rightest, loves everything Farías now writes against the leftists. Although I was ready to find Farías a fake, based on Hernán's diatribe against this German-trained "philosophy major," I had to admit to myself that his piece was very clearly and convincingly written. I could not help but agree with him that Dawes seemed to represent the typical U.S. academician enamored of Marxist critical thinking, as when Farías remarks that Dawes is one of the frequent "salon leftists in the States, who thanks to their lush salaries can criticize and vociferate against the system that indulges them punctually every month." (Again, this was written long before I would be beholden to Greg Dawes for seeing my *Hallazgo* book into print, for which I remain so deeply grateful.)

Irene had been complaining about the Santiago bus system and was then praising Farías when Francisco Véjar arrived for our planned meeting. After Irene left, Francisco asked me if she was a good friend of mine, which I assured him that she was. He obviously could not believe that I was so close to an obvious rightist, or *momia* (mummy, as they are called by leftists), but he did not understand that I am basically apolitical. When I read Ignacio Echeverría's response to Farías, I could not help but find his writing uncharacteristically muddy and lacking in any real argument other than unfounded accusations against Farías. My position was and is that whoever makes a strong, logical case, which is not based on a blind acceptance of just one perspective, is the person whose thinking I am more inclined to accept and to respect.

Francisco had arranged for me to meet Leo Lobos, a poet-artist with whom I had corresponded by e-mail and who had promoted on his web page my translation of Enrique Lihn's *Figures of Speech* from 1999. When Leo arrived, he proved a most pleasant, enthusiastic fellow. He had brought with him a copy of *Archipiélago: Revista Cultural de Nuestra América*, with his illustrated article on the artworks of Chilean Roberto Matta. (In Austin, María and I had met Matta's first muse, Lillian Lorca de Tagle, a friend whose memoir, *Honorable Exiles: A Chilean in the Twentieth Century*, the University of Texas Press published in 2000, after María had insisted that she write her autobiography and I had put her in touch with Press editor Theresa May.) Leo also wanted to show me a brief notice of my Lihn book that he had been surprised to find in *Archipiélago*'s book review page. Francisco, as usual, was drinking in our conversation with all eyes and ears. He is always so attentive, enthused, and ready to introduce me to writers that he thinks I should know.

On March 4th, Francisco and I had already met at Tavelli for the first time on this trip. While we were catching up on each one's latest projects, Francisco looked up to see Enrique Lafourcade enter the café, and he immediately went to invite him to join us. Francisco had been telling me of Enrique's new novel, *El Inesperado*, based on the life of Rimbaud during the poet's final years spent as a trader or gun runner in Africa. Francisco had a copy of the novel with him and had told me that I should read it, that it had been ignored in Chile. Enrique was happy to join us and discuss his novel, informing me that his daughter Nicole had translated it into English and that she and her husband and three daughters were moving to Austin. He was interested in my looking over Nicole's translation, and promised to give me a copy of a special edition of the book, but in the meantime he signed Francisco's copy for me, at Francisco's insistence. That night I would begin reading the novel, and found it grippingly written. María's sister loves Lafourcade's *Crónicas* (Chronicles or Stories), which had appeared frequently in *El Mercurio*. Dressed in a kind of official-looking dark jacket and wearing a blue cap with braid around it above the brim—sort of a navy-like outfit—he was a distinguished elderly man, with a slightly stooped posture and the jowls of the aging—the latter of which I myself have begun to develop. Enrique said that he wanted to phone and talk with me, which he did the next day.

After Enrique left, Leo, Francisco, and I chatted about poetry for a while and then visited a bookstore called TAKK, next door to Tavelli. I had told Francisco that I wanted to break down and purchase a copy of *Poesía chilena desclasificada (1973-1990)*, a 2006 anthology edited by Gonzalo Contreras, which I had seen at TAKK the day before when he and I had browsed its shelves of Chilean poetry. Leo knew that during my stay in Chile that I would be traveling to Chiloé, the second largest island off the coast of Chile, after Isla Grande de Tierra del Fuego. On hearing me speak of the Contreras anthology, Leo told me that two poets from Chiloé were included in the book, and he wrote down their names for me: Mario García and Carlos Trujillo. I had found the *Declasificada* anthology reviewed in the literary supplement to *El Mercurio*, when María and I had been in Chile the year before, but I had been unable to locate a copy. The price was almost $60.00 in paperback, but it was worth it to me because it covered the years of the military junta headed by General Pinochet, a period that I knew less well than I did the pre-coup era of the mid 1960s to the early 1970s. I had kept up with poets of that earlier generation, as well as Parra and Lihn, and newcomers like Raul Zurita, but I had read little of the work of poets of the mid to late 1970s like Juan Luis Martínez, and nothing by poets from Chiloé. For me, collecting books like the *Declasificada* anthology of poetry from the 1970s and '80s is always an important part of any visit to Chile.

While we were in TAKK, I asked if by any chance they had a book on jazz in Chile by an author whose name I did not quite have right, calling him Álvaro Amenanteau, when it was Menanteau. Again, I knew of this work, entitled *Historia del Jazz en Chile*, from the previous year, but it had been out of print at the time. When I had visited Pepe, I had seen that he had a new edition of the book, but he seemed to think that it was not available except through the author. The cashier at TAKK looked up the title on the computer and at first did not find it, but then there it was on the screen, and the store did have a copy, which a clerk brought down from the second floor. Having seen the book at Pepe's the previous year, I knew that among the Chilean jazz musicians mentioned or discussed were friends of mine like Pepe, who plays piano, drummer Paco Deza, trombonist Luis Artigas, pianist Manuel Villarroel, and his brother drummer-bassist Patricio Villarroel, with the last three of whom I had performed on trumpet in 1966. Pepe and Manuel are both pictured in the Menanteau book. Having this volume was and is very special to me, for many reasons, but primarily because it recalls that eventful year of 1966 when María and I met and married. María had been with me on one occasion when Luis Artigas and I were playing with a group that is described in my poem entitled "Music History," in the section subtitled "The Goodly Company in Chile."

During the first days of our stay, I thought a number of times of Bobby Knight, the basketball coach who at the time was the winningest coach in NCAA history. When he was celebrated for his achievement, he dismissed all the hoopla by saying that anyone who had been around as long as he had would accumulate a number of victories. This may have been false modesty, but there is a certain amount of truth in his assertion. It struck me that having lived long enough to have returned to Chile so often over a period of forty years, that I myself had become part of the history of Chilean poetry and Chilean jazz, at least as a listener, reader, observer, translator, and editor. The poets in the Contreras anthology include many prominent and lesser figures who were in my *Road Apple Review* anthology of 1972, and in the case of Parra and Lihn, I had continued over the years to translate their work. Erick Pohlhammer, a poet not in my *Road Apple* anthology, I had met in Santiago in 1977 and did include him in the special issue on Chilean poetry that Richard Carlisle and I had compiled and translated in 1980 for the Texas magazine *Cedar Rock*.

Reading in the Contreras collection I was especially impressed by poems by Jaime Gómez Rogers, whose work I had first known in 1971 when he gave me a sheaf of his poems for consideration for my *Road Apple* anthology. The occasion was my visit to the University of Chile's Pedagógico (teaching division), where a meeting was taking place of the editorial board of the then newly inaugurated *Revista chilena de la literatura*. I had found Rogers a retiring, modest person, and upon later reading his poems I discovered that I liked them very much and translated one for the anthology. In 1999, I believe it was, on the way back from visiting Parra at Las Cruces, Francisco and I tried to locate Rogers in his town of El Tabo, but without success. Unfortunately, he died in 2005 without my having been able to see him again.

Both Erick Pohlhammer and Rogers are well represented in the Contreras anthology, along with the following poets that I had translated in earlier years: Parra, Lihn, Jorge Teillier, Floridor Pérez, Jaime Quezada, Heddy Navarro, Carmen Berenguer, Diego Maquieira, Tomás Harris, and Andrés Sabella (mentioned in Contreras's introduction to *Poesía chilena desclasificada* but not represented by any poems, although in Contreras' 2007 *Poéticas de Chile / Chilean Poets on the Art of Poetry* he does have a poem by Sabella, which I had translated for that anthology). In the case of Juan Luis Martínez, I had not included any translations of his work in my 1972 anthology, but I had translated a poem of his for Contreras's *Poéticas*. I had also translated poets who wrote while living outside the country during the Pinochet years: Oliver Welden, Alicia Galaz, Gonzalo Millán, and Cecilia Vicuña, but none of those poets appears in the 2006 *Desclasificada* anthology and only Millán and Vicuña are included in the 2007 *Poéticas* volume. I feel fortunate as a translator, writer, and editor to have had even a small part to do with the Chilean tradition of world-renowned poets, and to have known so many of them personally, especially Parra and Lihn.

One thing that I found unfortunately ironic about the Contreras anthology of 2006 is that even though he asserts that early on Chilean poetry resisted the military coup and dictatorship, carrying on the struggle for a better life for all, and especially the workers, there is no way for the messages of the poets to reach the hands of the proletariat at $60 a copy. Francisco, who was teaching a few classes here and there and from to time would write pieces for *El Mercurio*, had told me frankly that he could not buy books because they were so outrageously expensive.

In the *Desclasificada* anthology, a poem by Floridor Pérez, entitled "La partida inconclusa" (The Unfinished Move), had really hit me when the speaker feels guilty that he has survived incarceration by the junta, whereas the Mayor of Lota, with whom he was playing a game of chess, was called out by the secret police and never completed his move, having been shot in the Regional Stadium in the city of Concepción. The Mayor, who had risen from being a worker in the southern coal mines to his political position, was playing with the white pieces, whereas the narrator, a poor country teacher, had the black. Years later the teacher tells a friend about the incident, and the friend's only response is, What would have happened if you had been playing with the white pieces? It was, as they say, the "luck" of the draw. (This was reminiscent for me of the Mier Expedition in Texas history, where white and black beans decided who lived and who died.) Lihn termed his country "horroroso [horrid] Chile," and as Ennio Moltedo says in his poem "Todas": "All these monsters [beasts] are from here, this beautiful place," alluding to the killings and disappearances during the military coup. The *Desclasificada* anthology, as critic Jaime Concho describes it in his prologue, presents a panorama of blood and death, of which the poetry is a constant and palpable reminder. Of course, those on the other side saw and still see Pinochet and the junta as saviors of the nation, and the opposing views live on, both in the memories of each side and in the writings by people like Victor Farías and Hermógenes Pérez de Arce, as in the latter's *Contra la corriente* (Against the Current), published in 2005 but comprised of columns that he had written for *El Mercurio* as far back as 1982.

In one particular column from September 22, 1982, de Arce reports on a visit to Chile by Sister Teresa, during which she did not condemn the free market system imposed by Pinochet. The author may have invented a leftist friend as his sparing partner in the article, but the two sides that he identifies and defines sounded only too familiar to me. For one thing, he says of his "friend" that once he embraced socialism he stopped asking questions, since socialism furnished all the answers, and left him with no doubts of any sort. At the same time, when confronted with de Arce's question as to why people wanted to leave countries where the state controlled everything and to go to those where free markets are the practice, the leftist had no reply. De Arce suggests that the reason Sister Teresa was deadly for the leftists was because she did more for the poor than they ever did, since they were against private capital and individual initiative. In another column, from August 1984, de Arce justifies the free market by reporting that from 1974 to 1984 Chile not only recovered from the catastrophe of President Allende's Unidad Popular, with its economics of debt, but in the four-year period of 1977 to 1980 "the free and open economy demonstrated that it could produce more employment, reduce the inflation more, make earnings grow, and augment the [gross national] product more than Chile had been able to do in any other four-year period of its history."

On the other hand, in a free-market country like the U.S.A., it is true that without the pressure placed on the captains of industry by unions, socialists, civil rights advocates, feminists, gays, and environmentalists, there would be no changes with regard to working conditions and pay, racist and sexist practices, or protection of species and plant life. Most governments and landlords and employers would not answer to the larger populace without strikes and protests against exploitation and unequal and unjust distribution of the goods and services, and neither would they yield to demands for a share of the benefits of "progress." Those in power are not self-motivated to improve standards of living, invest in medical and technological advances, reduce the dependence on immigrant labor, and reward the contributions of minorities and other groups denied their natural rights through discrimination.

Chiloé

On March 7th, María, her sister Coneja, and I flew from Santiago to Puerto Montt in the south, rented a small red Fiat "Fire," and drove to Puerto Varas, where we took a cabin on Lake Llanquihue at the Cabañas del Lago. We were on our way to the islands of Chiloé, but would spend the night in Puerto Varas before driving the next day to the channel of Chacao, which separates the Chilean mainland from the main island of the archipelago. At lunchtime, after having checked out a high-priced restaurant called Govinda, we ate instead at Restaurant Los Colonos, a pleasant, inexpensive café. I had the same *merluza* that I had eaten the year before at the café near Nicanor Parra's home at Las Cruces. Coneja ordered crab and María had rice and stir-fried veggies. Afterwards the sisters looked in a few shops while I walked around the downtown area in search of bookstores.

The first *librería* that I came upon was only a store for paper products—notebooks and school supplies. Another shop had typical bestsellers and touristy coffee-table photography books. A third shop, tucked in a side street and reached through a sort of garden area, had a section of poetry that included copies of Lihn's Ahumada poems, as well as thin volumes by a few poets unknown to me. The surname of one poet was unusual: Herling. I forgot the poet's first name but learned that Herling was a young female born in Llanquihue, who had earned a doctorate from Michigan State and had been living in the States for eleven years, teaching there at the time that her book was published by Humboldt State University in California. I glanced through some of the poems but did not find them that appealing, even though some did refer to her early life in Chile. I was hoping rather to find an anthology of poets of the region, but Herling was the only local poet whose work that I saw, and it seemed to me that she had been "tainted" by too many years in my own country. Obviously that was not a fair or valid basis for judgment, especially since I have continued to follow the careers of other Chileans who studied abroad or were "exiled" in the States or Canada, among them Oscar Hahn and Gonzalo Millán.

After one night in Puerto Varas, we headed for the channel of Chacao where we would take a ferry across to Chiloé. This trip was the first time that I had driven in Chile since 1965; the highways in the south I found to be excellent and the traffic not heavy. After crossing on the ferry, I had no problems making it to our destination of the city of Castro, the "capital" of Chiloé, founded in 1567. In 1834, Darwin had visited the city of Ancud, to which we crossed on the ferry and then drove 120 kilometers to Castro. While on the ferry we had watched sea lions along the way and had learned that a thirteen-year-old girl, Sirenita Milenka, had just swum from the mainland to Chiloé and now figured in the Guinness record as the youngest person to cross Lake Villarica and the channel of Chacao. It took the ferry a good thirty minutes to cross the channel and it amazed me to think that a young girl could swim in the cold Pacific for an hour or more, and, as reported, surrounded by sharks.

In Castro we had reserved a cabin overlooking an inlet of the Pacific on the east side of Chiloé, which separates the Castro-Nercon coast from a peninsula with towns like Puyan and Curahue. In some ways the view reminded me of the English Lake District, even though the body of water is part of the ocean rather than being freshwater. Dramatic cloud formations of seemingly unmoving pure white and dark puffs were punctuated by lighter and deeper blue patches of sky, with light pouring through to highlight the hills on both sides of the inlet. The landscape—of tall trees with limbs shooting straight up (perhaps some eucalyptus but mostly alamos), cleared fields, and grazing sheep—was as peaceful looking as anything imaginable. It was so far from the nightly TV scenes showing sand and palm trees, with pools of blood from roadside bombs and suicide attacks in Iraq's endless war between feuding Islamic sects and those battling the interference of Bush's neo-con nightmare. Chileans come to Chiloé to rest and relax, mostly during summer vacation in January and February. In preparation for our visit, María had been studying the "attractions" in the area—its wooden churches and the handiwork of the native peoples, although the original islanders, the Chonos, had essentially died off through European disease or had intermingled with the "invading" Spanish or with native peoples like the Mapuche.

In the evening, I would meet Mario García, one of the two poets whose name and information Leo Lobos had given to me. I had contacted Mario by e-mail before we left Santiago and had told him where we would be staying in Castro. He had phoned the cabin owner's home and she had walked down to let me know that he was waiting on the other end of the line at her house. Mario and I agreed that he would come to our cabin at 8 p.m., and he arrived at that hour with copies of his own books, one by a fellow poet, and an anthology of local workshop poetry. *Aumen: Antología poética* is the title of the workshop's 2001 anthology, and the word *aumen* in the native Huilliche language means "echo of the mountain." The poetry produced by the Aumen workshop had resounded not only throughout Chiloé but Chile as a whole. I was delighted to add this well-conceived and nicely printed volume to my collection of Chilean anthologies.

Carlos Trujillo, the other Chiloé poet with poems in the Contreras *Descalificada* anthology, was a professor and the co-founder of the Aumen workshop. In his introduction to the Aumen anthology, Trujillo recounts the trials and tribulations of the publication, including the fact that he was fired from his teaching position, along with four other workshop professor-participants. The difficulties with the authorities during the Pinochet period—or dictatorship as Trujillo calls it—included being deprived of their meeting place in a secondary school by the Mayor of Castro, even though the workshop had been held there for eight years, from 1975 to 1983. The Mayor declared the participants a bunch of Communists, which they may have been, but even so, it is clear that they were doing a wonderful job of teaching poetry to young students. The Aumen workshop introduced the participants to the history of lyric poetry, from Catullus to Nicanor Parra. Each member criticized the writing of his or her fellows, and some had been published in national magazines as well as abroad, and several had won national poetry prizes. It was most interesting to me to learn that in the first meeting in which the students read their work aloud, the co-founders provided them with copies of Parra's *Obra gruesa*, a 1969 collection of his antipoems, which the novice writers dismissed as lacking in traditional beauty and form. From that time forward the young poets-to-be developed into sophisticated writers with an appreciation for the art of poetry in all its historical eras up to their own day and in their own region, which is known for its rain and rainbows.

One young boy, Sergio Mansilla, found his life's work through the workshop meetings, since he himself later became a professor of literature, after having earned his doctorate from the University of Washington in Seattle. The whole story of the workshop is inspirational and most laudable on the part of Trujillo and his co-founder, Renato Cárdenas. During the typing up of my travel notes, I discovered mention of Renato in Wikipedia: "Chiloé has been described by Renato Cárdenas, historian at the Chilean National Library, as 'a distinct enclave, linked more to the sea than the continent, a fragile society with a strong sense of solidarity and a deep territorial attachment'."

Mario García was only twelve or thirteen when he joined the workshop, but he would ultimately figure among the five Aumen poets collected in the Contreras anthology. Along with Mario and Carlos Trujillo, the other three in the *Descalificada* anthology are Sergio Mansilla, Aristóteles España, and Rosabetty Muñoz. Black-headed, with a few silver hairs, somewhat stout, wearing a heavy woolen sweater, and not fully shaven, Mario spoke at length about his love of the wind, rain, and sea of the islands. He had gone to college in La Serena, in the arid north of Chile, and experienced severe depression from the desertic climate and lack of rain. Even though he was born in Chaiten, on the continental coast across the channel to the east of Castro, he had grown up traveling from his home in Chaiten to all the archipelagic islands between Chiloé and the Chilean mainland. A grandfather, I believe it was, had a business that delivered foodstuffs and household articles to the various smaller islands that make up Chiloé, and Mario had accompanied him on his trips.

Mario's poetry speaks of the wind, rain, sea, and the wooden piles of the harbors—called *palafitos*, the title of one of his books, which treats of this common sight in Chiloé and serves as a type of symbol of a life half in and half out of water. He lamented the destruction of the *palafitos* by the Pinochet government that sought to modernize and make the areas near the city of Ancud more attractive to tourists. He also criticized the salmon industry in Chiloé, contrasting it with that of Norway, which, after feeding and processing the salmon farmed commercially, returns the water to its original state. In Chiloé, he said, the companies pollute the channel by dumping unconsumed fish food into the sea, letting it sink to the floor, where it kills the flora and fauna. Mario's poems capture the look, feel, and way of life of the islanders, in particular their dependence on the sea and on the abundance of wood of the land areas. Drownings at sea, the threat of storms, the voices as if from the deep—these populate his poems and lend them a reality of place that made the islands come alive for me.

Two days later, María, Coneja, and I drove to the north of the main island, first to Quemchi and then to the Island of Aucar, where its wooden church was reached by a footbridge across the surrounding water. While I sat in the car, the sisters crossed the wooden walkway raised on *palafitos* and visited the church. In front of me were sheep grazing on a grassy area in the midst of smooth, grayish, rounded stones and beside a stream rushing into the sea. An oxen-drawn cart, apparently with groceries, came behind me down a car-wide stone path, as two young men, one tapping a pair of oxen with a stick, walked beside the cart across a wide muddy beach with patches of standing water. Where they were going I could not see because the walkway blocked my view once they angled toward the bay. Houses on stilts dotted the hills, some with bay windows, all with smoke pipes for burning wood for heat. Out in the bay a rowboat made its way along the shore of the island, while a larger fishing vessel sat in the water near what may have been nets in a type of swimming pool within the sea. Mario had described such nets to me, and had said that they were used in the raising and feeding of the salmon. Seagulls were thick along the shore, the sky overcast, light rain intermittently falling, and the sheep either yanking out the grass or kneeling on their folded legs as they stared straight ahead and chewed their cuds. The whole scene was so peaceful and perhaps accounted for the humble natives' unhurried routine, which would bore me to tears.

The most interesting "event" occurred when a small hawk hopped up on the back of one of the sheep and either pecked at bugs or, as it appeared from a distance, plucked out bits of wool. The truth is that I would find it difficult to live in this mostly gloomy region. Mario's wife, he told me, tends to hate everything that he loves about Chiloé, since she is from the sunnier central valley of Santiago. My brother-in-law Sergio would not come with us; he said that he would not even come if they gave him a free plane ticket. He is originally from the La Serena area and therefore drawn to its desertic climate and environment, whereas Mario had gone to school there and had experienced a shock to his rainy system.

My first experience of Chile's south had been in 1966 when I visited the city of Valdivia at the invitation of the Universidad Austral. I found the constant wetness not at all to my liking, but each to his own—where one is born largely determines one's preference in terms of climate and landscape, and it forms one's comfort zone, even perhaps one's character. It is clear in the case of Neruda and his early life in the southern town of Parral that it had inspired his identification with the humid earth and its fecundity. In a sense Chile's south made Neruda the fertile poet that he was, and accounted for his writing, which remained efflorescent and fruitful to the end of his life. The same can be said of poets of the arid regions of the world as well, beginning with those of Sumer and the biblical lands. West Texas poets are also enamored of their dry and wind-blown semi-desert. At 74, Walt McDonald chose to stop writing his fine Llano Estacado poems, whereas Robert Burlingame, though not a native to the dry El Paso area, has continued to write poems inspired by what he early on called "Desert, Not Wasteland." In more recent pieces, Bob has celebrated such fauna and flora of the El Paso area as a mountain lion, the Joshua lizard, the netleaf hackberry, and a thirsty woodrat—the last described in a poem Alejandro Cerda and I translated for the *El Navegante* mini-anthology of 2006.

On March 10th, Chiloé's wind howled and whistled around the picture windows of our rented cabin, rain splattering and streaking the glass, a rainbow forming over the channel before us as I looked out on the swaying foliage and rippled sea. Probably I would not have been writing this if the weather report had not discouraged the sisters from going out to see more churches like the ones that we had visited the day before in Chonchi and Vilupulli. The one in Chonchi, named after Saint Carlos, was called "the end of Christianity" by the Spaniards, presumably because it was so far south, or perhaps because this was as far as Christianity had reached at the time. In any case, the carved figures of Christ interested me more than the church itself, which was originally built in 1769, with the present building dating from the end of the nineteenth century. At Vilupulli, the church was closed, but María requested the key from a contiguous home, so we could enter and even climb up into the tower that is typical of all the historic churches of Chiloé. To me the inside of the Vilupulli church was not so interesting as the columns in the vestibule, which were impressive from the smooth fitting of planks that formed their rounded shape. The supporting beams in the tower were also rounded and were amazingly thick and solid, apparently of cedar, and of recent construction. But again, what struck me more were the carved Christ figures, which were intended to convert the natives to the new religion. Viewers would surely have felt compassionate toward the thorn-crowned Jesus, with blood running down his face and his eyes turned in agony to the heavens where the better life was promised for all believers in his resurrection. I wondered if perhaps the Spanish priests had offered through the suffering of Christ a paradise without wind or rain. If they did, how could the Chilean Indians, the Chilotes, have preferred such a life to the one they, like Mario, so adored.

Among the Chiloé poets in the Aumen anthology, there were two who surprised me the most—surprise being an essential quality of the best poetry, in the sense that we recognize something true that we had never seen expressed so effectively and/or so movingly. Both of the surprising poets were women, Rosabetty Muñoz and Jeannette Hueitra; the former says in one poem that she has had no reason to save anyone, and in other poems that she has run away from the flock and no longer believes in the old paradise, even though the words of prophets "were as divine as the night." She goes on to say that there are no prophets, and that she and others like her listen to the words "with the terrible conviction / that pain is the only language / that will pass beyond history." As for Hueitra, she speaks of the wind writing a prayer of smoke, rising from a cane hut to appeal for bread for all men, "But / the prayer of smoke / is not enough / to burn the newspaper with the horoscope / that God is reading." Even more interesting to me are the latter's poems on photographs, especially one entitled "Trapped," which says

> I am here . . .
> awaiting your arrival
> to implore you
> (even though I know
> it will be in vain)
> to understand me
> and at last that you decide
> to tear up this photograph
> in order to escape from it
> because I am
> that part
> facing the camera
> that you have lost.

The poet who impressed me above all others was Sergio Mansilla, although I did not read his work in the anthology until after I had seen some of his books at the Writers' Archive in Castro. His poems on scenes in Washington state where he earned his doctorate really impressed me, even though they were written after his time as an apprentice poet during his Aumen years. One poem from his Washington period is entitled something like "Homeless Jazz" and captures the life of the down and out. His writing in that and other poems is completely natural, seemingly effortless, and yet penetrating in observation and idea. His poems in the Aumen anthology reveal that even then he was aware of and identified with the difficult life of the underdogs, as indicated in his poem inspired by the death of Peruvian poet César Vallejo, with its title including the biblical phrase in the title of Vallejo's poem, "España, aparta de mí este cáliz": "Spain, take this cup from me." Here are a few lines that describe a famous photo of Vallejo taken in 1929:

> A half-breed face you have, your eyes cannot be seen
> above your walking stick,
> but your face is more beautiful
> and your hair prouder
> than that of Miss Universe.

On Sunday, March 11th, we drove north for a second time to Dalcahue, a town whose name means "place of the boats" or "canoes" that were created by the Chono Indians. After looking over the local crafts, mostly articles made of wool, the sisters left the roofed market with its wooden tower and shopped in an open area where two ladies were selling woolen dolls. The salesladies were talking about a large doll—María had already purchased several smaller dolls along with woven baskets, a blanket-rug, and other handicrafts—and I said to one of the ladies, while pointing to María, "this is my baby doll," and the saleslady acknowledged my remark with a warm smile. Another lady passing by said that María looked like a government or municipal official, but that she was more attractive, and that I should stick with her. Still another lady said that María, if she were that local official, would not be going with such a friendly man, since that official was rumored to be lesbian. All laughed and enjoyed the exchange that I had initiated, never thinking it would lead to so much commentary and even to a bit of politically incorrect gossip. Before I had shown up, as I learned later from María, she had been commenting to the ladies that the big doll had no panties, and they were all giggling that none of the dolls had any. Like all the people we had encountered in Chiloé, these were extremely friendly and jovial. I had noticed that Mario García would often find something funny, and on the phone he frequently laughed at most anything that I said. María could not get over how warm and cordial the Chilotes were, contrasting them with the "heavy" and humorless Santiaguinos.

We were lucky with the weather on our second visit to Dalcahue, for the sun was shining and there was no sign of rain, which helped change my whole attitude toward the island. Probably, had it not been good weather, I would not have had an opportunity to meet Héctor Véliz, one of the Aumen poets, born in Lemuy in 1960 of a Huilliche mother. Next to the ladies selling the dolls, Héctor was selling his little 40-page booklets, with stapled spines, for $4.00 each or so. As I was passing by looking down at his booklets spread out on a cloth covering something of a sidewalk, he gave me a sales pitch, pointing at one title on Huilliche myths and legends. I had seen similar booklets at the market in Castro, where María bought our son Darío a woolen cap, several skeins of wool, and a number of other items. Then Héctor asked me pointblank if I was a writer, and when I said yes, he began to discuss his own work and how he had written all the booklets that I saw on the cloth. Some of the booklets were bilingual editions, and he wanted me to read a text in English, but I told him that I preferred to read it in the original. When he asked, Then you can read Spanish? I replied that I could, I did, and that I was a translator of the poetry of Enrique Lihn, to which he had nothing to say. He then started explaining to me that his mother was illiterate, and yet when he was about eight, she had said that she wanted him to be a writer, since no one in their family had ever written anything. He said that this stuck with him, and the only thing that he wanted to be was a poet, which he acknowledged in Chile was totally insane. I commented that it was true, perhaps, in all parts of the world, at least if one was interested in earning a decent living by writing poetry.

Héctor mentioned that he had read or dreamed of—I do not remember which—a wind that had blown away all the pages of a manuscript, perhaps his own. Instead of being unhappy about this, he saw it as emblematic of his writing. He explained that having his poems and myths printed in booklets of 40 pages made it easy for visitors to the Crafts Fair to carry them off, the same as the wind had the manuscript pages. Shoppers, he said, bought them readily. I looked over the translations of his poems in English and they were, I thought, quite good. Héctor said that they were done by a local Chilean who had never left the country. At some point, I asked him if his poetry had appeared in the Aumen anthology of Carlos

Trujillo, and he affirmed that it had. I thought that I remembered his name among the contributors but was not for certain. I then told him that I had met Mario García, to which Héctor responded that Mario had written a poem (as I understood him to say) about his, Héctor's, work, and in it had claimed that Héctor had taken it all from a French writer and had translated it into Spanish. He assured me that the people in Dalcahue and in his own town of Lemuy did not think that he himself could write anything. He was not exactly indignant but simply told me of others' doubts about his writing as a way of indicating the disbelief within which he created and sold his work. I found him a fascinating fellow and was delighted to have come across him accidentally, or perhaps fatefully. I have often happened upon poets unexpectedly, but only, I believe, because my eyes and ears are always attuned to the possibility of meeting them whenever and wherever I have traveled, and especially in Chile.

On Sunday night, I phoned Mario and told him of my encounter with Héctor in Dalcahue. He laughed immediately, and at most everything that I reported about our conversation. He kept saying that Héctor was a character, and his laughter seemed to mean that little of what Héctor had told me was true. At that point I said that I would like to meet other poets before I left Castro. Apparently, he was quite happy to hear this, for he immediately said that he would contact another poet in the Aumen anthology, Nelson Torres, and see if we could meet him at his work. I was to phone Mario on Monday around 5:30 in the evening and he would let me know if we could meet with Nelson. On Monday the 12th, after we returned from a full day on the road, visiting little towns with their historic wooden churches, I called Mario again, as we had agreed that I would. He told me that he would call me right back, as soon as he had checked with Nelson, who had not been at work when he had tried to get in touch with him earlier. In no time Mario phoned me back to say that he would come pick me up so that we could join Nelson at his work at 6:30. I had assumed that Nelson, like Mario, probably taught school, which it turned out that he did, but he also served as a "collaborator" for the Chiloé archives in the city's cultural center in downtown Castro. The archives are dedicated to publications related to or written by the city's natives or immigrants.

As I learned after meeting Nelson, María's longtime librarian friend, Isabel Gómez, had come from Santiago to Castro to use the local archives. She was trying to find a quote used by Christian Buracchio Domke, her daughter Talia's photographer husband, who had died in a plane crash before they could complete a book of their travel photographs. The quote that Isabel was seeking was part of the book's title, *Chiloé: el jardín de las iglesias* (Chiloé: Garden of the Churches), and her daughter wanted her mother to find the source, which she did, in a work from the eighteenth century included in the Jesuit Archivo Romano: *Noticia breve y moderna del Archipiélago de Chiloé, de su terreno, costumbres de los indios, misiones, escrita por un misionero de aquellas islas en el año 1769 y 70*. The full quote that Christian had planned to use was: "Logra empero Chiloé en su natural desdicha la excelencia de ser un Jardín de la Iglesia" (Yet in its natural misery Chiloé attained the preeminence of being a Garden of the Church). Talia would publish the book nine years after her first husband's death.

When we climbed the stairs to the second floor of the cultural center, I could faintly hear someone practicing on a piano. The double doors to the archives both swung open as Mario and I each pushed on one and entered a room with chairs and tables for patrons, the materials on shelves behind a counter to the right, as well as in glassed-in shelving. Toño, as Mario called Nelson, was at the far left of the reading room, apparently straightening out in preparation for closing up for the day. Although born in 1957, Nelson looked older than I was at the time, even though he was almost twenty years younger. His dark tan face was somewhat drawn and appeared to bear the marks of a life of hardship, or at least that was my impression.

Chilotes that we had seen walking on the unpaved road, which we had driven on along the eastern coast from Dalcahue to Quemchi, were all, it seemed, living a difficult life, most of them walking for miles on rough terrain and often bare-headed in the rain. In Dalcahue we had asked a man walking toward the outskirts of the town if we were going in the right direction to San Juan. The man spoke with enthusiasm of the area we were heading for and informed us that he was from there and was going home. He explained that we needed to go back to the main part of Dalcahue and take another road because the one we were on would become too steep and difficult to climb. He offered to show us the way, so María invited him to come with us. She moved to the back seat with Coneja and the man joined me in the front. As soon as he shut the passenger's door, I could smell his clothes, probably soaked by sweat from hard work. He talked so loudly that it hurt my sensitive right ear that was facing him.

María asked the man where his bluish eyes came from—was he part German? No, neither German nor gringo, he said. His father was Spanish, but he had no idea from what part of Spain. I wondered aloud if he was Basque, but he assured me that he was not. Later the three of us thought that perhaps he was of Galician extraction. He spoke very clearly, and loudly, which made it easy for me to understand every word he said, but also painful. He was quite an interesting man, probably in his late 50s. To María's question as to his occupation, he replied that he farmed, although years before he had been a sheep shearer in Punta Arenas and on the Argentine side of the far south. María asked him why Chilotes did not use umbrellas in the rain, and he answered that it was not the custom. We had seen them walking with rain running down their faces. María then asked if he was born in the area and he said in the same tiny town where he lived, but I did not catch the town's name. One town that we passed bore the man's own name, Santana, and he said that it had been named after the Mayor, a relative of his. He explained exactly where we were to turn and that we were to go always to the right in order to reach San Juan. Shortly before we reached the place where we would turn, he indicated that the next intersecting road was where he would be getting off. He thanked us profusely and seemed a totally happy man. He would have walked all the way, which was at least 30 minutes by car on an extremely rough, rutted dirt road. He had nothing with him, no packages, nothing. Why he had gone to Dalcahue we failed to ask him. His life, like that of most all the country people we encountered, seemed to involve walking for great distances, apparently never hitchhiking, somehow content with their place and position, on their beautiful, fruitful island.

Neither Nelson Torres nor Mario García looked the part of

intellectuals, and yet both had spent their lives, after being introduced to poetry by the Aumen workshop, in writing and publishing and promoting other members of the group. At one point they both emphasized this idea to me—that they saw themselves as part of a group, a collaborative effort, unlike so many writers in Santiago who would, they said, knife one another in the back. This may have been true from their experience, but mostly I had associated with poets like Francisco Véjar and Leo Lobos who always seemed to me generous in promoting others.

In seeing a review of an anthology entitled *Diecinueve (poetas de los años noventa)* (Nineteen [Poets of the 1990s]), edited by Francisca Lange Valdés, I had noticed that the editor had collected almost all the same poets as Francisco had in his earlier anthology, *Antología de la poesía joven chilena* (Editorial Universitaria, 1999), and yet no mention was made of this fact in the review. I asked Francisco if he felt plagiarized, and he responded that indeed Valdés had ripped him off. In-fighting has always been a part of the poetry scene, in every age it seems, but there have also been groups like Aumen in which the poets have supported one another, and although one member may succeed more fully than others, there is no or little petty jealousy. I myself have always been more of a loner in many ways, and yet I have tried to promote my fellows, while at the same time cultivating my own particular kind of poetry. Chile, in general, it seems to me, has perhaps been more characterized by groups or generations than in the States, but in both countries there have been individual voices that eventually rose above the rest. As a small country, it is perhaps easier for poets in Chile to know one another than in the States, but since the country differs so much from the north to the central valley to the south, there are great differences in subject matter and attitude, especially through the influence of the native peoples in the south, where they are more populous. Chilotes see themselves as almost a separate nation from Chile, and this is naturally reflected in their poetry that focuses on a climate and culture peculiar to the islands.

Nelson told me that poets of his generation were not influenced by Neruda and Parra, because those giants did not attract them so much as a figure like Jorge Teillier, whose nostalgia for the southern region of Chile was more in tune with their own Chilote way of seeing and experiencing the lake district, or Lars of the South. I had brought Nelson a copy of *Figures of Speech*, my translation of Enrique Lihn's poetry. He said that he knew that Lihn was popular with younger poets, but he was not interested in what he called Lihn's metapoetics, his obsession with language in and of itself. I then pointed out to him Lihn's poems on the Galician landscape and its people and asked him if he had seen such poems, and he said that he had not. I suggested that he read two of them, and after doing so he agreed that they were unusual for Lihn in focusing on the lives of people rather than linguistics, but he still did not seem that impressed. He knew Lihn's book on his time in New York, which reminded both Nelson and Mario of García Lorca's *Poet in New York*. The two Chilote poets thought Lorca's New York book something totally new, not the customary Gypsy or folk songs of the Spaniard's earlier work. Unfortunately, Nelson had to leave, and so I was unable to pursue any further discussion with him, as I had hoped that I could, especially with regard to his own poetry. I had liked very much his "Letter to Lautaro," the figure in Ercilla's *La Araucana* who still remains a native hero. Mario later noted that the poem was in reaction to the dictatorship, which is evident in the lines "the blood / that burst forth against the duress of this soil / made enormous trees to awaken." The poem goes on to say, in an allusion, it seems, to censorship and the discouragement of poetry publications, that "the hatred came from fear / on those ships that I imagine you remember.../ tell [God], as well, that it erases you from history's books...." The ships referred to were infamous from having been used for holding political prisoners during the Pinochet regime.

One night María came into our bedroom where I was reading and with an anxious voice urged me to get rid of a horrible slug that had crawled into the cabin. I picked it up with a paper towel and tossed it outside, and returned to my reading, thinking no more about it. The next day—Tuesday the 13th—we visited a local museum of Chiloé history, which included wooden implements, steering wheels and rudders from ships, oxen harnesses, and stone points shaped by the Huilliche, Chono, and Mapuche peoples.

All of this was informative and of interest, but what attracted my attention most was a piece by Pablo Neruda, tacked on one wall, a prose-poem dedicated to the story of trains in southern Chile. Neruda's father had worked for the railroad, and as a youth the poet had known the rainy south intimately. The prose-poem on the wall was entitled something like "The Giant Slug," and later I could remember the following lines (in rough translation), which Neruda had written in Castro in September 1925: "a slow rainy train crawls by the mountain, stops to smell the railroad ties." María had told me in her distress that a "babosa" was in the kitchen, and I asked what's a "babosa," which she thought was so funny in my Texas twang that she kept repeating my question on any occasion. She only wanted to get rid of the slimy slug and I just wanted to go on with my reading. Neruda, on the other hand, had observed the damp slug with his ever-sensitive eyes and had found metaphorical connections to his father's profession and to the rain that makes things eternally green in Chile's south.

The next day, Wednesday the 14th, we visited Ancud and saw the site of one of the last two bastions of Spanish rule in South America. Founded in 1770, the city features a fortress built in 1778-79, with its rusty cannons mounted on the walls and aimed out toward the Pacific harbor. But once again, what drew my attention was information about Neruda that I read on the wall of the Hotel Nielssen: he had lived there in 1925-26, during the period when he wrote of the train-like giant slug taking time to sniff man's intrusive railroad ties that no longer serve Chiloé. To know where a poet was born and grew up, as in the case of Neruda, may help one to understand and appreciate his or her work, even though knowing next to nothing of Shakespeare's life in England would seem to make little or no difference in responding to his writings, which, except for the sonnets, are not autobiographical. Even so, most poets tend in their writings to reflect in some way their upbringing in a specific place.

The poet of the Aumen group whose poems evoked for me many of the salient characteristics of the Chiloé that we visited was Sergio Mansilla, who was born in Achao in 1958. On our trip to Dalcahue on March 11th, we had taken the ferry and crossed to the island of Quinchao, on which Achao is located. We had driven there to see the oldest church of Chiloé, dating from 1767, and considered the most beautiful of all the wooden churches. We sat for a while on the beach and watched the sea tumble in before visiting the church. Inside, to the left of the altar through a side door and in a hallway behind the altar wall, we found a museum that displayed musical instruments, created by a local craftsman, from mandolin, violin, and cello to a bass viol. There I read a text on various types of wood and their metaphorical qualities, such as *alerce* (larch), whose soft, light wood was compared to the smile of the Chilotes and described as huge and resistant to time and rain, noble in doors and windows, and as wooden shingles protective as a poncho. The text was in the form of a prayer of thanksgiving to God for the kinds of timber that sprout in the forests "for the benefit of your servants on these islands." María loved this church especially, with its recording of Gregorian chant, or some similar a cappella music, being played for visitors like ourselves and for local citizens, like a young couple huddled closely on one of the wooden pews. In the plaza across from the front of the church, two white goats were chewing on a small tree or shrub as the people gathered to watch them, the larger goat rubbing its horns ferociously against the branches with their pine-like needles.

In reading the poetry of Sergio Mansilla, I found references to so many of the scenes that we had witnessed, brought to life on the page by the poet's intimate address to his people and their island culture. One poem entitled "Life" speaks of the people erecting their houses the best they could: "juntamos piedras.../ tijerales y miles de tejuelas partidas a machetón" (we gather rocks... / timbers for trusses and thousands of small roof shingles split by a large machete). In another poem, addressed to his people (or perhaps a specific "brother"), Mansilla alludes to the difficult road to town, which is "dark beneath the rain." This poem seems to contrast country and city, an almost universal, timeless theme, with its subtle preference for the former and its simple comforts of a warm fire and corn cakes, as against money and sugar in the city. Many of Mansilla's poems speak of the dead, who are ever present if unseen. In one piece, a boy hears a knock at the door but finds no one there, only a vague "solitary landscape where one barely / hears far off the song of nocturnal birds." (I thought, of course, of Poe's "The Raven.") A piece entitled "Buried Poems" reveals that the poet, like many during the dictatorship, suffered from repression, and that even the air was bewitched, the seeds sown did not bear fruit, and at farm markets there were no sales to be made. He then resolves to bury a few of his poems for the future, and these will be "the real / fugitives of the real prisons." Once again, rain enters the picture, but here it is a symbol of hope, since the buried poems will germinate and await "the first / rains for lifting the forefinger to the sky." Death and the future are both the subject of Mansilla's poem entitled "Death of a Relative," where the poet reports on a type of epiphany, as he realizes through another's death that his time will come. The funeral takes place amid thunderstorms and hail, which become symbolic of fear and trembling that make one more alive on contemplating one's own mortality.

The impact of the habitual rain of Chiloé on its poets is epitomized by a section of Carlos Trujillo's poem, "Written on a Seesaw," from his 1979 book of the same title. In this piece of nostalgia for his Castro boyhood, section 7 declares:

> My verses are soaked with rain
> as I am
> because we have lived all these years
> crouched down
> like wild beasts on the lookout
> in these winters of Chiloé
> which—you know it—
> are no more than one winter
> —the one of life—
> with few interruptions.

I could not know Carlos personally since he had left Chiloé in 1989 and moved to the States, where he received the doctorate at the University of Pennsylvania in 1993 and became a professor at Villanova University. On returning to Texas, I contacted him by e-mail and he sent me several of his books, including a book of photographs by New Yorker Milton Rogovin, with poems by Carlos based on photographs that Rogovin had taken in Chiloé. Entitled *Nada queda atrás* (Nothing Remains Behind) and published in 2007, the year of our visit to Chiloé, this work captures the people, places, produce, baskets, and artifacts of the island. Carlos's poem entitled "La cantina" describes a bar with its bottles behind a smiling woman who tends to her customers. The poet says that it is not the bottles of liquor that make for a fiesta but that a single bottle of Chilean *chicha*, red or white, is party enough if "the barmaid who has known us forever / Continues laughing at the same stories / Repeated for all night after night / And always applauded / As if they had never been heard before." A poem on clothes hanging on a line contains once more that ubiquitous Chilote image: "They fell on me / as the rain falls."

Our cabin had been comfortable and offered a wonderful view of the inlet, but what I recall most about our stay was a pair of *queltehue* birds (Chilean lapwing) that I would see on the ground outside. They would run from me a short distance on their very long legs and then stop and watch me. I found them and their shrieking calls fascinating, and years later I discovered that Pablo Neruda had written a poem about this bird, whose call he describes as a "piercing tero tero." I somehow thought that I had written in my journal about the *queltehue*, but I must have thought that I would do so later on and then never did. In any case, here is some of what Neruda says of this Chilean bird:

> The lapwing flew glittering
> of white snow and black snow
> and opened his suit of light,
> a full silver morning:
> costly was the fan
> of his two nuptial wings:
> rich was his body adorned
> by morning and plumage.
>
> ...[a]nd I thought: Where is he going?

To what celestial reception?

To what weddings of water with gold?

To what salon of pure purple,
among columns of hyacinths,
where only the well-dressed clouds
may enter with him?

By Friday the 16th, we were back in Santiago, and on this day I took a bus downtown to the National Library to look up Tomás Harris, a poet who worked there and with whom I had spoken on a previous trip. Part of Tomás's job was to serve on the editorial board of the journal *Mapocho*, named for the river that runs through Santiago. I had translated one of Tomás's poems for *The Dirty Goat* and wanted to give him a copy of the magazine. In addition, I was interested in searching the collections at the Library for books by Sergio Mansilla, but I had gotten a late start and with the bus being packed it had stopped so often that it was nearly noon when I reached the Library. Tomás and I talked a bit about poets of Chiloé, and after I told him that I would like to purchase copies of Mansilla's books, he referred me to the Fondo Económico de Cultura, which sold poetry collections at a thousand pesos apiece, or less than $2.00. He also gave me the address of a branch or office of the Universidad de Concepción, where he said that I could find back issues of *Atenéa*, the journal that I had mentioned to him that I was also interested in finding. It turned out that the office of the journal had moved from downtown to an address on Apoquindo Street, which I always passed on the bus.

On both of my visits with Tomás I had trouble understanding him, since he spoke so softly that I missed many of his words, but he seemed not to notice and just talked right on. My occasional interjections or questions elicited responses that I only partially understood, since he would barely open his mouth and his voice would drop so low at the ends of sentences that I could not catch his final words and therefore often lost the point of what he was saying. In the end, however, thanks to Tomás, I did find and purchase two books by Mansilla at the Fondo Econòmico: a critical work on the teaching of literature, *La Enseñanza de la literatura como práctica de liberación* (2003); and his collection of poems entitled *Cauquil* (2005), the title a reference to the phosphorescent jelly fish washed up on muddy beaches. Unfortunately, the office of the Universidad de Concepción proved not to have back issues of *Atenéa*.

On this trip I felt at times that I understood more and better than ever in carrying on conversations, with the exception of my visit with Tomás, or in overhearing people conversing. At other times, however, I became depressed that I understood so little. At the market at Los Dominicos on Saturday the 17th, I could hardly catch a word on listening to people buying fruits and vegetables. On the other hand, a sister of Raffa, the husband of Coneja's daughter, Jimena, spoke so clearly that same evening at the birthday party for their son Domingo that I could follow her word for word. Francisco is wonderfully patient with my stammered Spanish, and I can usually catch everything that he says, and if I question a word or phrase, he will stop and attempt to explain its meaning.

On Sunday the 18th, Francisco and I met again at Tavelli. In our discussion of poetry and poets, he mentioned that Parra had said of Gonzalo Rojas's erotic poetry that it was simply "un rio de semen" (a river of semen). At first I had not understood the words "de semen," having heard them as one word, "desemen," and so had not caught Parra's witty phrase until Francisco repeated it a second time. I knew of Rojas's erotic poems only because I had read an article, just two days before, on Spanish and Chilean poets of the 1950s, in a copy of volume 60 of *Mapocho* that Tomás Harris had given me when I visited him at the Library. In the article, critic Naín Nómez quotes from some of Rojas's poems, in which I found the erotic imagery quite striking. Here are my translations of the lines quoted by Nómez:

> Give me again your body,
> that from your dark clusters the light
> may flow, let me bite your stars, your fragrant clouds,
> the only heaven I know, permit me to move over you and
>   touch you

> as a new David touches the strings,
> that God himself may go with my seed
> like a multiple pulse through your precious veins
> and burst on your marble breasts and
> destroy your harmonic waist, my zither, and lower you to the beauty
> of mortal life.

Parra had said to Francisco that it embarrassed him to read such poetry.

In the article by Nómez, I was pleased to see his reference to *El espejo trizado*, a book from 1992 by Jacobo Sefamí. I had been on Jacobo's dissertation defense at UT-Austin when he presented his study on Rojas before the committee members, who were all in the Spanish Department, except for myself. At the defense, the other committee members were not familiar with what I recalled was a long essay on Rojas by Mario Benedetti; Jacobo also said that he was not aware of such an essay. It was Jacobo himself who had asked for me to be added to his committee; at the time I was then a lecturer in the English Department. After Jacobo had graduated, he sent me a copy of his book, *El destierro apacible y otros ensayos*, published in Mexico in 1987. He remembered that I had been right about the Benedetti essay, for he had found and read it, and afterwards had revised his dissertation.

Also on the 18th, I had seen an interview with Rojas, who was to celebrate his 90th birthday in December 2007. The interview revealed the poet's attitude toward prizes, homages, and Parra, who he said was dying to win the Nobel Prize, for which Rojas had also been nominated. But Rojas asserted that it meant nothing to him, let Parra have it. Rojas confessed that as a student he had not been outstanding, that he was a "lentiforme" (slowpoke) because he took a long time to do his work, but that even so, he advanced right along, "swimming deeply."

In traveling to Chile I have always looked forward to visiting the various bookstores in search of new books of poetry and criticism. The trips have also provided me with an opportunity to acquire journals and magazines containing information on new and established writers, and to read articles on poets and reviews of their books in the culture section of Chile's main newspaper, *El Mercurio*. In the same issue of *Mapocho* that Tomás Harris had given me, I read an interview with Roberto Alifano, an Argentine writer and editor, who had served as the amanuensis of Jorge Luis Borges during an eleven-year period, from 1974 to 1985. In 1988, two years after Borges died in 1986, Alifano revived *Proa*, a magazine begun by Borges and others in 1922. Interviewed by Marcelo Rioseco for volume 60 of *Mapocho*, from 2006, Alifano impressed me by his entirely lucid yet colloquial form of Spanish. He spoke of first coming to Chile in 1965, the same year of my own first trip to this delightful land, and he recalled having taken a walk at the time with Jorge Teillier, the poet from southern Chile mentioned earlier—a favorite of Francisco Véjar.

During Alifano and Teillier's walk near Moneda, the Presidential palace where Salvador Allende would die in 1973, the Chilean mentioned to Alifano that nearby were the rooms where Nicaraguan poet Rubén Darío had lived in 1888, when his first book *Azul* was published in Chile. The two men found the building, and since Darío's old rooms were vacant, Alifano rented them, only to discover after spending his first night there that the mattress was full of bed bugs. Even so, he declared that he was happy knowing that he had slept where the great poet had laid his head. Other anecdotes and self-reflections abound in the interview, such as Alifano's notion that all who dedicate themselves to literature are, like Borges (according to the writer's own mother), a little bit crazy. Alifano asserted that "the accepted position is that people dedicate themselves to making money and living well. We [literati] take another route. Someone who lives all the time working in literature, or thinking literarily, has to be a little crazy. When someone has that type of obsession there is some insanity involved." He observes of Borges that he lived in a tiny, very Spartan room, and had a reduced library, with none of his own books, since, as he told Alifano, he was no one to be mixing his books with those by the likes of British authors Chesterton, Kipling, or Stevenson.

It was quite uplifting to read Alifano's words, and his recollections made me even prouder than I had been in 2004 when

I had a book review published in *Proa*. In 1988, in the first issue of that revived magazine, Alifano had published work by Enrique Lihn, who would die in that same year. In 2003, Francisco had asked me to review his book *El Emboscado* for *Proa*, and so I wrote a review in Spanish and it was published in the issue of January-February-March of 2004. As a result of my review, the publisher who was going to issue Francisco's *Bitacora del Emboscado* asked me to write an introduction to the book, but the volume so far as I know has never been printed. Nevertheless, my introduction, translated into Spanish by Claudio Giaconi, was published in issue number 59 of *Mapocho*, and so I owe in part my appearance in that journal to my having first been published in *Proa*. My association with Francisco has been invaluable, for he has been an open sesame to the world of Chilean poets and to publications like *Proa* and *Mapocho*. (Later, in 2019, my introduction to Francisco's apparently unpublished book would be included in my collection of essays and reviews, *Hallazgo y traducción de poesía chilena*.)

On Monday the 19th, I met Irene Rostagno at Tavelli, and from there we took a taxi to the campus of the Universidad Metropolitana, where I was scheduled to speak to her English classes studying British literature. The campus looked familiar but not exactly as I remembered it from my first visit in 1965, or even from more recent visits. (I have described the campus somewhat in my *Harbingers of Books to Come* of 2009.) I had sent Irene an e-mail asking her to bring along a textbook with some Chaucer and some sonnets by Shakespeare, but she had not checked her e-mail and arrived empty-handed. She said that we could see if their library might have an anthology of selections of the two authors, but she warned me that the collection was pretty bad and the librarian not much help. In the hallway of the English building, on our way to the small library room, Irene reminded her students to come to class. I found it unfortunate that she would have to say anything to them about attendance, but she explained that they were not dependable, although better under the new departmental administration, which had supported her flunking students in the prior semester, unlike the previous director who never allowed her to do so. Irene said that the former director had even changed the grades that she had given, from failing to passing. Some of that sort of thing I had myself experienced when I taught at Voorhees College in South Carolina, so I was already aware of such unprofessional behavior.

The librarian was sitting at her desk, talking on the phone, with two or three persons seated with her; the latter appeared not to be there to use the library but just to chat. Irene explained that we needed a volume containing Shakespeare's poetry, and the librarian went to a shelf but found nothing that she was looking for, so came back to her desk. In the meantime, I glanced at the books on the same shelf and was almost horrified to see nothing but out-of-date texts with no authors of the "canon." Finally, the librarian found a textbook for American readers of British literature, and allowed us to take it to the classroom. Fortunately, the book proved quite sufficient for my purposes, since it included a good deal of Chaucer and plenty of Shakespeare sonnets.

My plan was to speak on the Wife of Bath, whose prologue and tale were both in the textbook. I began by suggesting that the Wife was considered by critics—I was thinking primarily of Harold Bloom—to be one of the most original and profound creations in British literature, along with Hamlet, Falstaff, and Iago. The students had read a bit of the Prologue to *The Canterbury Tales*, but they were only going to study the Reeves tale. I went over a few lines of the Prologue, pointing out the meter and rhyme, showing how the language had changed—for example, from "strondes" to present-day "strands" —and noting how in the case of "folk" for people the word was close to the German "volk," as in Volkswagen. After this, I touched on the Prologue's description of the Wife and pointed out that "gap-toothed" was an indication of her lusty nature. Next I summarized her tale of the knight who had been condemned to death for rape, but whom Queen Guinevere allowed to live if he could provide her with the correct answer to the question of what women want most in life. Along with this background information, I provided the students with some details regarding the Wife and her five husbands. I mentioned her anger when anyone else got ahead of her at church and the obvious fact that she liked men. I then asked each of the male students what he thought women wanted most in life, to which they at first said they had no idea. I also asked what kind of woman they thought the Wife was. One student said that she was poor, but I asked him how that could be if she could afford to go on the pilgrimage, pay her way, and be away from home for a number of days. Also, I pointed out that she was probably left well-off by the deaths of five husbands. Some students began to see that the Wife was unusual because they knew that in the Middle Ages a woman married only once and if her husband died she was a widow for the rest of her life.

After one male student suggested that women want to be treated equally, we discussed how this was a rather modern concept. In regard to modernity, I pointed out that Chaucer was ahead of his time, and that it is partly for that reason that we read classic authors who still speak to us on issues of our own day and age. Moving to the female students, I asked them what women want most, and after several offered some of the same ideas that had been suggested by their male classmates, one young lady said that women wanted to control their own lives. I said that she was warm. (I asked the class if the Spanish word for warm, *tibia*, could also be used to mean being on the right track, and the students said that the word would be *entibiarse*. Later, Irene told me that *tibio*, not *entibiarse*, was the word used for getting close in searching for something or for answering a question, but she thought that it was only used in that sense in Chile.) Eventually I explained that the Wife in Chaucer's tale wanted control in the marriage. A young married man in the class said that women do have control, even though men think that they are in charge. It seemed clear to me that the students came to understand quite well the ideas that we discussed, since I had spoken to everyone in the class and had given each one a chance to express him or herself in English. They were obviously challenged and intrigued by Chaucer's character and her "feminist" mindset.

We next took up Shakespeare's sonnet 73, but on the whiteboard I wrote with a marker only the first line of each quatrain and the first line of the couplet. This allowed me to have the class focus on similarities in the lines: thou-thy; see, behold, perceiv'st; time of day, year or season; and how a fire burns itself out by consuming the fuel that feeds it. Slowly they began to observe the patterns, repetitions, and variations in vocabulary and imagery and how all relate to the projected death of the speaker, which makes the person addressed in the poem more loving toward the speaker, or so the latter asserts. I pointed out the metaphor of sleep as "Death's second self," but avoided in the last line the problem of "leave," which has always seemed to me should say "lose." Happily, the students were delighted with my presentation and applauded long and loud at the end of the class, and several came up to ask questions or simply to thank me. Irene was pleased, and later reported to me that everyone in the class was present. Despite the handicap of the students not having the complete text of the Shakespeare sonnet, and not having read the Wife's tale beforehand, the ideas of the two works came through even better than I would have expected.

On Tuesday the 20th, I took one of the much maligned Transantiago buses from Las Condes to the downtown area, getting off at the Moneda street stop and walking to the Instituto Chileno-norteamericano. I had worked at the binational Institute for a year in 1966, teaching English conversation and American literature classes and editing the literary magazine *Tide*, which I had started for the Institute and the Catholic University where I was also teaching. Passing the presidential palace and the same plaza across which I had so often walked during that momentous year of María's and my courtship, I felt free of the insecurity that I had experienced in those days from having understood so little in Spanish and from being always painfully aware of sticking out as a foreigner. On this trip, especially, I had felt more comfortable than ever, being better able to ask questions and to comprehend the answers. As for the Institute, it had changed in some ways, but the library where I first saw María was very much the same. And there was Magaly, María's coworker, who was now in charge. After greeting her, chatting a bit, and donating to the library copies of my translations of the Lihn and Welden books, I went on to the National Library at the other end of Moneda. There I gave another copy of the Welden book to a person in the section devoted to book deposits. The room was filled with boxes of books and loose volumes everywhere. I wondered if Welden's thin *poemario* would ever end up where patrons could check it out or read it in the library. My final stop was the bookstore of the National Library, where I asked if there were any past issues of *Atenea*. The woman at the desk immediately arose and went to a low shelf and from it took out three issues of the magazine, all from the late 1990s. Right away one issue caught my eye, even though it was not one of the issues on Neruda and Parra that I had come looking for. The issue was number 476 from 1997, and it featured on the cover a photo of Gonzalo Rojas, in a cap with a short brim and braid, like the one that I had seen Ernesto Lafourcade wearing at Tavelli. Looking at the contents page, I found an article on Neruda as a translator, which, together with an address given by Rojas, convinced me to buy the issue; later, once I had read both pieces, I was quite happy with my purchase.

Entitled "Neruda: humilde traductor" (Neruda: humble translator), the article by Darío Ulloa Cárdenas compares Neruda's translation of *Romeo and Juliet* with a version by Spaniard Luis Astrana Marín and with Shakespeare's original English. It was clear to me that Neruda's translation was superior to Marín's, which Cárdenas characterizes as pompous, rigid, and academic, versus the Chilean's direct, colloquial, simple language—a "plebización del lenguaje" (a plebicizing of the language). In rendering Shakespeare, Neruda outlined his own approach as one in which he would abbreviate the Bard's play, make the speeches more direct, and eliminate passages that described what had already been seen or heard. Cárdenas had consulted the edition of Shakespeare's play that Neruda had used and marked, a Yale University Press printing obtained by the poet in 1959 and preserved at La Chascona. Neruda also attempted to be more faithful to Romeo than to Shakespeare by cutting out comments by Juliet's family that are critical of her husband, though at the time her parents do not know that the lovers are married. Most impressive to me was Neruda's dropping part of a speech by Juliet in which she, through Shakespeare, alludes to figures in Greek-Roman mythology (Phoebus and Phaëton) and creates what Cárdenas considers the Bard's "concession to baroque preciosity," having placed such an unnatural allusion in the mouth of his tragic heroine, a teenager whose knowledge of such literary references may be questioned. As Cárdenas suggests, Neruda manages to improve the play by "suppressing" passages that do justice neither to the drama nor to the poetry.

The address in the issue of *Atenea*, given by Gonzalo Rojas in the southern city of Concepción, includes a reference to Harold Bloom's Western Canon, since the subject of the poet's "Discourse" is the impact of books on him and his writings. This was particularly valuable to me since I had been involved during the past months in recalling my own life as it related to reading and writing, which would result in my *Harbingers of Books to Come*. Rojas begins by declaring that even though he has lived since childhood in dialogue with books, he does not entirely know what the book is. He does know that for him it is not a bestseller but rather a source, like headwaters, written by destiny or fate, which permits him "to be and grow, since simultaneous interweaving of sense and senselessness provides [him] with a glimpse of the primordial chaos." Reminiscent of Wordsworth's famous line, "the child is father of the man," Rojas asserts that "the man is the son of his writings and one spins out his own book." Rojas asks pointedly, What would we do without books? Without them, where is memory? He declares that he himself is his own incomplete or unfinished book.

In the course of his talk, Rojas mentions a question posed to him in the Chiloé city of Ancud by a student of eleven or twelve years of age, to the effect that when Rojas finished writing something, did he feel like he still had not gotten to the end? Rojas replied by saying that the boy had enlightened him more deeply than any critic, by causing him to recall that Goethe, who was a boy to the end of his life, had said "That you may not be able to get to the end: that is what makes you great." Rojas continues, "Yes, children live the enigma more than their elders." Relatedly, Rojas does offer one definition of the book: the most beautiful instrument invented by man. He also asserts that it is preferable not to come to the end of a piece of writing in order to reach a place where one can look out at the inconclusiveness of the eternal. In his conclusion, Rojas recalls Borges, who had said in 1978 that to reread is more important than to read, "except that in order to reread one must have read." To Borges' idea, Rojas adds his own thought that each time we read, everything changes, and that we ourselves change *if we are*. This enigmatic addition means to me, if any enigma can be translated, that if we are readers we are changed by the book. Or he may be positing a view that only if we exist can we change, and that we only really exist through books, which, as he finally infers, is the world that we all need to reach and reread.

I have often wanted to translate critical writings by Chileans on literature, for they would enable readers of English to see how well-read, insightful, and articulate they have been and are. This, however, would take up a considerable amount of my time, which I prefer to devote to translating their poetry, which allows me to participate creatively in attempting to bring into English the poets' artistic writings. For a special issue of *The Library Chronicle*, devoted to articles on the holdings of the Benson Latin American Collection at UT, I did translate Peruvian Julio Ortega's essay on the manuscripts of Julio Cortázar's novel, *Rayuela*. I enjoyed doing the translation and felt that I had managed as faithful a job as I could of rendering Ortega's Spanish into English. Even though I found Ortega's prose "easier" to translate than poetry, I nonetheless still prefer to spend my time and effort on the more difficult and, as many have said, impossible task of bringing poems from one language into another.

On March 22nd, Francisco and I met at Pepe's home to chat and listen to jazz. After I asked Pepe to play something by Fats Waller and he put on "Lulu's Back in Town," this reminded Pepe of a version by Thelonious Monk, which he had on a vinyl disc, a Columbia album entitled *It's Monk Time*. The "Time" in the title is an allusion to Monk's appearance on a *Time* magazine cover, just as Dave Brubeck's *Brubeck Time* refers to his own *Time* magazine feature story. On "Lulu's Back in Town," I found Charlie Rouse's tenor better than on any Monk recording that I owned or had heard. Monk's piano is, of course, different from Waller's but owes something to the latter's stride style, though of the two versions I still prefer that of Fats. The Monk recording reminded me of his solo piano performance of "I Love You (Sweetheart of All My Dreams)," but I could not recall the parenthetical part of the title, and so when Pepe looked up the words "I Love You" in his computerized catalog, he did not find it. He then thought to look on his copy of *Monk Alone*, a two-CD set, and there it was. I had not thought to tell him that the piece was on that CD set, which I also own. There are two versions of the piece, and both are amazing—Monk's time is so perfect that it is uncanny, whether on the slow or the somewhat faster take. The sound is sui generis Monk, full of flawlessly executed runs and dissonant notes resolved beautifully in his renderings of the original melody and harmony. Pepe also played a more recent recording by the Dizzy Gillespie Orchestra as directed by Slide Hampton, with a couple of guest-appearance solos by Waco-born trumpeter Roy Hargrove, which were okay but nothing special—they did not change my mind from my brief comment in *Texan Jazz* that Hargrove's work for me is rather retrograde. The Monk sides were the highlight of our listening session, after which Pepe drove us to downtown Santiago for the production of Enrique Lihn's unpublished play, *Las Gallinas: Corral de mujeres*.

All three of us had looked forward to the Lihn play that was apparently first presented in 2006, but not in Santiago, or not in a large public venue like the theatre of the University of Chile at Morande 750. We left a bit late and there was a traffic jam on the first major street we entered. Francisco and I both worried that we would not arrive in time to pick up the tickets that Pepe had reserved, which would only be held until fifteen minutes before the performance. Pepe's driving is a bit nerve-wracking, as he forces his way into traffic where I never would, but he manages somehow to maneuver his way through the capital's congested streets with no problem. Although we were fifteen minutes late, our seats were still available, though not in front of the stage but off to the side.

The set consisted of a type of chicken wire, through which the "gallinas" (hens) would from time to time peer out at the audience. The actors and actresses could be seen clearly throughout the play, but I had a difficult time making out the soliloquies of the main character, a female who owns the house inhabited by three younger women and a maid (apparently), and visited by perhaps her eldest daughter, played by Lihn's own daughter, Andrea. At times I would catch a complete sentence, but the conflicts between the characters were only evident through gestures, tone of voice, and a few key words now and then. A photo of Lihn hung on one wall and another photo was on the floor, smashed at one point by a male character who seemed to oppose the matron and the other women. A few other props consisted of a single armchair, in which the matron sat during her opening soliloquy and from time to time thereafter, and a wheelchair, in which she was rolled in from off center stage through the only entrance from other parts of the house or from the outside, none of which was ever revealed. A man with a type of document—inheritance papers, a will, ownership of the house, or whatever—was played by an older actor whose lines I could understand somewhat better and whose part as acted was the stereotype of an unsure, fearful accountant, or perhaps a lawyer in need of a signature, or it may have been that he was entrusted with the task of evicting the old lady. A younger fellow I could also understand better, but his was a limited part. In general, I found the situation unappealing and the acting unconvincing. Pepe later said that the plot reminded him of García Lorca's *The House of Bernarda Alba*, whose title I knew but did not believe that I had ever read, only remembering have read his *Blood Wedding*, which is a powerful dramatic work.

    After the play ended, Francisco confessed that he had not understood even fifty percent of the dialogue or of the main character's soliloquies. Pepe said that he understood only about thirty percent and the play without the text was nothing he found engaging, but he could not judge the whole work because the characters' lines were so badly delivered. The revelation that even my Chilean friends could not understand much of the play was a great comfort to me, even though it did not let me off of the hook for my Spanish being as pitiful as it is after decades of reading the language and trying to speak it. Of the little that I did seem to understand I recalled especially a statement by a female character, who was at one point scantily clad, with her boobs prominently displayed: "I have known a thousand men and they're all the same." A male figure announced that "In this country people are all swine" (or perhaps just "unlucky," "wretched," "unhappy," or "unpleasant"). At the reception I met Andrea and gave her a copy of my translation of her father's *Figures of Speech*, which she really seemed to appreciate, saying that she only had one copy. I had had the publisher mail her ten copies, but they came back after never having been picked up at the post office in Santiago, probably because they charge so much for imported books. I also chatted briefly with Cristián Warnken, who is related to Lihn and is well thought of as a literary columnist and was at one time a popular talk-show host. Cristián was at one time the director of literature at the Universidad del Desarrollo and worked with Armando Roa Vial on the editorial committee of *El Navegante*.

We were all three quite disappointed in Lihn's play, but I was content with having attended the performance, so that no one, as Coneja always says, can tell me stories about how wonderful it was. I was also happy that I had attended Lihn's one-man performance at the Institute in 1977 when he came on stage and, as he spoke, began putting on make-up in front of the audience, slowly changing his appearance and his voice as he turned into the character he called Pompier. That performance was remembered at the reception after *Las Gallinas* by Pepe's piano tuner, who said that he still had the poster from the Pompier event. I had loaned my own copy of the poster for reproduction in a special translation section of David Yates' magazine *Cedar Rock* and never got it back. I do still have the little brochure from *Las Gallinas*, with its photo of Lihn and the actress who played the lead role of the domineering matron.

On March 21st, I spoke to Francisco's class at the Universidad del Desarrollo, at its branch location at the corner of Lastarria and Villavincencio streets. At that time I met Ernesto Pfeiffer, a fourth-year student who was doing his thesis on the Chilean poet Braulio Arenas. Ernesto must have heard from Francisco that I had been to Chiloé and so he showed me a collection of poems by Arenas that included a piece on Ancud. Later I tried to find the Arenas book, but only located a different, more recent collection, which did not include the Ancud poem. After we returned to Texas, Ernesto sent me a copy of the book, entitled *En el mejor de los mundos*, from 1970, and I discovered that the collection also included poems on Castro and Achao. The poem on Acud mentions Caleuche, the Chilote myth of a ghost ship that sails off the coast of the island, and also alludes to Ercilla's *La Araucana*, saying that

> Don Alonso arrived. Saw your immense
> panorama of skies and forests.
> Ercilla sang you: that was sufficient
>   for your heritage.

The source for this passage in Arenas' Acud poem is Ercilla's *La Araucana*, Part II, where the Spaniard describes the archipelago of Chiloé and praises the city. In Canto XXXV, the conquistadors have been abandoned by their native guide, who has left them starving in the middle of dense, unknown woodlands. Here are my unrhymed translations of two of the poet's eight-line stanzas, numbers 40 and 41:

> Seven days we wandered lost,
> opening with steel the impediments,
> having in all that time nowhere
> to recline our wearied limbs.
> At last one morning we came upon
> Ancud's spacious, fertile clearing,
> and at the foot of the mountain's rugged slope
> an extensive lake and grand shoreline.
>
> It was a wide archipelago, populated
> by innumerable pleasant islands,
> swift boats and canoes crossing
> from one side over to the other.
> No desperate sailor in the midst
> of fluctuating waves ever saw
> the nearby port with greater gladness
> than we welcomed that open way.

Ercilla goes on to describe the delicious *murta* berries, also mentioned by Arenas in his poem, and in Canto XXXVI Ercilla praises the sincere kindness of the people they meet, whereas he charges his fellow Spaniards with planting their standard of greed and cupidity.

    To me, the best of Arenas's three poems on Chilote towns is "Achao," with its unusual and quite beautiful sound pattern.

Although all three poems are constructed in the same three-and-a-half-line stanza form, "Achao" contains at times rhymes that bind together one or more stanzas through the repeated sound of "ante": in *elegante, anhelante, alucinante, distante, purificante, vibrante, instante, errante,* and *habitante.* The poem describes Ercilla crossing from the main island of Chiloé, at Dalcahue, to the island of Quinchao, on which Achao is located, just as María, Coneja, and I had done when we visited the town and its wooden church. Reference to the church appears in the following stanza of Arenas' poem:

> I was dying of sleep. But the church
> seemed to want to question me.
> Water-color church, in the morning,
>   so elegant.

Later in the poem, there are three stanzas that I have translated to suggest something of the poet's panegyric to Chiloé, in part through a native Chilote word:

> These islanders have a magic,
> *quelcun*, word of vibrant love.
> And for whoever says it, this word
>   is a key.

> It is enough to say it, in the middle of the night,
> beside a house, and this house will open.
> On being pronounced, the fire will be lit
>   in the poorest home.

> . . .

> I have arrived in Achao with my dream,
> leaping among the islands, errant heart,
> and when I said the word love,
>   I was an inhabitant.

Without having visited Chiloé and without knowing Ercilla's *La*

Araucana, I would not have been able to appreciate Arenas's poetry as much as I now do. And of course, without having met Ernesto, I probably would never have learned of Arenas's poems on Chilote towns. In this instance and in many another, my limited travels have made possible a greater appreciation for the places, people, and poetry that I have encountered and that have enlightened me. Finally, I must not forget that it was María's idea to visit Chiloé that led to all three, as has so often been the case, even with travels in my own home state.

Knowing that I wanted to see Nicanor Parra again, Ernesto offered to drive me to Las Cruces. I do not recall the day that he picked me up at 9 a.m. and we headed for the coast, but as we were chatting along the way, Ernesto pointed out the property where his family lived, in an avocado-groved area near Pomaire. Around 10:30 we arrived in Las Cruces and walked around near the beach, since Ernesto said that we were a bit too early for Parra. About 11 we drove to his house and parked on the same side of the street on which, just in front of his palm-tree shaded home, Don Nicanor's Volkswagen Bug was parked. We knocked at the closed front door, with its black spray-painted "antipoeta."

Parra, dressed as he had been the previous June, with round khaki hat, yellowish work boots, and baggy pants, opened the door and welcomed us in. He directed us into the same living room area with its view of the bay out the back and Las Cruces across the way. The furniture was arranged differently, with two couches, one against the side window facing the interior door to the room and the other against an interior wall facing the sliding glass door that looked out on the bay with its beautiful blue, white-capped waves rolling onto the beach. Sitting on the couch facing the sliding door, I saw for the first time on a visit to the house a green blackboard with math equations and the antipoet's distinctive printed handwriting. Parra sat on the couch with me, and on removing his hat, he looked healthier and younger, at 93, than he appeared in June of 2006. I tried to gain his permission to photograph him with his hat off, but he objected and replaced it on his head immediately. Next to me was a CD player, and after I mentioned that Ernesto had shown me a poem by his brother Roberto, he put on a disc of Latin-style music while he searched for a tape recording of Roberto playing the guitar. Once he had found the tape, he put it on, and the first piece, which I found quite good, had blues in its title. Don Nicanor explained that the song was called "jazz huachaca," and at first I thought it was based on Euday L. Bowman's "Twelfth Street Rag," but later I realized that it must have been "In the Mood." There was a history of music in Chile lying on the table next to the CD player, and I looked for the brother's name in the index, and there it was. Parra highly recommended the book, but I forgot to look for it before we left the country and no longer remember its title.

Another book that was lying among a pile of publications on a coffee table in front of both couches was a volume of the literary essays of José Victorino Lastarria, the 19th-century writer for whom the street in Santiago was named. Parra had been reading this work and praised it as an essential text. I picked it up and began to read in an essay heavily underlined by the antipoet. The ideas were certainly familiar, since they were those Parra himself espoused, such as the injunction to create a truly Chilean poetry based on the language of the everyday man. The day that we departed for Texas, I would meet Francisco one last time, on Lastarria Street, and we would walk over to Merced 345, where, in the bookstore El Cid Campeador, I found the original 1878 edition of Lastarria's *Estudios Literarios*, but it was far too expensive for me at about 120 U.S. dollars. However, the lady who helped me found a 1912 edition for about 30 dollars, which I took. Here is my translation of a few passages from Chapter XIV, entitled "Noticia de la Sociedad.— Discurso inaugural," Lastarria's address to the Sociedad Literaria (Literary Society) that he had helped to found in 1841:

> It is said that literature is *the expression of society*, because in effect it is the source that reveals in a more explicit manner the moral and intellectual necessities of the peoples, it is the frame in which ideas and passions are consigned, the tastes and opinions, the religion and the preoccupations of an entire generation....Literature, finally, comprehends, among its numerous materials, elevated concepts of the philosopher and the jurist, the

irrefutable truths of the mathematician and the historian, the freshness of familiar correspondence, and the raptures, the delicious ecstasy of the poet....I must tell you that we have very little to imitate, our literature should be exclusively our own, it should be entirely national. There is a literature that Spain bequeathed us with its divine religion, with its heavy and indigestible laws, with its pernicious and anti-social concerns. But that literature should not be ours, because on breaking the rusty chains that tied us to the Peninsula, our nationality began to take on a very different dye....There are no peoples on earth who may have, as the Americans do, the most compelling need to be original in their literature, because all their modifications are peculiar to them and they have nothing in common with those that constitute the originality of the Old World. (pages 122, 127, 136)

I am not certain that this was the address that Parra had marked in his Lastarria book, but it contains many attitudes characteristic of the paragraphs that I read at his home in Las Cruces.

My principal object in visiting Don Nicanor on this occasion was to obtain his permission to publish my translations of the five long poems that constitute his *Discursos de sobremesa*, which had been published in 2006 by the Universidad Diego Portales. I had sent him a contract from Joe Bratcher's Host Publications, but he had told Ernesto that the $2,000 the publisher offered was too little. Yet almost as soon as we arrived, Parra recounted a conversation that he had had with James Laughlin of New Directions, concerning, I presume, the 1966 publication of Parra's *Poems and Antipoems*, edited by Miller Williams. Laughlin had told Parra just to go on and sign the contract because neither of them was going to get rich from his poetry. This seemed to be an indication that Don Nicanor was now willing to sign the Host contract, but I did not bring up the subject until late in the afternoon. In the meantime, we had tea, and later his maids served lunch, which consisted of delicious, hot *humitas* (ground corn heated in shucks) and some slices of a meat roll, both with strings around them to hold the leaves and the meat together. We also had tomatoes and wine, over which we talked of Shakespeare. One idea of Parra's that I thought I would easily remember, I failed to jot down at the time, and regrettably it has escaped my memory—an object lesson that I have never learned. Later Don Nicanor began to write in one of his notebooks, partly about topics of our conversation, such as his granddaughter Cristalina Parra, who once declared that her name was Lina Paya, shortening her first name and mispronouncing her last. Don Nicanor showed me what he said would be a new book entitled LAS, an anti-title, he observed, since under that feminine word for plural "The" the rest of the title continued: "Genialidades de Lina Paya" (Ingenuities of Lina Paya), which he noted was a line in hendecasyllables. Above the "i" and the first "a" in the granddaughter's names he had drawn a star.

After a full day of conversation, I at last asked what we were to do about the contract. Parra said to give it to him and he would sign it. That was it, no comment, except to say that I could do whatever I wished. Ernesto added that there were other discourses not included in the book published in 2006. I suggested that it would be good to include the unpublished discourses in my translation, and Don Nicanor was enthusiastic. Ernesto offered to find them for me, but apparently he never did, and so they are not included in *After-Dinner Declarations,* my translated version of Parra's *Discursos de sobremesa.* Before we left, Don Nicanor gave me a shrink-wrapped copy of his *Obras públicas* and allowed me to take a photo of him with Ernesto, which the student had hoped that Parra would permit since he did not have a picture of the two of them together.

When Ernesto had been in another room during our visit, Parra had confided that he was a bright kid and that he was quite fond of him. Ernesto had set up Parra's computer system so that he could keep track of his bills and paperwork. On the way back to Santiago, Ernesto told me of his interest in studying in the States once he graduated at the end of December. I promised to supply him with information on the graduate program in Spanish at UT, which I did, but he never followed through, probably because he became engaged to a very intelligent young lady and they married soon afterwards. This trip to Chile had been a huge success, not only because Parra had signed the contract but because I had met so many fine Chileans like Ernesto, and had spent time with old friends like Pepe and Francisco, as well as Alejandro Cerda, who would come from Viña del Mar the following Tuesday. Alejandro and I would be giving a talk at the main campus of the Universidad del Desarrollo on the translations of poems by Texas poets that we had worked together on in 2006, which would be published in the University's journal, *El Navegante*.

On Saturday evening, the 24th, Francisco, his companion Kuki García, and I met at the home of writer Enrique Lafourcade and his wife. For dinner we were served a most delicious spinach lasagna, prepared by Mrs. Lafourcade, who paints and also acts as her husband's computer expert. Enrique's wife had transferred onto a CD their daughter's translation of his novel on Rimbaud, which he wanted me to take to Joe Bratcher at Host Publications. After dinner, we chatted at length, with Enrique and Francisco "pelando a Don Nicanor" (peeling Don Nicanor), meaning they poked fun at his egocentric view that he was the greatest of all Chilean poets. Francisco apologized to me, openly, for dressing down the antipoet, and later confided that he had a love-hate relationship with Parra, admiring him but resenting that he expected him to write in his shadow and to forego his attachment to the poetry of Jorge Teillier. Enrique told an anecdote about having taken Nicanor on his moped and the two having been scraped up when Parra, fearing that they would not make it across the bridge at the San Carlos Canal, loosened his hold around Enrique's waist, slid backwards, and caused the bike to leap forward and spill the two of them. Parra's then Scandinavian wife had accused Enrique of almost killing Nicanor.

During dinner, Francisco had mentioned that he and I had enjoyed listening to jazz together at Pepe Hosiasson's home. Enrique did not realize that I knew his longtime friend Pepe or that I was knowledgeable about jazz. He asked his wife to put on some jazz on their CD player, and she selected several Billie Holiday recordings from the 1940s that I had not heard before. Afterwards, Enrique turned his chair around from his place at the table and began playing a tune in jazz style on an upright piano. He was not bad, but the longer he continued the less pleasing it became. Once

Enrique stopped playing, he showed us a porcelain rose that he claimed he had removed from Rimbaud's tomb. I believe that Kuki called the rose "una maravilla" (a marvel), a phrase she often uses in praising something she likes. The way she would say the word "maravilla," emphasizing the "villa," was itself quite marvelous. Not long afterwards, we would say our good nights, having passed a fascinating evening of fine food, beautiful Billie Holiday songs, and some entertaining literary table talk.

By the time that we were ready to begin packing for our return to Texas, I had accumulated so many books that we worried about the weight of our luggage. I decided to carry all the books in my carry-on bags, which meant that my briefcase and a small suitcase were bulging and extremely heavy. I was concerned not to damage several of the books that were particularly dear to me, including *Historia del jazz en Chile* and the first volume of Parra's *Obras completas y algo +*, the latter of which I had purchased in Castro. It is always the most gratifying part of a trip to Chile to be able to bring back the poetry books that have come to form part of my rather large and special collection. I could hardly wait to dig into my many new volumes, and above all the history of Chilean jazz.

After we had been back home for ten days, María was looking on the internet for paintings and art works by Francisco Otta, a man who worked at the Instituto Chileno-norteamericano in 1966 in the office adjoining my own. Born in Bohemia, Czechoslavia, Mr. Otta was Jewish and had fled Europe during the Nazi invasion and had settled in Chile in 1940. He once invited me to his home across the street from Cerro Santa Lucía, and at work he was always very good to me. I wondered why I had never asked him to design the *Tide* issues that I edited for the Institute. Perhaps I felt that it was not proper, since he worked part-time and was always busy with signs advertising new Institute exhibitions or programs. When Francisco Véjar and I had visited Pepe on this trip, I had seen on his living room wall the drawing of a jazz musician done by Mr. Otta, which Pepe had commissioned. On the internet, María found scenes that he had painted in Chiloé, including one of the *palafitos*, which I thought was really quite wonderful, as were other works that struck me as more appealing than anything that I had seen of

On waking with the shaking of the plane, I raised the window blind and saw a perfectly clear sky with countless stars, never so visible from our home in Cedar Park. When we awoke for good, about 6 a.m., we were two hours from landing and an hour before the very friendly hostesses served breakfast. I could see through a window facing east on the other side of the plane from us that the sky was becoming orange-pink from the rising sun. Below on our side, mountain peaks seemed to poke up through the solid white layer of clouds. Slowly we could see more of the higher mountains ringed by clouds that covered a view of the cordillera of the Andes. I was reminded of my first trip to Chile when, in 1965, I had caught sight of the spectacular Andes. Little by little we could make out what I thought were roads—though María thought they were just trails—on the mountain ridges and in the valleys below. At one point I saw what looked like two cars parked on a space that may have been a scenic viewing area, but there were no houses anywhere in sight and the mountains were almost entirely brown and barren. As we approached Santiago, cultivated fields came into view, in between patches of low-lying clouds. Nothing of the city could be seen, since the new airport is now quite far from the populated sections of the capital.

After we entered the terminal, María, as a citizen, went one direction, while I lined up as a visitor who had to pay the reciprocal fee. That is, since the U.S. and other countries began charging non-citizens for entering their territories, Chile in turn imposed an entrance fee on visitors. On an earlier trip I had paid the $100 as a visitor, and as long as my passport had not been renewed, I was not required to pay it again on subsequent visits. But my passport had expired and now I had a brand-new passport that lacked the official payment receipt that had been stapled in my old one. On paying the fee, I found that it had gone up to $132. In the meantime, María had passed through Customs and had already located our luggage.

When I found her, an airport worker was loading the bags on a cart as she pointed out which bags were ours. Only on arriving at her sister and brother-in-law's home did she discover that she had mistakenly had the worker pick up a piece that was not hers, but was exactly like her duffel bag with two wheels. Her brother-in-law Sergio then had to drive me back to the airport to return the bag and retrieve María's. On phoning ahead, we found that the baggage claim office was open until 4:30 p.m. We arrived before 3:30 but the door was locked and no one in sight. We then went to a ticket booth and asked why the baggage claim office was closed when the sign clearly said that it was open until 5:00 p.m., not 4:30 as the woman on the phone had told María. Repeated phone calls did not locate the baggage person, so I went to the main American Airlines office where a man said that the baggage employee was at lunch—it was now 3:30. Because no one else had the key to the claims office, we waited about ten or fifteen minutes and finally the woman showed up, unembarrassed by the inconvenience she had caused. Of course, we were at fault for having taken the wrong bag in the first place.

On our trips to Chile, my primary interest is always to meet with poets and writers, but I also look forward to spending time with María's sister and her brother-in-law in their very cozy home. María's sister's name is María Eugenia but is called Coneja by the family, just as Sergio has been nicknamed Checho. Coneja is essentially a very shy person, but she is a wonderful cook and extremely artistic. Her meals are prepared with loving attention to both their gustatory and their visual appeal, for they are delicious to taste and a delight to see. Her meals are designed with colors and shapes in mind so as to form on each plate a culinary artwork. Not only is it pleasing to eat Coneja's meals but it is a joy to do so outside under their arbor with its green grapes hanging down in clusters and green lemons on tiny trees against the house and along the walls that enclose their small city lot. Plants of every type grow on all four sides of their property, in pots or in beds, including tomatoes, peppers, herbs, flowers, various fruit trees, an almond tree, and many other types of trees. Best of all, there are no mosquitoes and the weather during March is ideal, never too hot and never too cold, with no rain, although the acequias still run full from the Cordillera's melting snow. Checho worked as an agronomist for a Swiss company, and in retirement he is constantly pruning and caring for their plants and trees, all of whose scientific names and characteristics he knows so well.

Inside their home, Conjeja's decorations are everywhere. A wall hanging made of scraps of cloth in a variety of shapes, all in subtle tones, is a domestic equivalent to an abstract painting, and another wall hanging is stitched with outlined and veined leaves in artful shapes and patterns. Box frames with butterflies line the walls of one hallway; elsewhere, there are photographs, reproductions of artworks, and collages of her own making, framed in pleasing, simple wood tinted gray or, in the case of a framed assortment of dried leaves, in attractive raw wood. Books in Spanish, French, and English fill several shelves, CDs line a lime-green tray, art posters hang on the walls, and jars, vases, and plates rest on shelves or the tops of tables. These and other decorations and objects make every room inviting and intriguing. Inside and out, their home and gardens present various forms of beauty, both man- or woman-made and natural. Only after looking more closely at the shower curtains in the upstairs and downstairs bathrooms did I realize that Coneja had also decorated those with her own designs. On a pale blue curtain, she had drawn flowers in white ink and under each had written in Spanish the phrase "solitary flower." On a white curtain she had drawn five images in a patterned design: a star, fish, heart, spiral, and flower, and beneath each image she had written its corresponding name in Spanish. Some of the hearts contained, within their outlines, freckles or diagonal slashes, while others were left empty. Through Coneja's household decoration she has turned their home into a gallery, a living space with painted, sewn, and collaged imagery that makes each room take on something of her own creative personality. It has always been a feast for the eyes to visit her home, and she will never allow María or me to lift a finger, to wash a dish, or even carry plates or glasses to the kitchen where she will do them herself.

As I sat in the living room listening to recordings of Schubert and Mendelssohn symphonies, I began to think of María and Coneja's mother, Gladys, or Gala as she was called by the family. My memory of her was evoked by watching the two sisters passing by on their way to the backyard where they carried on their animated conversations. Seeing them seated in the lawn furniture while Coneja smoked and María listened intently to her dear *hermanita*, I could see their mother again before she had suddenly passed away at age 65, turning her head just so, thinking seriously about whatever topic was being discussed, or relishing to the fullest a game of cards, a book she was reading, a piece of fruit that she would hold with her fork and carefully slice with her knife. Too bad, I thought, that she did not live to see all her grandchildren grown, married, and with children of their own, except for Diego, Coneja's second-born son, and his wife Amelia, who have had no offspring. Gala's health had not been good for years, and she was living in pain, so in some ways it was a blessing that she had passed away with a smile on her face, in her sleep, in her own bed, with no sign whatsoever of struggle or resistance to the natural end, which apparently came without her even knowing it. Although she had not suffered from a debilitating illness or a loss of her strong mental presence in our lives, she had not been with us for as long as any of us would have wished. I most regret that she did not see how well María's and my life together has endured, how we still return to Chile and maintain close ties with our Chilean side. I remain grateful to her for having made possible our meeting, since it was she who convinced her younger daughter to attend with her my literature class at the binational institute. And so it all comes back once again to my literary life, to which I am so indebted in every way.

On Saturday March 21st, I once again took a bus up Colon street and got off at Tobalaba, walking from there to Pepe Hosiasson's home at Unamuno 696. There I enjoyed with my old friend a jazz listening session, before we would later visit a jazz club in the Bella Vista section of Santiago, near the Mapocho River. Pepe received me warmly, as ever, and we ascended to his music room on the second floor of his and his wife Gaby's typically tasteful Chilean home. I had brought along a CD of Ferde Grofé playing on piano his arrangements of 1920s songs recorded during the same decade. The recording had been issued by my Austin friend Karl Miller, a music librarian at UT, under his own Pierian label. Pepe admitted that when he first began to listen to jazz that he would have rejected such jazz-influenced work as below him, as inauthentic, and corny, but now he could enjoy it as a style that can no longer be heard and perhaps cannot even be performed. I find it happy and infectious music, and even amazing, played in Grofé's type of technically perfect version of early swing. For his part, Pepe wanted to share with me some recordings by Dena DeRose, a white singer born in 1966, whom he had met in person on one of the jazz cruises that he regularly takes in order to hear live jazz performances, many of them with musicians who were stars of earlier years. He showed me a photograph of Dena and himself, he with his right arm in a sling from having broken his wrist in a fall at a concert in Buenos Aires. Other than Billie Holiday, I have never cared that much for jazz singing and was not that enthused by Pepe's new discovery. DeRose certainly had fine control of her voice, and her piano playing was impressive, especially after she herself had recovered from carpal tunnel syndrome.

Pepe also played for me a CD of Wynton Marsalis at the House of Tribes. This recording, he said, was one of his favorites, but Wynton still did not convince me as a jazz musician. A wonderful person, an outstanding classical trumpet virtuoso, and a knowledgeable promoter of jazz, Wynton, to me, can play in a jazz style but his solos lack continuity. Too often I find his notes and phrases are more for show than for the purpose of any real development of a musical train of thought. The alto player, Wes "Warmdaddy" Anderson, developed his ideas more fully, yet none interested me that much. Pepe did say that he knew that Marsalis was no Armstrong and could not measure up to the other giants of jazz. He then showed me a new book by Wynton, just out in 2008, with a warm inscription and a note from the publisher saying that Pepe's credit card was not being charged because the copy was a gift from Wynton. Pepe said that the trumpeteer does so much for jazz, and he greatly admires his energy and devotion to the music. He also assured me that he did not allow his long friendship with Wynton to cloud his judgment as to his level of achievement as a performer of jazz. I told Pepe that I admired his classical trumpet work, and his response was that he knew few jazz musicians who could perform both types of music as well as Wynton.

In thinking of musicians who had performed both jazz and classical music, Pepe mentioned that Friedrich Gulda had played and recorded jazz, which was news to me. I own recordings of

Gulda playing Bach and Beethoven, but had known nothing of his interest in jazz. Pepe said that of course Gulda's version of jazz would interest no one who did not know his high level of performance as a classical pianist. He was reminded of George Bernard Shaw's comment on a dog walking on his hind legs, that it was nothing great but amazing that it could be done at all. Pepe then put on a long-play record of Gulda performing with two black Americans, Tootie Heath on drums and Jimmy Rowser on bass. Gulda definitely managed a jazz feeling, and of course displayed his considerable technique, but it was, as Pepe said, nothing one would buy for itself.

We then listened to a newly issued re-recording of the King Oliver sides from 1923, with Armstrong's first recorded solos on "Chimes Blues" and his second cornet part in the first version of "Mabel's Dream." The work and devotion put into trying to capture on CD the original speed and sound of the original recordings are a testament to the importance of what Pepe considered the beginnings of jazz as an art form. Armstrong's solo and his second-cornet part are still remarkable in their originality and enduring ingenuity. Pepe did remark that we do not know much about what came before 1923, not counting the Original Dixieland Jazz Band's repetitious patterns, but I doubt that even an unrecorded Buddy Bolden had played anything of the caliber of Armstrong's improvisations, for not even the great King Oliver could approach his protégé's breakthrough solos. In many ways, no other player in jazz history has exhibited Armstrong's genius for swing and rhythmic invention. I asked Pepe if he would play a rare late 1930s recording of Jabbo Smith, but he said it could not compare with Jabbo's playing of the early 1930s, and so put on two earlier sides that were impressive in their power but lacked Armstrong's control. Without Louie having come before Jabbo, the latter would not have been possible. The Oliver sides—with Armstrong, Johnny Dodds' clarinet, and Honore Dutrey's wonderful counter melodies—remain a high point in the music's history rarely matched by succeeding generations.

Around 10 p.m., two friends of Pepe's arrived to drive us to the jazz club named Thelonious, after, of course, the great pianist Thelonious Monk. Álvaro was an artist and his wife Andrea worked as a coordinator of articles for *El Mercurio*'s supplement called VD, for Vivienda y Decoración (House and Decoration). Álvaro I found quite sociable; his wife said very little. During the evening I asked Álvaro if he knew the work of Álvaro Oyarzun, whose art I had seen on exhibit at the Blanton Museum at UT-Austin. Álvaro said the name rang a bell and promised to see if he could find out about his *tocayo* (person of the same name), since I had said that I would like to meet his fellow artist from having written a poem on a piece of his entitled *El autodidacta*.

When we entered the club, a group was performing Brazilian music, with a singer in a black sleeveless top and black, silky pants moving to the rhythm and then delivering lyrics of a song in Portuguese. Álvaro commented that she sang well, but Pepe said that she merely sang. After this group ended their part of the night's program, they were replaced by the jazz musicians Pepe had come to hear, especially two musicians in their 70s who to Pepe were among the best in Chile. The youngish bass player was outstanding, but Pepe hated the drummer's timekeeping and informed me that he was the one who got the jobs for the others, and so he had to be endured for that reason alone. The main musicians were the pianist and the saxophonist, and from time to time a young female vocalist joined the group, as did for one tune another young woman. I had heard the pianist, Giovanni Cultrera, on another occasion, reported in my journal for 2006 when Pepe invited me to hear a group that he had gathered for a session at the Hyatt, on the occasion of a visit to Chile by Canadian engineers who enjoyed jazz. At that time I heard Melissa Aldana, as also reported in my earlier journal. The saxophonist for this night was Alfredo Espinoza, whom I had also heard that night in May 2006, when he played, as now, both tenor and alto. I was struck more than ever by the many tunes that practicing musicians know, with their melodies, chords, key changes, and bridges, which they manage it seems so effortlessly. The bassist took wonderfully well-constructed solos and exhibited a superior technique—I believe that someone said that he had first trained as a classical cellist. The pianist could handle any tune and often his solos were quite wonderful.

During the group's break, Giovanni sat at our table and talked with Álvaro about Italy. The musician reminisced about his life during World War Two when, in 1942, at age eleven, he was in Rome, living in the same neighborhood as Mussolini. From that time on Giovanni had witnessed the war in the city, although apparently it was not bombed the way other parts of the country were during the German retreat. Álvaro said that he had visited a number of sites where paintings miraculously survived, and he asked Giovanni many questions about the war, which the pianist answered but rather matter-of-factly, treating it as an experience totally unrelated to his present life. More of interest to Giovanni was his health, his diet, and obviously playing jazz. Álvaro apparently had high blood pressure, or perhaps he suffered from high cholesterol, so Giovanni recommended little or no red meat, no alcohol, and I fail to recall what else. In any case, Álvaro was smoking and drinking the whole time, neither of which could have been good for whatever condition he was suffering from. Giovanni neither smoked nor drank, whereas Pepe like Álvaro smoked incessantly. I not only found Giovanni a fine pianist but was impressed by his blunt manner that was neither condescending nor presumptuous—he seemed a no-nonsense fellow who at 78 (Pepe's same age) was living life with gusto, but healthily.

Before the jazz musicians had taken the stage, Pepe introduced me to Erwin Díaz, the young club owner, whose work as a poet and anthologist I already knew, having read a review of his poetry in *El Mercurio* in 2007, and whose anthology, *Poesía chilena de hoy: de Parra a nuestros días*, I had bought in 2006. I told Erwin that I owned the anthology and had tried to find his collection of poems but without success. He immediately said that he would give me a copy, and went behind the bar and picked up a plastic sack with probably half-a-dozen copies of his *Nieve en el fondo* (Snow at Bottom) and inscribed a copy to me as "uno de los pocos lectores" (one of the few readers), presumably of his poetry. The book was a lovely edition with a simple black and white cover, but with a wood engraving printed in brown and gold tones and the title in large and small red caps. A photo on the inside flap of the cover is a close-up of the poet's unshaven face, with one eye in shadow, which, after reading the poetry and looking at the photo, made me think of Erwin's poem whose first line is "A la hora del sexo Tatiana es invisible" (At the hour of sex Tatiana is invisible) and whose last presents an image of the moon staring at the speaker "Con su ojo de pirata" (with its pirate's eye). On thumbing through the book, the first piece that I read was entitled "Posdata," one of Erwin's many three-line poems: "El recuerdo / Del amor / Es el amor" (Remembrance / Of love / Is love).

After the jazz group's break, they returned for the second half of their session. The vocalist, who had earlier sung a few songs, joined the men again and sang such tunes as "Bye, Bye Blackbird," "Easy Living" (Billie Holiday's version being one of my favorite songs by her), "My Romance," "Sometimes I'm Happy," and "You'd Be So Good to Come Home To." There was nothing special about the singer's performances, but on one tune she reminded me of Nancy Wilson when the latter recorded with Cannonball Adderley, especially the tunes "A Sleepin' Bee" and "Happy Talk." The vocalist who only sang one tune rendered her version of "What a Little Moonlight Can Do to You," not in the style of Billie Holiday's moving rendition but quite wonderful in her own very happy manner, punctuated by her ooh-ooh-oohs and a fetching smile. Later on, I approached her and asked if she would write her name on a piece of scrap paper, since I could not hear well with the musicians playing; she then wrote: BÁRBARA WILSON. I mentioned Nancy Wilson to her and she seemed to know the black singer but I'm not sure that she did. The jazz musicians continued to create many excellent solos, and before I knew it, the time was almost 1:30 a.m. I did not arrive at Checho and Coneja's house till 2 a.m., and they were unhappy that I had not phoned, but I really had not realized how late it was and did not think to ask Pepe to call them on his cell phone, since I have never owned one.

The days were flying by and on Monday the 23rd I met with poet friends Francisco Véjar and Sergio Rodríguez, at Tavelli in Providencia. As mentioned in other of my journals, Tavelli is the favorite coffee shop of writers, with tables inside and outside and in a passageway in a mini mall of little shops and bookstores. I showed Francisco and Sergio my translation of Parra's *Discursos de sobremesa*, and Sergio gave me seven chapbooks by various poets published through his own imprint, *ediciones Santiago inédito*. Francisco wanted me to have Parra sign the copy of *After-Dinner Declarations* that I had brought for him, but he begged me not to let Don Nicanor just sign with his initials NP, as he tended to do. Both poets wanted to help me find a way to distribute the book in Chile, and Francisco asked for a copy to give to the woman at *El Mercurio* who was in charge of book reviews. We agreed to meet again the following Friday when I would bring a copy for the newspaper and the signed copy for Francisco, after María and I had visited Parra at his home in Las Cruces, which would take place the next day when my friend Ernesto Pfeiffer would drive us there in his car.

On March 24th Ernesto picked us up at 9:30 a.m. and we arrived at Parra's home on Lincoln Street at about 11:15. A maid opened the door and asked our names, then closed the door; she soon reopened the door and invited us in. Don Nicanor was sitting and reading in his living room, with its view to the Pacific. I entered and greeted him as he got up from a couch, telling him my name, since on an earlier visit in 2006 with my UT students, he had not known who I was until we had been with him for fifteen or twenty minutes. This time I believe that he knew me but I cannot be for certain that he did until I had given him my name. I then introduced María, who had never met him and had very much looked forward to coming with me on this occasion. Parra seemed aware that we were expected, although again I cannot say for sure that he was. In any case, he seemed genuinely glad to see us, and especially happy to meet María, who almost immediately asked him if the box of hardback *After-Dinner Declarations* had ever arrived, and he said yes, that the box was in the house. I then noticed a copy of the book on a coffee table covered with publications. María wanted to know if he had had to pay much to Customs for the box of hardbacks—we knew from a telephone call that we had made to him from Texas that he had not had to pay for a box of paperbacks—and he replied that the hardbacks only cost him 70 dollars, which he implied was nothing.

He told María that he was totally surprised at what a handsome production the book was, that he had not expected anything so impressive from a small press like Host Publications. He also remarked that this book—meaning *Discursos de sobremesa*, the original Spanish volume that I had translated—was *the* book for him. He explained that in this work he had captured or recovered his real voice, even though, as I noted to him, he at times speaks in the book in the voices of Huidobro, Oyarzún, and Rulfo. Francisco had told me that the book in Spanish was very important to him but that in Chile not much attention had been paid to it. At this point, I gave him the check for $2,000 that Joe Bratcher, the publisher, had sent in accordance with the contract. Parra said, no, this is for all the work the translator has done, but María insisted that it was for him. He laid the check on a bookshelf and it lay there until later Ernesto pointed it out to him and the antipoet then put it in his shirt pocket. I wondered at the time if he would ever bother to cash it. Years later I asked the publisher, Joe Bratcher, if Parra had cashed the check, and he said that he never had.

We talked for a good while in the living room, with Don Nicanor showing us a class photo from his time in Barros Arana, his high school mentioned several times in *Discursos*. Mostly he wanted us to hear a tape recording made by his sister Violeta, of a folksong entitled "Las tres pollas negras" (The Three Black Chicks). We climbed the stairs to the second floor and there Parra connected a speaker attachment to his computer for listening to the song. Even María could not understand much of the lyrics because Violeta would lower her voice at the end of a verse, but certain words we could both catch, like *pavo real* (peacock) and the rhyming words *crianza* (rearing) and *matanza* (killing) in reference to the three chicks that were raised and then killed. Parra had already asserted that after this song there was nothing more to say, that this was a Greek tragedy in three stanzas. He played the recording again and we could hear a bit more, but still María wanted to see the lyrics written down; the antipoet admitted that it was difficult to transcribe them. María already had a CD of Violeta singing some 22 different songs and with Nicanor reading his poem entitled "Defensa de Violeta Parra," which are all very clear on that recording.

After this we went back downstairs and Parra took us out on a balcony reached from the living room. We could see—as I had seen on several previous visits—the waves in the bay rolling in on the beach at a short distance from his house. Cats were everywhere, and one sneaked into the living room, with Parra explaining that they were a nuisance because they hid under the furniture and did their business. Food was furnished for them outside, and they reproduced prolifically it seemed. We then descended to the ground level by a stairway and stood among the ruins of a castle, as Parra called it, with stone columns and a Mapuche sculpture given to the antipoet in recent days. The ruins, columns, and sculpture were all on the edge of an area with clotheslines and clothespins hanging on the lines, as described before in my visit of 2006. Later, when we were leaving for lunch, Parra took down two clothespins and gave them to María and me, and when we reentered his house I asked him to sign mine with NP, which he did—adding a plus sign after his initials, as in his book of "complete poems" and "algo +" (a few more).

While we were still outside underneath one of the clotheslines, María and Don Nicanor sat on a kind of park bench and she asked him many questions about his life after he left his boyhood home in Chillán and came to Santiago for school at Barros Arana. She also asked him about his time at the University of Chile and his travel to Brown University and Oxford for further studies. Parra spoke a bit about his time at Brown, but mostly he recounted his experience at Oxford, telling a story that I feel certain he had told many times before, but that I had not heard directly from him. I had read a bit about his not really attending classes in physics at Oxford as he was supposed to do after receiving a scholarship from the British Council. He told us that about three months after his arrival in England that he was called in by three representatives of the Council, who confronted him with the fact that he had not attended classes, nor turned in any papers, and, worst of all, had not gone to see the Dean when he had been summoned to his office. Parra acknowledged that it was true that he had not gone to classes and had not written any papers, but he said that he did not know that the Dean had sent for him. He was told that he was to pack his bags and return to Chile. He accepted this order to leave and said he would be happy to do so, but he did want to explain his reasons for not attending classes or fulfilling any assignments.

Parra explained to the representatives that on arriving in England he had found that he had made a mistake in coming to study physics, that after he discovered Shakespeare, he had realized that nothing else mattered. He then proceeded to quote Hamlet's "to be or not to be" speech, until the committee told him that was enough, that he would be hearing from them. Soon he received a phone call telling him that he could stay at Oxford and do whatever he wished. Later he was informed that he could stay for a second year. Originally, in 1954, when he was preparing his book, *Poemas y antipoemas*, he had entitled the work *Oxford 1950*, in recognition, it would seem, of the place and time of his discovery of Shakespeare with its profound impact on his own poetry.

At some point in our visit, Parra spoke of his first book, *Cancionero sin nombre*, which won a prize and was to be published, but once he saw the galleys he declared that the book was no good and he did not want to see it printed. The publisher, however, went ahead and published it. Parra disowned the book and would not allow its contents to be reprinted in his *Obras completas y algo +*. He said that he knew that it was imitative of García Lorca. None of this was new to me, except for the part about seeing the galleys and realizing the poetry was for him worthless. That had been in 1938, and the first volume of his *Obras completas,* which had appeared in 2006, covers the period 1935 to 1972, and it does include *Cancionero sin nombre*, but at the back of the volume. The dedication of *Obras completas* reads: "Opera Omnia / basura parra todos / A Dios / exista o noexista" (Complete Works / trash for all / To God / if [He] may exist or may not exist). The word "parra," instead of "para" (for), is another example of the antipoet's witty play on his own name, mentioned in my previous journals.

At about 4 p.m., María was starving when Parra finally decided that we should eat lunch. We walked to the same restaurant, Puesta del sol, where I had eaten a couple of times before, once with my UT students in 2006. Although there was little on the menu that María could eat, with her vegan diet, she could order rice, with a salad of palm hearts and lettuce. I had fried *merluza* again, a very delicious fish that for some reason was the most inexpensive dish.

Parra had *congrio a la plancha* and Ernesto another type of fish. Before Parra could pay, I went to the register and charged the meal with our Visa, which he said that he did not like, but nevertheless I think that perhaps he was pleased.

During our visit he explained at length that he would write no more but would only write down what children said, since "ahí está la cosa" (there is the thing), meaning that they speak the truth and express themselves spontaneously. He had quoted his poem on the sea "written" by his granddaughter that I have recorded in an earlier journal, about the sea floating, its bathing in itself, and more sea lying underneath the sea. María was fascinated by all the antipoet's gestures when he would quote the children's conversations, blowing out his breath, placing his hands on the sides of his head, and exclaiming "chupalla," which means a straw hat but is used as an expression of amazement.

Earlier, I had asked Parra to give me a definition of quantum physics, since I know almost nothing about science. He said that Newton thought light passes in a straight line through the atmosphere (or ether), whereas a later British physicist, Thomas Young, thought that light moves in waves. Now, however, Parra said, physicists think it does both, or they don't really know how it behaves. In speaking of Newton, he commented on how important it had been for him to study English, saying that he found the language full of clarity, concision, and information, in contrast to the rhetoric and arabesque convolutions of Spanish. He also spoke of Andrés Bello as not being Venezuelan, as he is generally considered to be, but Colombian, and then went on to say that he was actually English in his thinking, and that as the father of Chilean letters he had brought the clarity of the English language to Chile. Parra was referring, as he spoke, to a biography of Bello on the coffee table, and in looking at it I found that the author was Luis Bocaz. I had first known of Bocaz's writing in 1966 when I visited the southern city of Valdivia and read his essay on the poetry of Enrique Lihn in a book entitled *Poesía chilena (1960-1965)*. Any visit with Parra is a master class in whatever subject, from science and history to language and literature. What a privilege it has been to know this man and something of his mind, which are exceptional not only in the annals of Chilean literature but in the history of mankind, along with Lucretius with his own combination of science and poetry. Perhaps I am exaggerating, but given Parra's achievements in both physics and literature he seems to me unique in modern times.

Parra mentioned a book that he had written on physics, which I thought that I had heard mention of before. Later, in searching for such a title, I only found a 583-page work published in 1969, which he had translated from English to Spanish: *Foundations of Physics* (1957), by Robert Bruce Lindsay and Henry Margenau. Parra touched on something of his work in the field when he recounted his experience while teaching as a visiting poet at Louisiana State University, at the invitation of Miller Williams, the poet whose translations introduced me to Parra's antipoetry in 1965. During his time at L.S.U., Parra had told Williams that he wanted to give a lecture on physics. Williams could not understand what he would be able to say on the subject; he told Parra that he would have to speak to the professors in the Physics Department. In a meeting with the chairman, Parra was asked what he would talk about. After the antipoet explained his own theory of whatever it was— he was not too specific and I would not have understood in any event—the chairman had said fine. During his talk, as I understood it, Parra was told by someone in the audience that a mathematical problem that he had used in his calculations could not be proven, but Parra showed them how he had solved the problem quite easily. The response to his talk was mixed: professors who were Japanese thought that he was crazy and did not know what he was talking about; the other professors wanted to hire him for a permanent position in the Department, but Parra said no thanks, that he would be returning to Chile.

Anyone seeing Parra either in his house or on the street would never know that he is a genius with money enough to buy fancy clothing, the finest furniture, and tickets to travel anywhere he would wish. Of course, he has been to Russia, England, India, Spain, the U.S., Cuba, and Mexico, as well as other countries in Latin America, but he seems content to stay at Las Cruces, which in fact he said is the place that belongs to him, or he belongs to it. He quoted someone who had said that when one finds the place

Nicanor Parra, María Isabel, and Dave in the antipoet's home in Las Cruces, March 24, 2009.

that corresponds to him or her, he or she should leave it and it will still remain within that person. Parra declared that he had found his place at Las Cruces, but that he could not leave it.

Parra talked so much and on so many subjects that it was virtually impossible to remember them all. I was worn out by the time that we would end our visit, but he was not ready to see us go, and asked us to have some wine. He had already given Ernesto and me some dark chocolate, which he said that he loved. María and I declined the wine, and with that he said it was bad manners not to accept a glass and for us just to play like we were drinking from it.

While we were sitting outside of the restaurant, I had asked Don Nicanor if he would sign a copy of *After-Dinner Declarations* for the publisher, and he replied that he would with the greatest pleasure. I also mentioned that Francisco Véjar would like to have his copy signed, to which he indicated a certain resistance. While the antipoet had gone back into the restaurant, I had asked Ernesto why he thought that Parra would not be willing to sign Francisco's copy, and he suggested that Don Nicanor might be miffed that Francisco had not come to visit him in quite some time. Earlier Ernesto had told me that Parra had recently "peeled" or criticized Francisco. Nevertheless, after Parra signed Joe Bratcher's copy and wrote a warm *dedicatoria*, he also signed Francisco's copy with a cordial note and a hope that he would see him again in Las Cruces. María was unhappy with me that I had not brought a copy of the book for Parra to sign for me, but I was satisfied just with the visit and with his having allowed me to translate his work for publication.

On returning to Parra's house from the restaurant, we had walked up a steep cement stairway from the beach, which in no way tired him as much as it did us. After we were sitting in his living room again, I had mentioned my forthcoming memoir. Parra asked the title, and after I said "Harbingers of Books to Come," he seemed struck with astonishment by the idea of "books to come." From that time until we departed, everything was "a book to come." He began to write on pages in a notebook and to tear out the sheets and hand them to me. On a page of the journal that I had with me, he wrote his thanks to (María) Isabel and me, concluding with "a book to come." Mostly he was entranced by the thought of a book

Travels of a Texas Poet

> Isabel & Dave
> amistad & poesía
> tenemos que volver a vernos
> Nicanor Parra
> 2009
>
> Promised!
>
> Gracias x todo
> a book to come

"A book to come" in Parra's handwriting.

we would write together: "Hamlet: un libro que está X aparecer [a book that is about to appear] / Dave Oliphant & Nicanor Parra / Host Publications." But he also wrote on another sheet: "Hamlet: a book to come / Dave Oliphant." From his enthusiasm for this new title, he urged us to spend the night. We could stay in his house, or if we did not want to be so close to the poet, we could stay in his daughter Colombina's house across the street, or he would pay for us to stay in a nearby motel. María was enthused but knew that we should return to Santiago. Also, we were expected for *onces* (teatime) at Ernesto's parents' home in Talagante, and it was already 8:30 at night. Parra was quite taken with María, especially after she told him that she had once met Violeta and had told her how much she admired her songs. She also told Parra that a cousin of hers, who was a carabinero, had given Violeta a ride in his jeep after finding her sopping wet with rain, walking in the mud to tape folksongs with her heavy recording machine.

I am now reminded that when Parra played the tape of his sister singing, he asked me if I recognized the number written in ink on the top of his computer table or desk: 1564. This number was the code for opening his computer files or documents, and although I knew it as the date of Shakespeare's birth, it did not dawn on me that the antipoet had chosen it for his password when signing in to his electronic files. A few days later, when I was teaching a class for Irene Rostagno at the Universidad Metropolitana, I would tell her British literature class about Parra's use of 1564 as his computer password. As an aid to remembering Shakespeare's dates, I would also say that I always think of the four in 1564 and the final six of 1616 as totaling ten, as a way of recalling the two years of the Bard's birth and death. When we discussed John Donne's Holy Sonnet, "Death Be Not Proud," I would tell the class that Parra had said that the English metaphysical poet's title was for him miraculous, that nothing like it exists in Spanish poetry. I will have more to say about my visit with Irene's classes, but for now I return to our farewell to Parra, followed by our visit with Ernesto's parents.

María felt sorry for Parra when we left him standing at his gate, waving to us. She thought that he looked frail, even though he had proven to be as fit and as full of mental stamina as someone half his age at 95. As we drove by him, standing at the front of his house, he continued to hold up his hand and looked at us with what seemed a rather disappointed expression, although I feel certain that he was probably relieved to be left with his own ever-engaged thoughts. He seems always to be working out some problem in poetry or the meaning of life, just as he had been doing for decades, whether seeking some scientific solution or considering the wording and significance of a Shakespeare line. I did not for a minute think that he needed us for any reason, but María may have been right in seeing in his look something of forlornness or even loneliness. As he had indicated to me when I visited him previously at his home in La Reina, he feels content to withdraw from the world to contemplate the larger issues that most of us are incapable of analyzing, from physics to philosophy, Greek tragedy, and Shakespeare. Surely his own thoughts keep him company more than his admiring visitors.

Ernesto's parents were waiting for us when we arrived around nine o'clock. They had laid out a spread for *onces*, with kuchen, avocado, cheese, homemade bread, round, thinly sliced preserved meat, and cups for tea. The father was born in Chile of German descendants and still spoke with an accent, having been schooled in German in Temuco, where María had lived as a child. The mother was Chilean of Spanish blood, but she had adopted Lutheranism and was totally happy, she said, with the change from Catholicism. She told María, when they talked alone in the living room, of the suicide of Ernesto's older brother, which had deeply affected Ernesto. No signs of the loss were apparent in Ernesto's manner, for he was a very enthusiastic, warm, generous person; of course, those qualities may have been the result in part of his brother's having taken his own life. The brother had shot himself while the parents were away from home; a maid had discovered him after hearing the gun go off. Again, no signs of ongoing grief were evident, for both father and mother could not have been more welcoming and outgoing in their reception of María and me. All the food was delicious, and especially the blueberry kuchen.

When we first arrived, the father insisted on showing us his property, using a flashlight to give us a tour of his avocado, quince, pear, lemon, walnut, and araucania trees. On one type of tree there was a *copihue* growing. According to the father, the *copihue*, which is a vine of the cooler, wetter southern region, had found that that particular tree, whose name I failed to catch, could support the vine's climbing and flowering even in the warmer climate of central Chile. After María made it known that ever since her childhood she had loved *membrillo* (quince), the father gave us an armload of the fruit to take with us. After we had eaten *onces*, the mother invited us to return and spend a day and night with them, which we would have enjoyed after finding them so hospitable. By then it was quite late and we needed to leave for Santiago, so we cut short our visit and thanked them heartily for having waited for us for so long after they would normally have served their afternoon tea.

By the time that we reached Coneja and Checho's home, it was 12 midnight. When I saw them, I joked that we had arrived before 2 a.m., referring to my night out with Pepe when they had waited up, concerned about my whereabouts. But on this occasion both Cony and Checho were clearly angry at us for not having phoned that we were on our way. They were so worried that they had called the carabineros. Checho chastised us for not phoning and for not thinking of their concern. The carabineros arrived shortly after we did and María apologized, explaining that we had been with Nicanor Parra until very late, which was enough said, since they were quite impressed to learn that we had spent time with the great antipoet.

The next day, Wednesday the 25th, I was to meet Irene Rostagno at Tavelli in Providencia—our usual rendezvous site—and then go with her to the Universidad Metropolitana, or UMCE. She had invited me to teach two of her classes, one an introduction to literature and the other on British lit, in particular on the poetry of Milton, including his sonnet on blindness. Once we arrived by taxi at UMCE and entered the English Department, where students are prepared for teaching the language, Irene told me that the introduction to literature class was also doing a poem by Yeats on old age, entitled "When You Are Old," which I looked at but was not that interested in discussing because it did not seem to offer that much for analysis. The one point that I made about the poem was that its image of a fire, before which the speaker is sitting, is central to the idea of aging. Now that I think about it, I believe that I was wrong, or at least that I was overly influenced by thinking about the fire consumed by its own ashes in Shakespeare's sonnet 73, which I had discussed on another visit to UMCE; in both poems, it seemed to me, fire is an image of old age and death. At any rate, I noted that the phrase "glowing bars" in the final quatrain of "When You Are Old" might be difficult for the class to understand and asked them what they thought was being described. It took them a while to realize that the phrase referred to the fire's burning logs. I then explained (but on hindsight should have asked them to explain) why the poet had chosen "bars" rather than "logs," and the answer is surely that he needed the rhyme with "stars," the word that ends the poem and vaguely relates to personified Love. There was, as I should have known, more to analyze in the poem than I had thought at first glance. Part of my lack of interest in the Yeats poem came from what I considered its vagueness and its rather weak ending, but also, as I told the class, from its forecasting the effects of old age, since such a theme would probably have little appeal for young persons with their whole lives ahead of them.

When Irene mentioned the Yeats poem, I thought to myself that I would prefer to analyze the Irish poet's even shorter piece entitled "Memory." I had not at the time realized that "Memory" and "When You Are Old" both concern aging, time, and love, but I still prefer "Memory" as a poem that is so tightly constructed that every word is essential to its development of the theme of enduring love. At first I was going to write the poem on the blackboard, but then it occurred to me that it would be better if I had the students write it down as I dictated it from memory—the only complete poem that I can ever remember! This worked well as an exercise that tested their ears in listening to my Texas accent.

After the class had written down the poem, I asked to whom did the first two lines refer: "One had a lovely face / and two or three had charm." It was difficult for them to answer my question because they were thinking in very general terms and not of specific women the speaker had known. Even more difficult for them was to make the leap from persons to the "mountain hare." We had already struggled with the spelling and meaning of "hare," since all the class had written "hair." I explained the meaning of the word by recalling for them the small vans that in previous decades in Chile, before the new bus system with its large and even two-car vehicles, had been called in Spanish *liebres* (rabbits or hares) for their speed and quickness in traffic. The image in the poem of the one person remembered because she had more than "a lovely face" and "charm" was also hard for the students to envision as it related to the "mountain grass." Slowly, however, they began to see that the "form" of the "hare" that was left imprinted in the grass was like the memory, in the title, of the girl or woman who remained in the speaker's mind. This poem definitely intrigued the class and they clearly delighted in its message of love's lasting impression, and perhaps also in finding, as I pointed out, that the rhyme scheme contains the poem's main idea: face / charm / in vain / grass (off-rhyme with face) / form / lain.

 Having known ahead of time that the class was doing Milton, I had come prepared to say a bit about the influence of the poet on other writers. I mentioned that a number of famous novels had taken their titles from phrases in Milton's poetry: Thomas Wolfe's *Look Homeward, Angel* (from "Lycidas"); John Steinbeck's *In Dubious Battle* (from *Paradise Lost*); and Aldous Huxley's *Eyeless in Gaza* (from *Samson Agonistes*), which related to the blindness theme in the sonnet that we would discuss. In the sonnet itself, which begins "When I consider how my light is spent," I called their attention to the final line, "Those too serve who only stand and wait," and told them that President John F. Kennedy, during the U.S.-Cuban missile crisis of 1961, had repeated the line when he called up the army reserve units. But on a "lighter" note, I mentioned that I had once read a parody of the beginning of the sonnet in *Mad* magazine; that, of course, was before their time, yet one student did know about MAD TV. I quoted the *Mad* version and explained the humor: "When I consider how my light is spent / I grope and wonder where the yellow went," an allusion to an ad for Ipana toothpaste that claimed that it could clean yellowed teeth.

 We then discussed the traditional contrast between light and dark, with the latter referring to Milton's own literal blindness. Irene also wanted me to mention the allusion in the word "Talent," and so I talked about the biblical parable of the talent (a piece of money symbolic of one's God-given ability in some field or other, such as poetry), as it related to Milton's struggle with the fact that as a writer he had lost his eyesight and yet the Lord still expected the poet to serve him through his literary talent. I also mentioned that each morning Milton had dictated his epic poem, *Paradise Lost*, to his elder daughter Deborah, speaking the lines that had come to him during the night, which she would then transcribe. (Later I read in Dr. Johnson's *Lives of the Poets* that Milton's three daughters were all illiterate, but that Deborah had acted as her father's scribe; how she could write being illiterate is a mystery to me.) We had managed to cover only a bit of Milton before we were suddenly forced, after about 15-20 minutes, to evacuate the classroom when the carabineros came to occupy the campus.

When we had been just about to start the class, Irene had been notified that we would have to leave, that everyone was being ordered out of the building, but she thought that we could go on with the class for a while. It so happened that at the end of the week there was to be a celebration of the day of *el Joven combatiente* (the combatant Youth), and so protestors were warming up for the big event: an observation of the day on which two brothers had been killed as a result of their opposition to the government, or the authorities. The two young men were anarchists or revolutionaries, one killed by his own bomb. In another context during our discussion of Milton, I had happened to quote the phrase from *Hamlet*, "hoist on his own petard," and had I known of the "victim's" death by having exploded his own bomb I could have applied Shakespeare's phrase to that particular historical incident. I said that the word "petard" is almost unknown to English speakers, but I learned from the students that *petardo* is quite familiar to Spanish speakers, but apparently used more for firecrackers than for bombs.

Students, or more often non-student outsiders, frequently come to the Metropolitana campus to disrupt classes and destroy property, and these persons wear hoods, so that they are called *encapuchados*, or those with hoods that hide their identity. The carabineros battle the hooded ones with tear gas, and so the university administration closes the campus, has the students leave, and cancels classes for as long as the *encapuchados* are doing their thing. As a result, students miss many classes, which seems such a shame. To me it makes no sense that the protestors in their frustrations with the political or economic system take them out on schools and universities.

The following week I would meet again with Irene and this time speak on the poetry of John Donne. As an example of his metaphysical style, Irene had chosen the holy sonnet, "Death Be Not Proud," but in addition, I would cover two other poems, which I had printed out beforehand: "The Flea" and "A Valediction: Forbidding Mourning." We did discuss the holy sonnet, but mainly I focused on the other two poems, first analyzing with the class the syllogistic arguments of the lover in "The Flea." We discussed the responses in the poem of the woman to the speaker, who is attempting to convince her that through the flea having bitten them, the two are already married; he even argues that the flea's body is a marriage temple in which they are united and that the three of them form a trinity: he, she, and the flea. I commented especially on the combination of religious or holy and sexual imagery (loss of maidenhead) as being characteristic of metaphysical poetry. One student understood the use of syllogism in argument and gave an example of this weakest form of logic: a rabbit is an animal; a human is an animal; therefore, a human is a rabbit. Even though the speaker's various claims are far-fetched and apparently rejected by the woman, this does not deter him. Even when the woman kills the flea with her fingernail, the man simply argues that it is proof that she is no weaker from the flea's death, and that therefore she need not fear any loss of honor in yielding to him. If witty, the argument is clearly not a convincing line of reasoning, but the class was definitely entertained by the male's typical attempt at seduction.

When we came to "A Valediction," I noted that in Spain people always use the word *vale* as a way of saying goodbye, and that "diction" relates to the Spanish verb *decir* (to say). In this way I introduced the argument of the speaker in the poem against "mourning," that is, an injunction to the wife that she not be sad when he parts from her on taking a trip, since they will not be separated spiritually. Once we had worked our way through the various stanzas, I asked the class to enumerate the types of images Donne uses to support the argument that the couple will not be apart in a spiritual sense but only in terms of physical separation. One young student, who Irene later explained to me was the daughter of a fundamentalist minister, or was active in such a church and had been to the States, easily understood the difference between physical and spiritual attachment, in that only the former is affected by the absence of the loved one's body, whereas spiritual love is "inter-assured of the mind." Most of the class caught on readily to the metaphors or conceits of spiritual union represented by "into airy thinness beat" and the twin feet of the compass. One student, however, could not quite comprehend the sense in the poem of the word "beat," since she was bothered by the word order for purposes of the off-rhyme with "yet," and therefore expected "beaten" instead. Eventually it was clear to all that "beat" meant that gold, as a malleable metal, could be worked or hammered until it was stretched out so thin that, like the souls of the couple being one, it was imperceptible yet still intact.

In teaching the poem in the States, I had found that some students, when they read Donne's word "compass," would think of the directional instrument rather than the one for drawing circles in geometry. The Chilean students, however, did not seem to confuse the two. They were quite able to picture the two feet of the compass leaning apart but still attached to one another, so that after the one has roamed and the other remained "firm," they grow "erect" on being brought together as the circle is completed and the feet of the compass are folded or closed. To illustrate the idea that the image of a circle as drawn by the compass is an emblem of unity—with Donne's gold and circle being metaphysical images and symbols for inseparable union—I held up my left hand to show the class my golden wedding band, purchased in Chile and with María's name inscribed inside.

Finally, to demonstrate Dr. Johnson's definition of metaphysical poetry as "the most heterogeneous images…yoked by violence together" and his assertion that "the metaphysical poets were men of learning, and to show their learning was their whole endeavor," I asked the class to list for me the various fields of knowledge that Donne brings to bear on his theme of true love. Little by little, the students came up with astronomy (including the contrast between "sublunary" love of the flesh and spiritual love that does not depend on the physical body), geography (the earthquake image of separation—"moving of the earth brings harms and fears"—a very familiar one to Chileans accustomed to frequent tremors and earthquakes), geometry, metallurgy, religion (the virtuous man passing away quietly in the first two stanzas and the couple not profaning their love by sharing it with the church laity), and weather (with its hyperboles of tear-floods and sigh-tempests). The class applauded enthusiastically, and several students came up to ask about other metaphysical poets and to thank me. Irene said that I had "outdone" myself, a pun on the poet's name; even though she had said in Spanish *te pasaste*, her phrase means the same as that English word. For me it was a most gratifying response, and a happy ending, as it was, to our too-short visit to María's native land.

Chile (March 2011)

It had been two years since our last visit to Chile, and María was more than anxious to be with her sister and back in her longed-for country, even though she hates Santiago—all big cities for that matter. While I too was eager to return to her long thin land, I was not perhaps as up for the trip as in previous years. Since I was deep into the writing of my verse biography of Kenny Dorham, I was not so ready to abandon the project for a whole month. Also, I did not have any pressing reason to return, no project in mind for writing or translating, but I did look forward to seeing old friends and just the country itself. Unlike María, I always enjoy Santiago, which I find endlessly interesting, so agreeable weather-wise, the vegetation, the houses, the Andes, the people, and of course her sister's house with all her decorations and with her husband Checho's outside plants.

The day after we arrived, on March 2nd, my friend Pepe Hosiasson invited me to go with him to an exhibit of photographs by the Dominican Republic photographer, Mariano Hernández, who specializes in people who participate in his country's Carnaval. The exhibit was held in Casas de lo Matta, a property belonging at one time to the family of Chilean artist Eduardo Matta. The one-time home, where the photographs were hung on white walls in a long building-length hall, had recently been repaired after having suffered in the 2010 earthquake. The grounds were well kept, with roses in bloom and a huge avocado tree with fruit hanging from its branches. The photographs featured the Dominicans dressed in colorful costumes and either wearing masks—of devils or other figures—or with their faces painted with designs or abstract drippings. One photo caption described a feathered woman as "she who steals from the hen." A young man with hair and face entirely black, including his lips, was painted with or stained with coal oil—*tiznado* it was called—so that against his white teeth the effect was quite dramatic. Another figure, with a wide-brimmed black hat and his face blackened, except for his lips being painted white and white rings around his eyes, looked like a black-faced minstrel. So many of the faces were like abstract drip paintings by Pollock, but alive with maskers' bright eyes and white-toothed smiles.

Not only was the exhibit impressive but so was a brief talk offered by the country's ambassador, a light-skinned, handsome black man with a colorful but tasteful necktie. He spoke without notes, his Spanish clear and his vocabulary elevated, and as Pepe noted, he never used a single cliché. The ambassador explained the origins of the Dominican Republic Carnaval, distinguishing it from the Brazilian, which follows from the forty days (*cuaresma*) of Lent when the flesh or body (*carne*) returns to its life after spiritual abstinence. In the DR, the celebration is more a politically-oriented event, marking the Republic's independence day of February 27. The DR Carnaval includes music, parades, and the largely African tradition of masks and painted bodies. One photographed figure had covered his entire body with a type of "clothing" made of painted, recycled plastic bottles, which the caption called a recycled costume. Devil masks always seemed to include prominent animal-like teeth and rather sinister-looking eyes. One young boy was painted entirely, except for his teeth, with his front two broken off to form an empty vee, just as mine had been and are, though capped since about age 17. I could certainly identify with his loss.

Drinks and finger food were served and music was provided through a CD player, which inspired one fellow to dance with several of the ladies, giving the exhibit a festive feel to go along with the Carnaval photos on exhibit. Pepe had some champagne, and a lady, to whom I had been introduced by an embassy employee who had invited Pepe to the exhibit, handed me a glass of wine, but I drank none of it and just placed it later on a serving tray as a waiter passed by. Pepe said that he liked to drink wine but not hard liquor. He smoked, as usual, and after I had shaken hands with the ambassador and thanked him for his fine history of DR's Carnaval, we took our leave. Pepe is not the best driver, and he even made a turn where it was illegal, but he always manages to arrive safely at his destination and so far as I know has never had an accident. I had not known what to expect at the exhibition but was pleasantly surprised to find both the photos and the ambassador delightful and informative.

We had arrived in Chile on a Wednesday, on Thursday I had gone with Pepe to the exhibition, and on Friday I met Francisco Véjar at Tavelli, our customary point of contact in Providencia. Although Francisco's friends call him Pancho, I never have used that nickname for this poet-friend whom I first met in 1998. The story of our meeting and its subsequent impact on me and my work as a translator I should have recounted long before now, but better late than never.

Probably in 1994 or 1995, a Chilean living in Florida contacted me about translating the poetry of a dozen or so Chilean poets of his post-1973 generation. I did translate the work of this group of Chileans, but the project never came to anything. In 1996, Jim Hoggard, my longtime poet friend in Wichita Falls, asked me to send him some translations for the Hawaiian magazine, *Mānoa*, which was running a feature on Chilean poetry that Jim was guest editing. I sent poems by four of the Chileans whose work I had translated for the poet in Florida, among them a piece by Francisco Véjar. The magazine did publish my translations of a poem each by Juan Pablo del Rio, Luis Ernesto Cárcamo, and Eduardo Vassallo, but none by Francisco. Somehow, nonetheless, Francisco learned of my forthcoming translations in *Mānoa* and got in touch with me through Irene Rostagno.

When María and I flew to Chile in February 1998 for the wedding of Vicente and Jessica, the younger son and the daughter-in-law of Coneja and Checho, I took along copies of *Mānoa* to give to the Chilean poets. Even though the magazine had not included Francisco's poems, he still wanted to get together with me. We met at a bookstore near the Plaza Mulato Gil, and not only did Francisco turn out to be a very friendly fellow but he would prove invaluable in putting me in touch with other Chilean poets, and in making possible my second meeting with Nicanor Parra, at his beach home in Las Cruces. (My first meeting with Parra had taken place in 1965 at his home in the La Reina section of Santiago.) Before we left Chile for the States, Francisco had suggested that I translate Parra's poem-speech dedicated to Luis Oyarzún, a friend from the antipoet's school days in Santiago. One of Parra's *discursos*, the Oyarzún poem of 47 sections, had just appeared in *El Mercurio*. After we returned to Texas, I did translate the Oyarzun *discurso* and it was published in 1999 in issue number 10 of *The Dirty Goat*, along with my translations of poems by several younger Chilean poets, including Francisco.

Parra was quite pleased with the publication of my translation of his Oyarzún poem-speech, and as a result, he recommended me to a committee organizing an international gathering of scholars and poets who would be paying homage to him and his long, productive, and influential career. Sometime in the spring of 2001, I was contacted by the University of Chile with an invitation to attend the homage to Parra, to be held in August 2001. I was asked to give a presentation and was informed that my plane ticket would be paid for by the Cultural Division of the Ministry of Education. By the end of that year, the talk that I had given on translating Parra's antipoetry, entitled "Un tejano descubre la poesía de Parra y la trata de traducir," had appeared in *Ciclo Homenaje en torno a la figura y obra de Nicanor Parra*, a beautiful publication of all the homage proceedings. After giving my talk, a Ministry representative handed me an envelope with about the equivalent of $200 in Chilean money for my expenses while in Santiago. Part of the funds I shared with Francisco for all the help that he had been in making possible the appearance of my translation in *The Dirty Goat*, my participation in the homage, and the then forthcoming publication of my talk in the homage volume.

In 2006 when I was preparing to take a group of UT students to Chile as part of the Maymester program, Francisco would give my e-mail address to Alejandro Cerda, a young poet living in Viña del Mar near the town of Reñaca where the class and I would be spending about two weeks. Alejandro had told Francisco that he wanted me to translate the work of poets of the Fifth Region, which includes Viña del Mar and Valparaíso. He also wanted me to collaborate with him in translating a selection of poems by Texas poets. During the students' and my stay in Reñaca, Alejandro and I worked together to translate the work of 15 poets from Texas, which would appear in *El Navegante*, the journal of the Universidad del Desarrollo in Santiago. In 2007, my translations of poems by the "port poets" of the Fifth Region came out in *The Dirty Goat*. Francisco also arranged for my students, Alejandro, and me to visit Parra at Las Cruces, and from this came my article in *The Texas Observer* on the Maymester course and our conversation with the antipoet. On the very day that we visited Parra, *El Mercurio* published a piece on his work and included sections from another of his poem-speeches, the one on his fellow Chilean poet, Vicente Huidobro. I would also translate sections from the Huidobro poem-speech and publish them in issue number 17 of *The Dirty Goat*, along with the selection of poems by the port poets that I had translated, including one by Alejandro, as well as my translations of poems by a number of Santiago poets, Francisco among them.

When María and I returned to Chile in March 2007, Francisco introduced me to his student, Ernesto Pfeiffer, who often visited Parra at Las Cruces, As mentioned previously in my journal for 2009, Ernesto drove María and me to Parra's beach home, where we spent all afternoon with the antipoet. Back in Texas, I received an e-mail from Gonzalo Contreras, whose important anthology, *Poesía chilena desclasificada (1973-1990)*, I had purchased in Santiago, and again, Francisco was responsible for this contact, since he had suggested that Gonzalo involve me in his second anthology, a bilingual edition of poems by Chileans on the art of poetry. For Gonzalo's bilingual anthology I translated poems by 15 Chileans, and I also recommended to him as a translator my friend Jim Hoggard, who contributed even more translations than I did. Jim, of course, had indirectly made possible my coming to know Francisco through the *Mānoa* issue. Within about six months of the time that Gonzalo contacted me, his *Poéticas de Chile / Chilean Poets on the Art of Poetry*, an impressive hardbound edition of 500 pages, came by mail to our home in Cedar Park.

Thanks to the Chilean in Florida, whose name I can no longer recall but who requested that I translate Chilean poets for his anthology that apparently never got off the ground, and thanks to Jim Hoggard's request for translations that I was able to send to him from that project that had come to "nothing," I met Francisco, who made possible all the connections and publications that followed from our first encounter at the Plaza Mulato Gil. As for this account of the entire series of events, María "made me do it," thank goodness.

When Francisco and I got together on March 2nd, 2011, he looked the same, attentive as ever and very patient with my poor Spanish. Without his knowing it, perhaps, he had improved my use of the language by explaining any word or phrase that he employed that I had not known before. For example, on this occasion, in referring to Ernesto Pfeiffer, Francisco said that "se le fueron los humos a la cabeza"—that is, the smoke went to his head, meaning that he had taken on a superior attitude after having founded an imprint with his own last name. I was reminded of Shakespeare's *Julius Caesar*, in which Brutus says of Caesar that he has become an example of

> a common proof
> That lowliness is young Ambition's ladder,
> Whereto the climber upward turns his face;
> But when he once attains the upmost round,
> He then unto the ladder turns his back,
> Looks in the clouds, scorning the base degrees
> By which he did ascend. (Act II, sc. 1, ll. 21-27)

This was part of our conversation that concerned Francisco's explanation for having distanced himself from Parra. He said that his staying away from the antipoet was partly due to Ernesto having repeated some critical comments that Parra had made about him. I had already known that in the past Parra had admonished Francisco for writing about his own experiences and for favoring the poetry of Jorge Teillier. Parra had told Ernesto that no one could remember a single line of Teillier's poetry. After I had finished a mineral water and Francisco had drunk his without gas, we walked around the corner to the Ulises bookstore.

According to Francisco, Ulises has the best selection of books in Santiago, and it certainly has a fine stock of Chilean poetry, as well as criticism, fiction, history, etc. Primarily I wanted to buy a copy of Francisco's *Los inesperados* (The Unforeseen or Unexpected), a collection of his *crónicas* or memoirs of his personal associations with twelve Chilean authors (including Parra and Teillier), a painter, and a filmmaker. Published by the Chilean press, Tajamar Editores, in November 2009, the edition is well produced and Francisco's prose is easy to read, moves smoothly, without quotation marks, from his own voice to the voices of his subjects, and reveals the character of each through anecdotes, references to their works, and in a number of cases accounts of their final days, especially in the entries on Claudio Giaconi and Jorge Teillier. A reader would benefit from knowing in advance something of the works of the fourteen figures, but it did not seem entirely necessary in order to appreciate Francisco's personal encounters with largely well-known Chileans. Without knowing anything of Giaconi's writings, I could certainly enjoy his anecdote concerning Thelonious Monk. From living for a number of years in New York, Giaconi recalled having gone to hear Monk in 1964 at the Side Stop Club. At the time, Giaconi was with another Chilean writer, Enrique Castro Cid, who went up to Monk during a break and told the great jazzman that he did not know how to play the piano, to which Monk replied, "But it sounds good." "*Divine, divine, divine*," said Castro Cid.

Francisco's memories of the various authors are recalled in an easy-going style that yet can be both dramatic and moving. His recollection of the death of Teillier is particularly poignant. As for Parra, Francisco does not pull any punches in speaking of the great antipoet. He confesses in *Los inesperados* that, in spite of Parra's egotism, he cannot deny that after having distanced himself from the antipoet, he misses seeing him. Francisco goes on to say that he becomes nostalgic when he remembers Parra having said to him that one has the right to be sad, even though sadness has been eradicated from poetry. With regard to Teillier's poems, sadness lies at their heart, but for Parra such writing is no longer valid.

At 96, Parra had told María on the telephone that those who want to die, die; those who don't want to, don't. There is a great deal of truth to this, since several of the poets in Francisco's book had obvious death wishes, including, it would seem, both Giaconi and Teillier, who drank themselves to early graves. Poet Armando Uribe, although still alive in 2011, had been trying for years to commit suicide by smoking four packs of cigarettes a day.

That last sentence turns out to be not quite right. At the time that I wrote it I had not read the *crónica* on Uribe but had based it rather on my conversation with Francisco. Only after reading the piece, entitled "En el Purgatorio," did I discover that Uribe had given up tobacco late in life, but as Francisco had indicated in conversation, the damage had already been done and his emphysema and other conditions were irreversible. As Francisco says in the essay, Uribe "has always been bitter, with a dark humor." In 1971 I had translated a number of the poet's short, epigrammatic pieces, one of which reads in part as follows: "Like a patient Job I bite / my nails and rub the ankles / of desperation, of desperation." For me, an especially interesting part of Francisco's memoir on Uribe is about the poet's mother, María Emelina Arce, who followed her son into exile after the military coup of 1973, fought against the violation of Human Rights, and habitually visited women prisoners. When she died, a number of prisoners who had been freed through her efforts attended her funeral. Uribe's wife, Cecilia, "calmed the waters" for her husband the best she could and "her presence radiated something angelic." Although Uribe had been embittered for years, after Cecilia died in his arms, he became calmer and placed photos of her on an altar facing his preferred armchair.

It was a pleasure to read Francisco's recollections of his writer friends—his memory for details and dialogues is marvelous. His book made me feel that this trip had been worthwhile just from having discovered and read his memories, which are so well and so often touchingly described. He lamented that *El Mercurio*, the newspaper that he has written for over the years, only gave his book a tiny notice, not a regular review, and neither was it reviewed in other publications, except for one, which he did not identify, other than to say that the review was good.

On Monday the 7th, when we visited Ulises, I also bought a book by Francisco's friend Armando Roa, whom I had known on other trips and one of whose poems I had partially translated for *The Dirty Goat*. While still at home in Cedar Park, I had read in *El Mercurio* of an anthology of English and American poetry selected and translated into Spanish by Armando, and this was the book that I found and purchased at Ulises. Entitled *Covers: 36 poetas en lengua inglesa*, the book includes the poetry of Louis Zukofsky and Lorine Niedecker. On a previous trip to Chile I had given to Armando a collection of the latter's poetry, having known of his interest in both American poets. Also in the collection is work by English poet Basil Bunting, whose name forms part of Armando's e-mail address. Although I was particularly curious to see how Armando would translate Zukofsky's poetry, and which poems he had chosen, I discovered the most surprising and delightful inclusions to be poems by W.S. Merwin and Gary Snyder, neither of which I had known before.

Merwin's work I have admired as a translator and at times, but not always, as a poet. However, his poem entitled "Berryman," included in Armando's anthology, really hit me. It is a wonderful tribute to the American poet John Berryman, whose *Dream Songs* I so much prize for their sound and sense within his own peculiar form of three six-line stanzas and their subtle rhyme scheme. Merwin's poem is also a well-told tale of Berryman's attitude toward poetry and anyone who would write in the genre. With regard to Merwin's question of the older poet as to "how can you ever be sure / that what you write is really / any good at all," Berryman replies:

. . . you can't

you can't you can never be sure
you die without knowing
whether anything you wrote was any good
if you have to be sure don't write.

The Gary Snyder poem, "Why I Take Good Care of my Macintosh," was unlike anything of his that I had read before, although my awareness of his work had been fairly limited to *Rip-Rap* (1959) and *Myths & Texts* (1960), and a later poem like "Old Pond" from *Axe Handles* (1983), analyzed astutely by Camille Paglia in *Break, Blow, Burn* (2005), her reading of *Forty-Three of the World's Best Poems*. In Snyder's poem about his computer, he writes on a subject far removed from his nature poetry, or so it seemed, until I came upon lines that offer reasons for his "good care" of his Macintosh:

> Because its keys click like hail on a boulder
> And it winks when it goes out,
>
> And it puts word heaps in hoards before me,
> dozens of pockets of
> gold under boulders in streambeds, identical seed pods
> strong on a vine. . . .

The boulders reminded me of rocks in Zen gardens, which certainly fit into Snyder's scheme of things, since he has long been influenced by Oriental philosophy. The entire poem is both clever and philosophical in its treatment of what I would have thought a very unpoetic subject matter, and yet it demonstrates artfully the range and depth of this poet's meditative mind.

As for Zukofsky, his poem, or rather his translation or transliteration based on the famous Catullus poem number VIII, seemed to me an excellent choice for its wonderful Americanization of the Latin, with words like "glowed," "spunk," "take it," "bother," and "bothered." This poem I had myself quoted from in my *Harbingers* memoir, with regard to kisses: "Bite whose lips?" Armando's translations of American and British poetry are quite impressive, even though his choice of poems is not always to my personal liking. Even so, I found his selection to be intriguing, including as it does poems by Robert Graves, Malcolm Lowry, Kenneth Patchen, Philip Larkin, and W.D. Snodgrass, among many others. The poems he chose by Robert Creeley and those of several other poets disappointed somewhat, but overall the choices are excellent and very representative. I was especially pleased to have learned through Armando of the Merwin and Snyder poems. Once again, the trip was already rewarding as a result of my having bought and read into the pair of books by two of my Chilean poet-friends.

Our visit this time would be taken up with more trips outside of Santiago than usual. This meant that it was harder for me to find free periods for writing down my impressions or accounts of our experiences from place to place. With John and Consuelo Anderson, Austin friends who had traveled to Argentina and then flown to Chile, we would visit Viña del Mar and Valparaíso for two days, with John driving a rental car that made the trip quite convenient and carefree. María had found through the Internet a bed and breakfast in Viña called Casa Olga, a house built in 1934 with a view to ships anchored in the bay. In the morning of our second day we could see what were probably destroyer escorts, or some other type of naval vessel, cruising just off the beaches and harbor areas, probably with Chilean sailors in training, since the Naval Academy is nearby. Carolina and José María, the owners of the B & B, were, to María's great relief, wonderfully hospitable. Carolina, a Chilean, and José, an Argentinean, welcomed us warmly, as did their two black dogs—one a huge schnauzer named Ché. The couple and their dogs were totally delightful and entertaining. José, in between making witty observations, prepared a delicious, healthy breakfast, and Carolina showed us the Renaissance-inspired masks she makes, decorates, and sells for operas and parties. The B & B was located at the corner of 18 de septiembre (Chile's Independence Day) and Pasaje Olga, and we enjoyed walking up and down in the neighborhood on its hilly sidewalks and streets. María had made a very fortunate find, for our stay was a complete success with the Andersons and ourselves.

Our tour of Valparaíso was most pleasant as well, with John keeping up a running commentary on the city's architecture—he is quite the observant and knowledgeable guide. In the downtown we had *onces* at Café del Poeta, with its photos of poets like Neruda, Huidobro, and Mistral on the walls, and with collections of their own and other poets' books for sale. After touring the downtown, we took the famous funicular or cable railway to the neighborhoods above and walked around for some time, viewing old houses and the many ships visible in the bay. We also visited various shops offering wool, souvenirs, books, and artwork. On descending to the main level of the city, we dined at the O'Higgins restaurant where I had first eaten with my UT students in 2006 and then with María and her sister in 2009. We all loved the restaurant's uniformed waiters, who were so attentive, and the food that was so delicious. John had ceviche and rare steak, Consuelo fish of some kind, a plate of corvina with rice for myself, and María with her vegan-limited diet had grilled veggies and rice. Afterwards we walked toward Independence Street, where María wanted to visit some antique shops. Along the way, in a tiny "junk" shop filled to its high ceiling with the kinds of old hardware María loves, she spied some Yale-type locks and other metal objects that are always so attractive to her eyes. She ended up paying the equivalent of $50 dollars for a lock with no key, because it brought back fond memories of her maternal grandfather who farmed and cared for his tools and implements.

While waiting for María, I read a newspaper article pasted outside the shop on a wooden board, the paper torn in places, and all of it faded by time and light. The subject of the piece was the first Irarrazaval in Chile, a family name well-known in the country's history and apparently related to the Aguirre side of María's genealogy—both family names are Basque in origin, as indicated by the double "r". The first Irarrazaval had come to Chile in the 1500s in the company of Alonso de Ercilla, the Spanish poet of the Chilean epic, *La Araucana*. María's own forebears on her Aguirre side had first come to Chile in 1540, and two are mentioned in Ercilla's poem. The owner of the shop was himself an Irarrazaval, and either he or a relative had produced two paintings stuck behind a bookcase outside on the sidewalk.

Above the paintings and the bookcase, there was a sign that reminded me of Nicanor Parra's *artefactos*, or "found poems." The sign concerned the amount of time the owner would allow to visitors, friends, or customers. Printed in black on a kind of white poster board, the times were given for each of a number of categories. Here is my translation of the information:

>   friends – 2 minutes
> friends when busy—1 minute
> friends with "luminous ideas"—0 minutes
> friends who invite the owner to lunch—1 hour 45 minutes
> those who come to buy something—24 hours
> those who come to pay—72 hours

The owner's list of times later brought to mind Parra's poem, "Se me ocurren ideas luminosas" (Bright ideas come to me), which seems to suggest that, as in English, "bright ideas" can be both good and bad. In Chile, or in Spanish generally, "ideas luminosas" is a popular phrase, which demonstrates Parra's constant use in his antipoems of colloquial language. On returning to Texas I would incorporate María's lock and the owner's "timetable" into my poem entitled "María's Antiques."

At the time of writing down the list of times, I recalled two other pieces of graffiti that I had noticed during the trip. One graffito I had seen in the Recoleta area of Santiago at the Franciscan church known for a Friar called Andresito. Born in 1800 in the Canary Islands of Spain, Andresito died in 1853 in the Recoleta section of the city where he had become famous for his saintly care for the poor and ill. The church includes a small museum devoted to the Friar, with implements that he had used, such as *escapularios* (religious scapulars, part of a monk or friar's habit), which he himself had made, and a daguerreotype of him taken in 1849. On leaving the museum I observed on a wall the handwritten graffito "No al aborto; sí a la pedofilia" (No to abortion; yes to pedophilia). This comment on the Catholic church's opposition to abortion but not to pedophilia was in stark contrast to the work of Andresito, who was credited by his followers with having cured their infirmities. One man, in fact, with whom María had spoken at the museum, had lived in the church's monastery and had been cured by Andresito fifty years before (through prayers to the Friar, I assumed, since he had died more than one hundred years before). The man had come that very day to offer a prayer of thanks in remembrance of the aid that the Friar had rendered to him.

The other piece of graffiti that I had spotted was in Curicó, a city to the south of Santiago. This was when María and I would later take the train to visit her longtime friend Gaby Concha and her doctor husband Pepe Muñoz, who live about 40 minutes outside of Curicó. While we waited for Gaby to drive into the city to pick us up at the temporary train station—the old one having been destroyed by the earthquake in 2010—I walked around the downtown area, since we had about an hour "to kill." I had not realized that I had bought tickets for the 7:30 a.m. train instead of the 8:30, and so Gaby was not expecting us to arrive an hour earlier. On one wall downtown I read the following graffito: "Me cago en tu país kuliao" (I crap on your asshole country). What was curious to me was that "your" was in the intimate form of the word, not the formal. Again, this reminded me, like the sign for time allowances in Valparaíso, of Parra's *artefactos*, or rather more specifically of the line that precedes his *Discurso* on Vicente Huidobro, entitled "Also Sprach Altazor." The line in Spanish reads: "Hay que cagar a Huidobro" (We have to crap on Huidobro). Another notable feature of the graffito in Curicó was that Chileans tend to drop letters in pronouncing certain words, and this was the case even in the written form of "kuliao," which would not only be spelled with a "c" instead of a "k" but would have a "d" between the "a" and "o"—*culiado*. I had first learned that word when María and I had just started dating and we had gone for a walk near her home, when a couple of male Chileans yelled at me "gringo curado" (drunk gringo), or that's what I thought they had said. On hearing María mention the name-calling, her sister explained to me that I had misunderstood, that they were saying "gringo culiado" (asshole gringo).

After having spent the night at Casa Olga in Viña on the 14th, we rode the next day with the Andersons to Isla Negra to see the Neruda home. Both María and I had been there on several previous occasions, so we did not experience anything especially new. However, the lady who conducted the tour was quite good, and we learned in talking with her that she was a native of the town. She told us that the Neruda Foundation, which ran the home-museum, hired local people to work at the area's biggest tourist attraction, thereby accounting for about thirty jobs for the Isla Negra economy. Since there was little else that people in the area could do, Neruda's home-museum rendered a vital service, that is, the wealthy Communist poet continued beyond the grave to support the poorer section of the community.

The tour of the house, with its various rooms and collections of sea shells, instruments, ship prows, etc., was still fascinating, and especially the view from the second-story bedroom with the Pacific's blue-green and white-crested waves dashing against the huge boulders on the beach below. At the end of the tour, when I walked toward the shore, I saw two peso bills lying on the sandy path and picked them up. No one was around, only John Anderson, who was following me. A group of visitors to the home-museum had gathered by the Chilean flag flying near the beach, but I did not know how I could ask who lost 15 thousand pesos (in bills of 10 and 5 thousand) and know for certain that they belonged to that person. Worth around $25.00 in U.S. currency, the bills had obviously dropped from someone's pocket or purse, but I simply kept them and walked on. John had noticed but said nothing. Later at Checho and Coneja's I reported the find, and Cony said of the person who lost them, *mala pata*, or bad foot, meaning tough luck for him or her. I felt a little guilty, but again, could not see how I could ever have returned the money to its rightful owner, and the bills helped pay for the gas on our drive back to Santiago. Even so, I felt it had not been right to keep the money.

My friend Pepe had loaned me a book by Clark Coolidge, entitled *Now It's Jazz: Writings on Kerouac & the Sounds*, and a copy of Mario Vargas Llosa's 2010 Nobel Prize acceptance speech. Before returning the two items, I wrote down my thoughts on both. Pepe had met Coolidge on his last jazz cruise, after he had noticed the book on the lap of a fellow jazz lover and asked him where he could get a copy. Coolidge said that he would give Pepe his copy, and he then signed and wrote a dedication. Until Pepe saw the signature and inscription, he had had no idea that he was speaking with the author himself. On reading the book, Pepe had enjoyed Coolidge's spontaneous bop prose in celebration of Kerouac's jazz-inspired, uninhibited, on-the-road riffs, which I also found quite enjoyable. I was especially delighted by Coolidge's memories of his first having discovered jazz. He had come to the music through recordings of the Spike Jones band and its various racket-making paraphernalia, from pistols, bicycle horns, "a baseball bat to knock over the teetering pile of pots and pans precisely on cue," washboard, klaxon, fire alarm, "gargled water," cowbells, etc. All of those I too had heard on Spike's recordings, long before I discovered jazz. I have always remembered hearing as a boy, at my Uncle Keetch's home in Oklahoma City, the Spike Jones versions of "That Old Black Magic," "Cocktails for Two," and Rossini's *William Tell Overture* (with the calling of a horse race won surprisingly by last-place Beetle Bom, while throughout the race it's Cabbage by a head and Assault passing Battery). When I was a teenager, I heard the Jones band live in Beaumont, but by then I was not that taken with parody, after having discovered real jazz through my orchestra teacher, Harold Meehan.

Coolidge's descriptions of bop drumming really knocked me out, in particular that of Kenny Clarke: "Consider [his] 'magic cymbal' which he 'kept level' and 'when somebody would sit in on drums and use his set, it would sound like the [lid] of a garbage can, but when he played on it, it was like fine crystal'." Coolidge did not identify, it seems, whom he was quoting, but it was his source that impressed me most. Still, Coolidge's own writing was at times even better than the Kerouac sentences he quotes and does identify. Here is a sample of Coolidge's own bebop prose: "Jazz, rare time. In a home attic turret, mind full of zinc tints and scents, whisking wire brushes across a phonebook cover, raking it to a graphite smear, sump of strataed exclamation, grinding down in all the grace of felt beats and tampers, willing music blaze[d] and shock[ed] me to actually shoot to my feet and stand amazed before the green vinyl Webcor Holiday suitcase phonograph...."

In reading Vargas Llosa's Nobel speech, I felt so very fortunate to be able to do so in his Spanish, with its special rhythms. The novelist recalls in his talk that he first learned to read at age five; he then lists the effects of that achievement: his love of his native Perú but also other places where he lived, including Barcelona, Washington, D.C., New York, and Paris; his admiration for writers from Hugo to Faulkner; his hatred of all dictatorships, whether political or religious; and his belief that fiction tells the truth, transforms its readers, expands their horizons, and stirs up their hopes and their ambitions to convert the impossible into the possible. As ever, I was grateful to Pepe for sharing with me not only the Dominican Republic exhibition and his vast jazz collection—this time a recording by Charlie Parker of "Body & Soul," when the saxophonist was just 22, which seemed to me beyond anything else of his that I had ever heard—but also his awareness of literature that he thought that I should know. How lucky to have had such a friend, one so generous and with a mind filled with both music and languages; his command of English ever amazes me, as does his knowledge of most any subject.

On this trip, Pepe mostly wanted to play for me a recording with Bud Freeman, the Chicago tenor saxophonist who had married a wealthy woman and come to Chile (sometime in the 1950s, I believe it was), to become a country gentleman. During Freeman's stay, Pepe spent almost every day with the tenorist and set him up with jazz gigs, until eventually Bud and his wife split up and he returned to the States, never having fulfilled his desire to become a gentleman farmer, mostly because the only thing he could really do was blow a kind of sophisticated Dixieland. I had never cared much for Bud's playing, and the album Pepe played for me, with Bud and His Famous Chicagoans, from July 24, 1940, did nothing to change my rather low opinion of his stiff swing style. But one of the "famous Chicagoans" was Texan Jack Teagarden, and on "Jack Hit the Road," Big T recorded one of his finest solos, in two parts, which I had never heard before. I wrote an e-mail to my jazz friend Morton Stine, and sure enough, Mort knew this piece, owned the recording, and agreed with me about Bud's unconvincing approach to the tenor sax. Pepe told an anecdote that only confirmed my general feeling that Freeman was not the real thing. After performing with a Chilean rhythm section one night, Bud came down from the bandstand and asked Pepe how he looked, which was more important to him than how he played. Pepe conceded that Bud was basically a dandy, ever concerned that he dressed the part of a cool British gentleman, complete with the appropriate accent that he affected.

While still in Chile, I ordered through Amazon the Charlie

Parker "complete 'birth of the bebop'" on Stash that Pepe had played for me—a used copy for $30.00. On arriving home the CD was awaiting me, and I put it on the player and found it well worth the price, especially all the tunes Bird performs with just Little Phil Phillips on drums and the rhythm guitar of Efferge Ware: "Cherokee" (with a typical quote from "Popeye the Sailorman"), "My Heart Tells Me (Should I Believe My Heart?)," "I Found a New Baby," and "Body and Soul." Here Bird's sound is never strident or harsh but smooth and lovely, especially on "My Heart Tells Me." The recordings of Bird on tenor cannot come close to the beauty of his alto tone and fluidity, even if they may offer some interesting pre-bop moments. Also while in Chile, I ordered several Charles Ives recordings, prompted by my reading of the final chapters of Jan Swafford's 1996 biography of the composer, *Charles Ives: A Life With Music*. I had contacted the author on several occasions to report my progress in reading his book. From Pepe, when I mentioned Ives and pointed out the composer's name in his copy of Julio Cortázar's "El perseguidor" (the short story based in part on Parker's life), I learned that the Instituto Chileno-norteamericano had established a prize for musicians, composers, or writers on music, named in honor of Ives. Pepe did not know much of Ives's music but once again he did know something that I did not know: Ives was recognized even in Santiago as a figure important enough to be honored by a prize named for him. Of course, the prize was probably the idea of the U.S. personnel who work at the Institute, since it is an arm of the U.S. State Department.

 The icing on the cake of this trip would come when Pepe invited me to the official opening of an exhibit of library materials on Pablo Neruda's 1950 *Canto general*, held at the National Library. At the exhibition reception I met up with Jaime Quezada, poet-friend and authority on Gabriela Mistral, and Manuel Jofré (with the same last name as María but unrelated), a scholar and promoter of the Nobel Prize candidacy of Nicanor Parra. Manuel I had met in 2004 when I participated in that year's homage to Parra. At the time, to use a phrase that I heard from sociologist and TV talk-show personality Fernando Villegas, Manuel had "ninguneádo[me] maravillosamente"—that is, he had patronized me wonderfully as a nobody, which of course I was and still am. But now Manuel seemed genuinely delighted to run into me at the exhibition. He called our meeting up a lucky happenstance, for he had a book that he wanted to give me and, as I would later learn, one that he wanted to sell me for $40.00. Just the day before when María, Francisco Véjar, and I had visited Parra in Las Cruces, I had seen the same oversized book that looked like a handmade portfolio tied by twine looped into a knot to hold the cover and pages together. It turned out that the book was a limited edition of a printed compilation of materials on Parra, introduced by a letter from Manuel and addressed to the Swedish Academy, for purposes of nominating the antipoet as a candidate for the Nobel Prize. This was not the first time that Manuel had nominated Parra—along with many other Chileans and even Harold Bloom of Yale University—but this latest nomination had been entered in 2010, when, as noted above, Mario Vargas Llosa had come out the winner.

On noticing at Parra's home the nomination volume, entitled on the cover *Nicanor Parra: Poeta del Bicentenario* (since the nomination coincided with Chile's two-hundredth celebration of its independence from Spain in 1810), I had not looked at the various materials contained in it. Only after Manuel drove to Coneja and Checho's home, to give me a copy of his book *Parrafadas* and to allow me to buy a copy of the limited edition compilation, did I realize that it included the introduction that I had written to my translation of the Luis Oyarzún section of Parra's *Discursos de sobremesa*, published in *The Dirty Goat*. Naturally, I was quite pleased that, thanks to Pepe, I had run into Manuel, since we were leaving for Texas the next day and I would not have acquired the publication. As a result of my conversations with Jaime and Manuel, I never got around to viewing the Neruda exhibit, but I remain happy with the trade-off.

Also at the reception, Pepe introduced me to Juan Agustin Figueroa, the director or CEO of the Neruda Foundation. When the director learned that I had taught at the University of Texas and worked at the Ransom Center, he wanted to talk to me about a problem that the Foundation was having. The director said that they wanted permission to see letters from Neruda to his second wife, Argentinian Delia de Carril; the Ransom Center held the letters but the Foundation had been unable to receive a response to their request for copies. I told the director that I would see what I could do. After returning to Texas, I contacted the Ransom Center and found that the regulations governing the duplication of letters had changed and that the Center could in fact now provide the Neruda Foundation with copies. It would simply be a matter of the Foundation writing again with a request for copies of the letters, and once I had communicated this information to the director and he wrote a letter to the Center, the Foundation did receive the copies and in turn I received from the director a warm thank-you note.

When I first arrived at the exhibition, I visited the National Library's bookstore and asked about another book that I had seen at Parra's beach home, a volume entitled *No leer* (Not to Read), by a young writer named Alejandro Zambra. The author had informed Parra that he was going to give a class on the antipoet's writings, and just before Zambra began to lecture, there was a knock on the door of his classroom and to the young writer's total surprise, there was the antipoet himself, who at 96 rarely appeared in public. The bookstore clerk could not locate a copy of *No leer,* but in the meantime I had spotted another book that I had not seen before, a gathering of pieces written by Adriana Valdés on Enrique Lihn and entitled, following his name, *vistas parciales* (partial views). In the translated words of Valdés: "'Partial,' because they are written from friendship and proximity, 'partial' because they do not pretend to tell everything about Enrique Lihn. These 'views' seek to be simultaneously an invitation to read his work and a contribution to future biographies."

A friend of Lihn, Valdés had reviewed for *El Mercurio* my collection of Lihn's poetry, *Figures of Speech*. Since she knew the bilingual edition of my book, she had included it in her own volume's list of Lihn's writings in translation. Consequently, instead of *No leer*, I bought the Valdés book, but then, while I was with Pepe at the exhibition opening, the clerk came up to me and showed me a copy of *No leer* that she had located, and so I purchased it as well. In reading Zambra's memoirs and essays on literature I found them wonderfully well written, enthusiastic, and insightful. They reminded me of Argentine author Alberto Manguel's *A History of Reading*, *The Library at Night*, and *Homer's The Iliad and The Odyssey*, three books that I had read with an all-absorbing pleasure. Zambra, as I later discovered, on mentioning his name and his book to professor-poet María Inés Zaldívar, was a student of hers and was doing his doctoral dissertation on Parra under her guidance at the Universidad Católica. The connections between one discovery and another were uncanny and had happened time after time on this particular trip.

The exhibition opening made possible yet another highly satisfying development during our visit to Santiago and my last visit with Pepe. Even before we had left Texas I had written to him to say that I had read about his early life in a book by Fernando Villegas, the writer and TV talk-show personality mentioned earlier. The year before, when Jessica Maralla, Coneja and Checho's daughter-in-law, had gone to Texas with her husband Vicente and their two children, María Beatriz and Catarina, Jessica had brought with her a library copy of Villegas's *Memorias dispersas, juicios erráticos* (2004). During their two-week stay at our home, Jessica loaned me the Villegas book and I found it fascinating, and especially when I discovered that the author was a friend of Pepe's and that he had written on Pepe's life as a jazz aficionado. After I had written to Pepe about his being in the Villegas book, he wrote back and wanted to know the title, but I could not remember what it was. Once we arrived in Santiago, I checked with Jessica, but she too had forgotten the title of the book. Later, after searching on the Internet, she phoned to say that the title was *Memorias de un amnésico*, which was the title that I reported to Pepe. Only a day or so before her phone call I had seen in Ulises a book with that same title that had just been published, but I thought it had to be a different book from the one that I had read because the author was not Villegas. Soon Pepe, somewhat irritated, let me know that this new book had nothing in it about him, and that when he spoke to Villegas at their regular Friday gatherings (of a group calling themselves the Toby Club, after Tubby, the cartoon character in Marjorie Henderson Buell's *Little Lulu*), Fernando had declared in no uncertain terms that he never wrote about his friends. Jessica and I both knew that we were not crazy, that we had read about Pepe in Villegas's book, so Jessica went to her local library and found the book, which turned out to be *Memorias dispersas, juicios erráticos* and not *Memorias de un amnésico*. She then made photocopies of the pages where Pepe appeared, and with great satisfaction, I handed the photocopies to Pepe at the Neruda exhibition and told him that we had the goods on Villegas, for he had written about a friend.

When Villegas was shown the Xeroxes of the pages on Pepe in his 2004 book, he said that he did not remember that work, for, as Pepe had told me, Villegas was totally uninterested in his earlier memoirs. The only thing that interested him at the time was to report to the Toby Club that he had been invited to the banquet honoring President Obama and First Lady Michelle Obama, who were in Santiago on the second leg of their South American tour. Villegas had been photographed holding hands with Michelle. With his extraordinarily puffed-out head of hair, Villegas holds forth each Sunday night on the capital city's popular televised round-table discussion of current events. The one show with him that I caught during this trip featured an interview with Alfredo Moreno, President Piñera's even-tempered, articulate foreign affairs minister, who spoke about the Libyan conflict. Villegas opposed any intervention in the Arab country, while other dictatorships were not being criticized or interfered with. At the Toby Club, as on TV, Villegas was obviously more into his public image (like Bud Freeman) than his seven-year-old book of memoirs that merely recounted the life story of a figure and friend like Pepe, whom he could see every week but not, through him, make the news that it seemed he craved. Pepe and his family had escaped from Poland during the Nazi regime, fled to Italy, and finally to Chile, where he would become a noted authority on jazz, and he and his wife Gaby would raise a son who became a physician, another who became an architect, and a daughter who became a professor of Brazilian literature. Yes, we had the goods on Villegas.

Always on our trips to Chile I would look forward to seeing our longtime friend Irene Rostagno, who has taught for over twenty years at the Universidad Metropolitana and who each time we have traveled to Santiago has invited me to speak to her classes. During this stay, Irene wanted me to meet with her first-year and third-year classes, the latter a British literature course. As I had in 2009, I would talk on the metaphysicals, at Irene's request. I prepared by checking once again to find the exact wording of Samuel Johnson's definition of metaphysical poetry, and also printed out before leaving home several John Donne poems, including this time his "Elegy 19: To His Mistress Going to Bed," which I ended up concentrating on, leaving only a bit of the class time to comment on Ben Jonson's "To Penshurst" as an example of another type of poetry of the same period. I asked Irene if the sexual imagery in Donne's poem might be too strong for her students, but she found no problem with my choice of the elegy, saying that, after all, they were college-level readers. Afterwards, she told me that the class had declared that now they understood the meaning of metaphysical poetry, since I had illustrated Johnson's "the most heterogeneous ideas are yoked by violence together" by pointing out the wide variety of images in Donne's elegy, from war to "flowery meads," from the "hallowed temple" of the bed to Mohammedan's paradise, from the new-found land of the Americas to the precious minerals and "empery" of his mistress, from "souls unbodied" to "bodies unclothed," from mysticism to a man's "flesh upright," from books' coverings to innocent laymen, etc.

In the first-year class, only one male student would answer my question as to whether or not we can go home again, answering no, since he said we and our view of home both change. The context of my question was a discussion of the plot of Homer's *The Odyssey* and of Joyce's *Ulysses* and other works based on the Greek epic, as well as the title of Thomas Wolfe's novel, *You Can't Go Home Again*. My point was in part that literature comes from literature, but each generation reacts to, usually against, the works by the previous generation or age. I used Parra's antipoetry as an example of his reaction to Neruda's florid style. In the same class a young female student asked if one could write poetry without having read literature, to which I responded with my standard answer, based on the Chinese novel, *The Dream of the Red Chamber*: that it is difficult to do so if a writer has not read enough. I should have encouraged her more by saying that one must start somewhere, even if one is not as prepared as one should be or would like to be, and that despite one's first poems not being that good, with more reading, and more writing, one will improve and be able to express one's own ideas more fully and effectively. It has always been a pleasure to visit Irene's classes, for I learn in the process of trying to explain or analyze the literature. It is also pleasing to discuss the written word without having to worry about grading papers and assigning a letter or number for the course as a whole.

Before leaving for Chile, I had been in touch with María Inés Zaldívar, who had earned the Ph.D at Rutgers University and had done her dissertation on Chilean poet Gonzalo Millán. I had translated the poetry of Millán for my *Road Apple Review* anthology of 1972, and had also, only the year before, translated a poem by María Inés from her book, *Década: 1996-2006*. The poem, entitled "La viajera" (The Traveler), I had read in a review of her book in *El Mercurio*. A Canadian magazine, *The Associative Press*, had published my translation and had put me in touch with the poet after the editor had contacted her for permission to publish the translation. Unfortunately, when I had sent a revised version of my translation to the magazine I had typed the word "sin" instead "skin." María Inés was not so upset as I was, partly because she knew that the translation would not be seen by many readers. In spite of the typo, she proved quite enthused about meeting María and me when we traveled to Santiago. She gave me her phone and address, and asked me to contact her as soon as we arrived, which I did. We settled on a date for us to come to her apartment, but María was not that interested because she knew that we would be talking poetry while she twiddled her thumbs. As it turned out, Mané, as María Inés signed her e-mails, had to change the date when one of her sons unexpectedly altered his travel plans and was to fly in from Brazil at the time of our gathering. This let María off the hook because any other date was filled in her jam-packed agenda of visits with friends and family. So I went alone to Mané's apartment building located on El Vaticano, near Pepe's home on Unamuno, both just blocks from Colon, but on opposite sides of that main thoroughfare.

Mané received me with great enthusiasm and we chatted for almost three hours, at the end of which time she invited me to come to the Católica and speak to translation and literature classes. Since

María's and my travel plans within Chile made scheduling difficult, I would have to visit the Católica on the same two days in a row that I visited Irene's classes at the Metropolitana. Preparing for four classes in two days was a challenge, after not having taught regularly for five years, but I even enjoyed awaking at 3 a.m. with a Shakespeare line in my head and getting up to double check it on Checho's computer. Only later did I remember that I had quoted the line in my *Harbingers* memoir and could have looked it up in one of the copies that I had brought to give to Pepe and Irene. The phrase I had in mind was Hamlet's "water-fly" in Act V, scene 2, line 82, although in the memoir I had not supplied the specific source of the quote. My reason for thinking about the phrase—or my subconscious continuing to do so while I was asleep—was that I planned to talk to the literature class at the Católica about Parra's knowledge of Shakespeare and his use of the Bard's writings in his own poetry, and also about Shakespeare in the poetry of Enrique Lihn.

For the class on translation at the Católica I planned to relate science and literature through Parra as a physicist, as well as William Carlos Williams as a medical doctor who, in his 1944 *The Wedge,* had defined the poem as "a small (or large) machine made of words. When I say there's nothing sentimental about a poem I mean that there can be no part, as in any other machine, that is redundant." I was also going to mention Lihn's "Larga distancia" (Long Distance), his poem on the telephone as a marriage of science and magic, as well as Vicente Huidobro's imagery of airplanes and parachutes, and his "squaring the circle" in *Horizon Carré.* With regard to the latter, I would speak of Parra's satire of his fellow Chilean in *Discursos de sobremesa,* where he says that Huidobro solved the problem of "perpetual motion" by never settling down anywhere (as he had constantly moved from one city or country to another). All of this science and technology was intended to appeal to Pablo Saavedra Silva's translation class, which the instructor had informed me by e-mail was comprised largely of engineering majors. In the end, I had little time to talk on all the ideas that I had planned on discussing and the class was too large to speak individually with many of the students. I came away disappointed with my performance.

The day following my presentation to the translation class, I had more success with the literature class, comprised of three different classes taught by professors Allison Ramay and Carmen Luz Fuentes-Vásquez, all assembled in the Católica auditorium. On this occasion I dealt mostly with the Hamlet passage with the word "water-fly," which Parra was so amazed by when he himself quoted the line on my visiting him at La Reina in 2001. I also worked in other lines in Shakespeare that had to do with flies, quoting in particular from *King Lear*: "As flies to wanton boys are we to the gods. They kill us for their sport." I mentioned another passage in *Hamlet*, a speech by Polonius, which also delighted Parra: "that with devotion's visage / And pious action we do sugar o'er / The devil himself" (Act III, scene 1, ll. 47-49). Finally, I quoted from Parra's "Also Sprach Altazor," his *discurso* on Huidobro, with regard to the latter's relationship to Pablo Neruda: "a little more than kin, and less than kind," taken from *Hamlet*, Act I, scene 2, line 65.

In talking about Shakespeare in Lihn, I quoted from his poem on a Hamlet-like cat, in his "Para Rigas Kappatos" (For Rigas Kappatos), where he calls his feline subject "a species of sage / who contrary to Socrates responds to the anti-categorical imperative: / Don't know thyself." While speaking of this poem, I was suddenly wishing that I had with me my Greek edition of poems by Kappatos that includes Lihn's drawing of the cat, Athinulis, to show the class the poet's skills as an artist. And then it came to me that I *could* show the drawing, since the previous day, after I had met with Mané, poet-critic Pedro Lastra, and several other professors to discuss various literary topics, Mané had taken me to her office and given me several publications, including a special Lihn issue of the Católica journal, *Taller de Letras*. That night I discovered in the Lihn number that the journal had published the poet's "1985 Farewell 2," claiming that it was appearing in print for the first time in the 2008 issue, whereas I had included it in my Lihn collection, *Figures of Speech*, in 1999. The title of the poem in *Taller de Letras* was "Para Sharon" (For Sharon), added by hand to an illustrated typewritten version of the poem with Lihn's handwritten corrections, all of which were consistent with my own printed version. I had remembered that the 2008 Lihn number also included a reproduction of his drawing of Athinulis, and I had the issue in my briefcase and so could hold it up for the students to see. This and everything else in my presentation seemed to please the congregated classes, and afterwards a student came up and told me in English "You made my day. I really enjoyed your lecture." As I told him, his saying so made mine.

The next morning, María and I went by taxi to the Metro station at Los Dominicos, carried our luggage down to the underground line, rode to the stop at Estación Central, and there bought tickets for our train trip to Curicó. We always enjoy going by coach, with its leisurely pace and its large windows that allow one to take in the scenery without worrying about keeping one's eyes on the road and watching out for other drivers. The views on both sides of the car were picturesque, with eucalyptus trees, vineyards, vegetables of various sorts in rows, houses, animals, people along the way, and on both sides, east and west, the parallel cordilleras. (I am now reminded of Parra's poem, "Viva la Cordillera de los Andes," in which the speaker opposes unreasonably, even absurdly, as we do so often in life, two different things; in this case, he shouts, "Long live the cordillera of the Andes!! / Death to the coastal cordillera!!") Arriving, as mentioned earlier, an hour before María's friend Gaby expected us, we waited at the temporary station, where one lady manned the ticket booth and another swept the floor with sprinkled sawdust. After a while, I walked up and down the street a bit, María continuing to sit in one of the dozen or so seats. Once Gaby picked us up, she drove us to an apartment her husband Pepe rented in Curicó for whenever he needed to stay the night for some late or early case of pediatric surgery. There, lying on a table, I noticed a book that, on reading into it, I found quite disturbing. We had only come to the apartment to use the restroom, since we had not been allowed to use the one in the temporary train station reserved for station personnel. Had we not stopped at the apartment I would not have known of the fate of a young priest who had been taken into custody by members of the military (or Navy) during the Pinochet regime.

My views on the military dictatorship had never been those of most poets who lived through the experience of censorship and even of the disappearances of fellow writers. Knowing that some writers had fomented attacks on the carabineros or on citizens opposed to Allende's government, I could not justify in my own mind such violent activities. The case of the priest, however, troubled me because the young man had tried to assist his poor community but was "disappeared" by the military. I cannot recall the name of this young priest, whose family I believe was English in background. What I do recall is that he was tortured by sailors under orders from three Navy admirals and died under mysterious circumstances, was said to have been buried in a mass grave, but had lately been discovered in a grave with no other bodies. According to the book, the case was still being investigated. Photos of the young priest were included in the account of his life and death.

Later, at Gaby and Pepe's home, on their property near the community of Palquibudi, I saw another book related to the Pinochet period. This was a history of modern dance in Chile—Gaby having studied modern dance in New York on a scholarship—but also of the period of repression when artists and writers for the most part protested against the military dictatorship. One dancer was a central figure in Chile's history of dance, and during the period of the junta, he had returned from exile, even under threat of death. He helped to create and produce dances that represented the violence inflicted on people associated with the opposition to military rule. Three professors involved in protest had been murdered, and the dancers had staged a type of memorial. All of this affected me in a way that much of the news of censorship and repression had not been able to, causing me to feel that I had never understood the depth of the suffering of those who opposed the junta. I had been unable to avoid the view that Chile was better off from having escaped Allende's form of proletarian autocracy that punished anyone who disagreed and that destroyed property, technology, and educational facilities for no other reason than revenge against those with a differing viewpoint. But now I felt that the price some sectors of society had paid, for a more open and apparently more productive and seemingly more equitable system, was not entirely justified by the resulting improvement of the condition of the majority. It was hard for me to face these issues, but the two books of Pepe and Gaby's had made me do so for the first time.

At the time that I was transcribing the paragraphs above, I happened to be rereading in Chapter X of Coleridge's *Biographia Literaria* and came across the following passage that relates in many ways to my views on the zeal of those who would support a humanitarian cause but end up doing so at the expense of the very principles for which it stands:

> I have seen gross intolerance shown in support of toleration; sectarian antipathy most obtrusively displayed in the promotion of an undistinguishing comprehension of sects; and acts of cruelty (I had almost said, of treachery) committed in furtherance of an object vitally important to the cause of humanity; and all of this by men too of naturally kind dispositions and exemplary conduct.

Traditionally, many if not most poets in Chile have been leftists, socialists, Communists or whichever side favors the welfare of the lower classes, although this may result more from a social consciousness rather than any political, ideological position. One example—and there are many examples to choose from—was the socialist poet known as Pablo de Rokha (the pen name of Carlos Díaz Loyola), who was born not far from Palquibudi in the town of Licantén, which we visited the following day when Gaby took us on a driving tour of the area. De Rokha and his wife Winétt were both socially *comprometidos*, that is, engaged in and committed to supporting an improved lot for the lower classes, even when Winétt at least had come from a well-to-do family and dressed the part inside and outside the house—wearing white gloves no less, as I later learned. De Rokha lived off his writings, but this meant that the family endured a difficult life economically, and yet they managed even so; this was admirable in itself, but nonetheless, I had never cared much for de Rokha's rather bombastic poetry. Still, I was interested in seeing his birthplace, and was quite impressed by a huge sculpture of the poet carved from some giant tree trunk by a local artist identified as Kako Calquín, who created the sculpture in 2002.

Along the river Mataquito, right on highway J60, outside of Licantén, the sculpture rises some eight feet above the pedestal on which it rests. Most impressive are the large workman-looking shoes the poet wears, with laces artfully rendered and the poet's legs seeming in motion as he appears to stride forcefully ahead. His huge hands, coat, tie, pants, his close-cut but curly hair brushed back, his large eyebrows, and his firmly set mouth, all speak of a determined figure, as he seems to have been from the little that I have read of him. His opposition to Vicente Huidobro and Pablo Neruda is partly the subject of Parra's *Discurso*, "Also Sprach Altazor." Neruda's name, like de Rokha, was a pseudonym, for Neftalí Ricardo Reyes Basoalto, whereas Parra and Huidobro only signed their work with their real names, a fact that Parra uses to satirize both Neruda and de Rokha. (Gabriela Mistral also went by a pen name instead of her birth name, Lucila Godoy Alcayaga.) In a way, both Parra and Huidobro represent antisocial poets in Chile, even though, as Parra says, Vicente dabbled in Communism but was never socially *comprometido*. My sense has always been that some of the social consciousness in poets is at least partly a pose (as María had said of Huidobro), or an expected posture, but that deep down they can be bourgeois as the next guy. The young priest and even the dancer mentioned above struck me as authentically committed to improving the lives of the less fortunate. Certainly they put their lives on the line for their beliefs.

Because connections tended to occur or come to mind during my travels only after a visit to a place or a meeting with a friend, it was hard not to jump around in writing my journals in order to take them all into account. Some ten days after our trip to Curicó, María Inés Zaldívar would invite me to come to her apartment so that she could interview me for issue 48 of the *Taller de Letras*. At that time she gave me a copy of a book for which she had written the prologue or introduction: Winétt de Rokha's *Fotografía en oscuro: Selección poética* (Madrid, 2008). It was in Mané's prologue that I read of Winétt's practice of wearing white gloves, and also of her poems written on Lenin, her anti-Franco rallies, and her poems to the leftist "Frente Popular" of 1937, as well as poems to proletarian children of the Soviet Union who, in her words, were owners of tomorrow and the happy roof with pigeons. Similarly, Neruda had written a poem in praise of Stalin. Pablo de Rokha spent much

Sculpture of Chilean poet Pablo de Rokha in the town of Licantén, by Kako Calquín.

of his energy attacking his fellow Chileans Neruda and Huidobro. When María and I later traveled to the "little north" of Chile, with its Elqui Valley, where Gabriela Mistral was born, we visited, in the town of Montegrande where she is buried, a Casa de la Cultura (House of Culture) named for the poet. There I found a book by de Rokha entitled *Neruda y yo*, in which he viciously criticizes Neruda's odes. Here is my translation of an excerpt from the book:

> These are "the odes," these very ones, and these, in their authentic virginal and demential state, without possible and viable justification: vulgar, idiotic, mangy with insolent imbecility, worn out and repeatedly palmed like counterfeit coins…with terrible badly cooked sausages and swindles.
>
> …

It is difficult to take such writing seriously or to see in the writer a person whose politics one can respect or believe to be based on humanitarianism or a concern for the views of others. This kind of criticism strikes me as characteristic of extreme positions that would deny to others a legitimacy or even a right to exist. For this and other reasons I find poets who are political activists suspect, and this includes Neruda in his guise as spokesman for the Communist agenda. His poems on workers and even to some extent those in his "Heights of Macchu Picchu" seem to me suspiciously self-serving and less genuine than his odes in celebration of life, despite their rejection by de Rokha, Lihn, and other Chilean poets.

In no way would I fault Neruda or the de Rokhas for championing the so-called lower classes or the workers. The issue is not whether their hearts were in the right places, but whether a writer can be as nasty as Pablo de Rokha is toward Neruda, while advocating for justice and respect for others. I question the sincerity of such poetry as that written by the de Rokhas, though of course life and writers are full of contradictions. Still, de Rokha's attack on Neruda seems beyond the pale and must give one pause when it comes to evaluating the integrity of his political views.

The only work of de Rokha's that ever impressed me is his

Epopeya de las comidas y bebidas de Chile (Epic of the Food and Drink of Chile) from which I heard him read on a tape recording broadcast on a car radio when I was riding with someone in Santiago. This "epic" celebration of Chilean food and drink is full of delightful gustatory descriptions, or references to typical dishes identified with different regions of the country, such as *curanto* in Chiloé, a combination of shellfish, meat, and vegetables cooked on heated stones. As for other poems by de Rokha, those written to Winétt can be touching but a tad overdone. In his "Círculo" he writes of missing his wife after her death, of the "the entire human species [being] lamented in [her] bones," and of her being like "popular pottery, / so gracious and so modest in their customary way." In "Soy el hombre casado" (I Am the Married Man), he speaks of going to the cemetery like a factory of infirmities that would make itself a salesman of roses. Often he presents himself as bigger than life, like his wooden statue, and in "Mordido de canallas" (Bitten by Scoundrels) he sees himself crucified by his enemies, though he drags along not a cross but a "torn proletariat heart / and the epic decision never to be defeated." He even ends that sonnet with the notion that he will found "a new religion" based either on his memory of human drama or perhaps his remembrance of his beloved Winétt (the interpretation depending on the date of the poem, in which he sees himself as a "calvary / dripping human blood").

In *Antología de la poesía chilena contemporánea* from 1968, the year in which de Rokha committed suicide, Roque Esteban Scarpa and Hugo Montes write that his last books show him to be a more serene, mature writer, especially in *Epopeya* (even though this work was originally published in 1949 and reprinted in 1965). De Rokha won Chile's National Literature Prize in 1965, but the anthologists conclude that his "fighting spirit" hindered him from creating definitive, "classic" works like those of Huidobro and Neruda, "his tall rivals in the world of letters."

Leaving Licantén, we headed for Vichuquén, where the sculptor Kako Calquín was born. Gaby wanted us to see Lake Vichuquén, and to reach the lake, we had to drive on dusty, unpaved roads through vast forests of eucalyptus and past clear-cut stretches on mountain sides where new growth was sprouting. The drive for me grew rather disagreeable with all the curves in the rough roads. Finally, we made it to an entrance gate, but Gaby was not sure that we could enter without permission or without paying. We heard some people in a nearby cabin playing very loud music, which turned out to be for exercise (or jazzercise). She was told to go on in, after which we drove for another fifteen minutes on dusty roads, with trenches across them that we had to cross slowly, before we reached the lake, a private area with only one public piece of property with access to the water. To me it had not been worth the effort and I dreaded having to return on the same bumpy, curving roads. María, however, thoroughly enjoyed the scenery, walking out on a pier to take pictures of the lake, of houses on the opposite shore, and of ducks floating about or sitting on docks. Owners of the rather grand houses, I later observed, had their own private landing strip for private planes, which made it possible for them to avoid the, to me, long, unpleasant drive. I thought of Ben Jonson's "To Penshurst" and its closing lines: "their lords have built, but thy lord dwells," in reference to absentee landlords versus the Penshurst owner who lived in his home full-time.

Leaving the lake, we passed the entrance gate and reached the top of the uphill road, where Gaby continued in a direction opposite to the one from which we had come. This took us around the lake, which is sort of S-shaped and quite extensive. We were now headed for the beach town of Llico. Arriving there, we walked on the shore, where I picked up a piece of driftwood and a few shells, while María and Gaby talked and watched a fellow with a fishing net as he pulled it through the incoming waves. We then started back to Palquibudi, or so it seemed. I had the feeling that we were going back toward Llico, but when, much later, I could see the town from above, and I asked Gaby if we had returned to Llico, she assured me that no, we had come to another town. Once we descended to the town, I saw a store sign that included in it Llico. Gaby could not believe that we had driven for half an hour or more and had ended up again where we began. Both she and María needed to use the restroom, so we looked for a national park indicated by a road sign, but the road went nowhere. Then we discovered that the park was across the main street of Llico but in the opposite direction. We crossed a long wooden bridge, over an inlet of stagnant water from the Pacific, and found the park, where a ranger allowed us to drive into the camping site and visit the *excusados* (toilets). All the facilities among the pine woods and the fenced off areas for campers were in excellent condition. This time Gaby asked for directions, and we started again for her home.

Along the way Gaby played a CD of a Spanish singer whose soprano notes pained my sensitive right ear, so I stuck a finger in it to endure the music. Gaby noticed and kindly turned down the volume, but certain of the singer's pitches were still painful. I should have been grateful for the trouble that Gaby had gone to in taking us to Lake Vichuquén and Llico, but I would have preferred to have spent more time walking on their property and chatting with Pepe about all the trees they had planted, including peach and almond. Earlier, when we had taken a walk around their meadows, where their three horses were grazing, we had passed through a large section of eucalyptus trees and along the edge of a grove of almonds. Among the almond trees we had spied a hen with her brood of chicks hurrying through the grass after her. We had also seen many quail scurry under the almond trees but never fly away. We tasted almonds, peaches, and some wild blackberries that were deliciously sweet. Pepe is a delightful fellow and obviously loves to be on his family's land after having lived, studied, and practiced medicine for many years in Santiago. Gaby no longer misses the city or her dancing and is quite content to be in the countryside. When Pepe asked if we had seen Llico, I replied, yes, several times. He smiled and seemed to know what I meant, for he went to Gaby, hugged her, and said something about his wife tending to lose her way. He kissed her on the cheek and called her his dear wife. Apparently, Gaby was known for taking wrong turns. I felt badly that I had even hinted at her having driven us in a circle.

When we returned by train to Santiago, we spent several days in the capital, and afterwards traveled with Coneja and Checho, in their comfortable SUV, to La Serena, Vicuña, and the Elqui Valley. Along the way we passed through many farm areas with vineyards, avocado trees, and fields of tomatoes, corn, and other vegetables, as well as olive orchards. The mountains on either side of us were sensational, and at times the Pacific coastline came into view with its gorgeous blue-green water and rolling, white-foamed waves. In La Serena we were fortunate to find a very nice and inexpensive "cabin" in a place called Las Añanucas, one of three such motel-like accommodations, this one not on the beach front but back a block from the main shoreline drive.

After settling our suitcases in the rooms, we drove to the downtown area and a shopping mall nearby. I was interested in making contact with Arturo Volantines, a poet whose name I had from Oliver Welden and also from having seen his poetry in the volume entitled *Antología de poesía chilena: periodo 80—2000*. I knew from Oliver that Volantines ran a small bookstore, but after visiting two bookstores in the mall, I could not find anyone who knew him or his whereabouts. One store clerk suggested that I ask at the mall branch of the city library, and there I found a librarian who knew the poet and gave me directions to his store, located in a shopping area called La Recova, in the old part of the downtown.

After we drove to La Recova and parked at a supermarket, I walked to the address of the bookstore, while the others shopped first in a grocery store and then in the many shops with handicrafts. Although there were innumerable small businesses, I had no trouble finding the bookshop, called Macondo. But unfortunately, on that very day, Volantines had traveled to Santiago. The shop was being tended by his wife, so I explained to her that I was a translator and would like to acquire some of her husband's books. She told me that she would phone him and see which books of his he would want her to give me. The next morning at 9 a.m. I showed up at the shop and she gave me a pile of his titles: his first collection of poems, *Pachamama* (1987); his *Lo que la tierra echa volar en pájaros* (2003), a beautifully printed and color-illustrated edition of his poetry published by Ediciones Universitarias of the Catholic University of the North; two anthologies of regional poetry that he had edited; and a book on a local military figure. I especially liked a poem in *Pachamama* on a teacher who had explained cells to his biology class. In *Lo que la tierra . . .* I liked most a poem entitled simply no. 7, where he compares his lovemaking to a crocodile in turbulent waters, to his digging into his loved one's subterranean caverns, and to a miner discovering his fortune in the dark. When we returned to Santiago, I wrote an e-mail to Volantines, but he never replied.

That same day we drove on to Vicuña, where Checho owns a *parcela*, a small piece of land facing Riquelme Street. Isabel Riquelme was the mother of Bernardo O'Higgins, the Chilean hero and president during the period of Independence. Just half a block from Riquelme, on the street named for Gabriela Mistral that ends exactly at Checho's property, there is a museum devoted to the poet's career. While the others looked at the *parcela*, I walked to the museum and found that it was closed for repairs. Nevertheless, I asked a workman if I could speak with the director, Rodrigo Iribarren, whose name I had from Mané, who had recently met him at an official gathering for the judging of a literary contest in Mistral's memory, for which Mané had been one of the judges. Knowing that we were going to visit Vicuña, she had sent with me an inscribed copy of her book *Década*, with a note explaining that the book was a gift on the occasion of my visiting the museum. The workman conducted me to the office of the director, who received me cordially, and after we chatted briefly, he offered to have a staff member give me access to the exhibit area, even though it was being renovated.

I hurried back for María and together we toured the exhibits, which were quite well done. I jotted down information from the display cases and noted that many of the quotes of statements made by Mistral were from *Beata mi lengua sea*, edited by Jaime Quezada. I had the distinct feeling that I had seen that book before, but only after we returned to Santiago did I find that in fact Irene Rostagno had given it to María and me on the first day after our arrival in the capital. Some of the quotes that I translated and wrote down were: "I have lived my years abroad carrying my own [people, loved ones] over me like a protective blanket or book cover"; "the mist plays like a child over [the mountain's] shoulders and knees"; and "there is no exile on the continent," the last statement a bit enigmatic, since there had been poets like Neruda who had been exiled politically. I also recorded the fact that Mistral's mother, as the poet had written, uttered few words, whereas those who came after her used "many words," which I took to be a criticism of garrulity, but maybe not. When Mistral was living in Naples in 1952, she wrote her *Poema de Chile* about the many parts of the country, but she noted that "my Elqui Valley is my only Chile from having been my childhood."

From Vicuña, we drove to Mistral's beloved Valley, passing a dammed, manmade lake, with no boats on it to disturb its lovely, extensive, almost unrippled waters. In the town of Montegrande, where Mistral spent part of her childhood and where she is buried, we stopped at the B & B where Checho had made arrangements for lodging. He had deposited a check in the owner's bank account, but there was no answer to our knocking on the door. We were assured by people at other rental accommodations in the town that the lady was completely honest, but still, we needed a place to stay and luckily found one among a wonderful collection of thirteen cabins, for the same price as the B & B. The next day Checho spoke with the B & B owner by phone, and she explained that she had had to leave for an emergency and had left a woman in charge, but the person had gone off before we arrived. The owner promised to refund the money to Checho's bank account, which she did.

While we were looking around Montegrande, I came upon a huge wine barrel with a Mistral quotation on it. The barrel had been turned into a type of kiosk, which was closed—that is, the door made from the barrel slats was locked. The quotation from Mistral read, in my approximate translation: "The true fatherlands are for me those [of] the entire radius that covered my childhood in the Cordillera valley of Chile. The rural life of happiness and my customary way of being are the two callings that my heart and soul are based upon." Later, when we toured the local Capel pisco plant, I saw other such huge barrels in a small cellar museum where we were given sample tastes of different flavored piscos; the one I chose was of cherimoya fruit and it was fantastically delicious. In Montegrande, María, Coneja, and Checho visited Mistral's grave, while I sat in a delightful plaza, listened to the birds, and watched the townspeople come and go. I felt that I appreciated Mistral's poetry much more after this visit to her beloved Elqui Valley and its towering mountains.

Driving back to Santiago the next day, we passed by Tololo with its sign pointing toward the observatory where international astronomers have such a clear view of the universe. I recalled that one of Nicanor Parra's grandsons is named Tololo, the one who once would not answer to that name but only to Hamlet—a tale told in my *Harbingers* memoir. We also passed a sign for La Chimba, the town where María had spent many of her summers at her maternal grandparents' home with its avocado trees, fruit trees like figs, vineyards, and fields, the latter cultivated by her grandfather. I tried to convince Checho that we should take a detour and see La Chimba, but he was not interested in going out of the way, and María in any case would not allow it. She has never wanted me to see her idyllic childhood scene because she always says that I would be disappointed and find it not worth seeing. She feels the same way about La Chimba that Gabriela Mistral felt about her own Elqui Valley. But how could María have ever thought that I would not have loved her La Chimba, since it was so much a part of her.

On Tuesday the 29th, María, Francisco, and I would take a bus to Las Cruces to visit the antipoet. María was more anxious to see Parra again than I was. I did not feel that I had any more to say to him, and it was always a bit difficult for me to keep up with his mind and speech. Francisco was perhaps even more eager than María to see Parra, for he had felt that Don Nicanor was displeased with him for not following his advice not to write about his own experiences and for his other "transgressions." As it would prove, Parra welcomed Francisco warmly and told him not to stay away for so long, which tickled Francisco pink. María found the nonagenarian as brilliant as ever, although a bit more fragile after two years that included surgery on his right ear that had resulted in hearing loss. He would pull his chair closer so that his right side was nearer María and me where the three of us sat on a couch. He had tea served to us but María did not drink any, and I took a few sips to be polite, having learned my lesson on the previous visit.

The first thing that I did was to give Parra Xerox copies of all the reviews that had appeared of my translation of his *Discursos*. He glanced at them and asked if he could have the copies, and María explained that they were for him. Immediately he said that there was a new development with regard to the title of my translation. A Mexican-American editor of a luxurious New York magazine had come through and told him that the title was wrong, that no such phrase as "after-dinner declarations" existed in Spanish, that the translation should have been "Closing Remarks," which Parra loved. Two years before, Parra had discovered in *Taming of the Shrew* the phrase "paucas pallabris" (few words), a corruption of the Spanish "pocas palabras," and he wanted me to change the title of my translation to *Few Words* (as in the case of Mistral's mother). María told him it was too late, that the book had been printed, as Parra had to know since he had some fifty copies in his house. Later, when we were leaving and I mentioned to him that thanks to Francisco I had been able to place copies of the book at the Ulises bookstore in Santiago, Parra declared that a *faja*, a paper wrapper, should be printed with *Closing Remarks* and folded around the book, to which Francisco readily agreed. I was quite disappointed that Parra seemed not to have appreciated all my efforts, but later Francisco dismissed this as typical of the antipoet and told me that I should ignore it. Earlier Francisco had confessed that he would never show Parra his *Crónicas: Los inesperados* because anything of his that he had shown him had been met with "this is all fine but here…" and he would object to the way Francisco had written a line or sentence. According to Francisco, Parra always found fault and would suggest that something should have said this or that instead of what it did say. In his *Crónicas*, Francisco praises Parra, but he also says of him, as noted before, that he had a tremendous ego or *egolatría* (self-worship). Of course, how could he not, given his achievements and the assertion in one of his poems that "poetry ends with me"! María also felt that Parra had been ungrateful, and she told him that all the copies at Ulises had been sold.

The visit added little new for me, since Parra repeated many of the same stories that I had heard before, including the one about the poem of his granddaughter Josefa in which water floats and there is more water under the water. Before we left I gave the antipoet a copy of my collection, *Backtracking*, in the first poem of which, "An Occasional Ode," he is mentioned, and a copy of my *Jazz Mavericks of the Lone Star State*, telling him that his musician daughter Colombina might find it of interest; he said that he would too.

At first Parra was going to go to lunch with us, but because his son Juan de Dios had disappeared after having greeted us on our arrival, Don Nicanor said that he did not have the key to his Volkswagen Bug and could not walk because ever since his surgery he suffered at times from vertigo. After walking with us for about half a block, he stopped and wished us farewell, returning slowly to his house as we descended to the beach and the same restaurant where we had dined with him two years before. It was not so satisfying a visit as I would have liked, but it was still good to see the great antipoet and to realize again how fortunate I had been to have met him and to have been able to translate his work. As I had written in the inscription in the copy of *Backtracking*, first discovering his antipoems and meeting him in 1965 had been life changing.

I was sad to think that this would probably be the last time that I would ever see Don Nicanor. But knowing how durable he had been, both as a poet and as a man, I could believe that he would be around for his 100th birthday in 2014 and perhaps even outlive me, just as he had his contemporaries, from Huidobro, Mistral, Neruda, de Rokha, Teillier, and Lihn to so many younger poets like Millán, Juan Luis Martínez, and Rogers. Just listing those Chilean poets reminded me that on this trip I had renewed my acquaintance with the poets' writings and even visited their birthplaces, some of their homes and/or museums, learned once more how beautiful their country really is and how lucky I had been to discover it, to form lasting friendships among its literati, and above all to find in a library in its capital city my dearest María, the love of my life.

María In Memoriam
(1944-2020)

María Isabel and Dave in their front yard in Cedar Park, Texas.
Photo by David Leonnig, 2015.

1

what good is going on without her here
well-meaning friends say live & write of her
but how can she be served by either act
cremation having with its heartless heat
reduced to ash her smiling lips & teeth
delicious were they once to watch or kiss
her soft brown eyes sweet ears & witty tongue
she now can read or hear or speak with none
whatever could be said to bring them back
not even bones for let her loved ones know
no casket no mortician's painted show
so why seek words to take her features' place
when those rely as much on artifice
as any makeup on her artless face

2

against the best advice I yet persist
in telling friends there just does not exist
a reason to remain with her not here
no hands to hold & never more to hear
her reassuring voice as when it said
with only me could she have ever wed
but now the kids both say she never would
have wanted me to fall apart & not
live on & in my grief I have forgotten how her wish had always been to die
before I did & not be left to lie
alone & how she wanted me to go
on writing & remarry too & so
be happy when with only her I could

3

the flowers she had planted still grow on
though weeds & ivy threaten all her beds
where happily I then would rake & dig
but if her salvia pinks & greggii reds
should not survive I shall not feel bereft
for no perennial is worth a fig
with her not coming back year after year
her beauty & her fragrance once so near
now never here yet friends say just go on
keep watering the potted herbs she left
but how can garnish help a frozen meal
so microwaved it smells & looks unreal
her dishes fresh nutritious never plain
no recipe of hers will taste again

4

unjealous strong & wise she was & bright
& yet had married me who never has
had any of her cleareyed qualities
could not conceive what she had ever seen
in me or how she left her land & came
with me to this has no respect for those
whose veins (as hers did) pulse with Latin blood
when asked at first she offered up the same
tired maxim "love is blind" unfazed in light
of flaw or fault but then had said she judged
that she should join with one could be as keen
as she on books & faithfulness in throes
of woe one stirred & soothed by verse & jazz
her absence though no word or note can ease

5

was all I ever could have wished for in
a friend a love a wife rolled into one
but on first sight thought none of that before
a book checked out from her had let me hear
her speaking with her fetching accent in
her second tongue my rare librarian
with skin so soft & smooth & after more
than fifty years with me still fresh & clear
those cozy chats with her were so much fun
until remembrance ceased & any word
except *Coneja* (sister hers so dear)
seemed even in her Spanish not to mean
a thing & to endearments lipped between
caresses no response since merely heard

6

too late to say the words I would have said
the heavy burden of unspoken love
although expressed so often not enough
no matter if in every different way
as "crazy over" "mad about" "adore"
yet never half the number due each day
in gratitude & homage ever owed
to her who blessed me with her selfless years
so full of warmth & wisdom & bestowed
upon the kids & friends she always touched
by insights shared & facts in books she read
in Spanish English French & far above
those three her own Chilean with its lore
she missed each day brings on remorseful tears

7

how lucky to have lived with her so long
though never had deserved to be with her
as one friend with a crush on her declared
agreed with him & told him so yet said
the choice had been her own if not of fate
since she believed almost that it had brought
together two from cultures poles apart
if differed in our speech were one in thought
a countryman she did for two years date
but in the end had not for him so cared
as for her foreigner she chose instead
who never would fit in nor quite belong
exiled herself for him aware could err
& he turn out unworthy of her heart

8

had never felt could measure up to her
& stood in awe of having been the one
directed to her door by destiny
design or accident or hook or crook
acknowledged each day's prize unfairly won
for knew the others sharp & gifted too
who clearly merited her hand much more
& yet throughout the years I saw I grew
in every way from having been allowed
to sleep with her & though unearned to be
night after night admitted to her store
of intuitions lessons learned from book
or life & taught to me through her own perfect bliss made me less cowed of her more proud

9

with her at home could feel the peace within
& all the joy she brought to every room
with prints on walls her knickknacks on the shelves
the photos of the kids & grandkids too
of us with smiles the posters from our trips
to Taos & my local Texas towns
would not have known if had not been for her
insisting we should visit them ourselves
take in a landmark or a famous tomb
the farmer markets with their cider sips
their blushing peaches & their country sounds
from fiddle bands until would come back then
to doors & floors meant more with her astir
now mean much less with only one of two

10

the happiest of all my days was when
she let me take her as my love for life
& not for being just a pretty wife
but one to urge us both to find within
the vital drive for each's highest aims
to reach them then as truly equal mates
united even though sex separates
yet not from fondness nor the newborn names
the saddest came when saw her eyes roll back
& knew she left me with my lesser self
to face the future with this deep regret
for time not spent with her & for my lack
of focus when I had & so much selfishness yet loved by her cannot forget

11

our life so wonderful & happy too
a fairy tale from her own point of view
to me beyond belief since hopes for such
had held so few till felt her magic touch
& knew had never been with one like her
for lacking common sense all others were
far less had they approached her loveliness
still less her sincere candid readiness
to take me with my own deficiencies
shortcomings she endured but did her best
to mend the worst while lived with all the rest
would tell our kids your father's idiocies
have been atoned for since he loves & respects
me so yet could not save her from disease

12

can take scant credit for contentment in
her life with me since her own happiness
she made herself in spite of my missteps
her few needs too conduced to that result
now painfully confess of wedding vows
I failed to cherish her in sickness when
(by then our past to her beyond recall)
she fought against a stranger washed her hair
& rinsed shampoo & brushed her teeth till all
my patience lost I yelled at her insult-
ing words a worse incontinence I swear
than hers with diapers changed in our own house
or kneeling worship-like on restroom floors
in filling stations & in grocery stores

13

the one unlucky number some believe
but this thirteenth resolved to look out for
an ending happier than hers had been
so hard to think of that along with loss
of all she was had made for paradise
yet in this grief now read again her note
inside the book she gave in which she wrote
how from the first she knew this love was real
not seeming so as in those times before
with soldier boy & others who had eyes
for her & she for them until had seen
the signs within her heart as in her thoughts
should wait for one would never once deceive
nor ever change as fortune's fickle wheel

14

o how could I have ever said to her
if you will marry me you ought to know
that always poetry comes first with me
why did she not reject me then & there
she would of course replace it soon enough
once all she was & made & said & loved
(as covers for the couches she would sew
her voices for each doll & Pooh the bear
our kids she bore & books she read again)
had filled my verses friends did all prefer
to those I wrote & thought my solid best
her quick assent remains a sweet refrain
reminding how she passed the true-love test
since foolish words were less to her than we

15

she wrote to them to introduce herself
but neither Mom nor Dad replied to her
too jealous of her place in my new life
Aunt Sis did write a slanted florid hand
was hard to read yet so endearing were
her words: Assure your mother everyone
will take good care of you & will demand
my nephew love & always treat you well
He's like a son to me I'm proud to tell
of his accomplishments His very best
will now be you o how could she have guessed
or known before she saw & heard the wonder of that face & speech of my own wife-
to-be whose depths I barely knew myself

16

had said that I would write of her no more
gave reasons why but then continued to
& in this stiff & worn-out sonnet form
a hypocrite I was when swore before
that I could never live without her near
& yet went on with her no longer here
except in lines that made me feel I knew
verse after verse she kept me company
now let the iambs count & rhymes perform
that words may bring again her quiet charm
that syllables may sing each absent trait
(though each still leaves an emptiness in me)
& may this language somehow reach my mate
to say I grieve for you my poetry

About Dave Oliphant

Born in Fort Worth, Texas, in 1939, **Dave Oliphant** has published over thirty books, including a dozen collections of poetry. In 2017, Alamo Bay Press published Oliphant's *The Hero's Fall I Fell For: Jazz Poems*, and in 2018 the Press issued a revised paperback edition of his *KD: a Jazz Biography*, originally printed in 2012 in a hardback edition by Wings Press. Previously ABP brought out three other collections of his poetry: *The Cowtown Circle* (2014; revised and expanded in 2016); *María's Book* (2016); and *Austin: a Poem* (2018). His poetry collections also include *The Pilgrimage: Selected Poems, 1962-2012* (Lamar University Press, 2013). In 2015, Wings Press published Oliphant's *Generations of Texas Poets*, a collection of 55 essays, articles, and reviews on Texas poetry. His most recent book is a collection of twenty essays, articles, and introductions on Chilean poetry published in 2019 as *Hallazgo y traducción de poesía chilena* by Editorial A Contracorriente at North Carolina State University. Oliphant's translation of Nicanor Parra's *Discursos de sobremesa* as *After-Dinner Declarations* was published by Host Publications in 2009 and in 2011 won the Soeurette Diehl Fraser book translation award from the Texas Institute of Letters.

www.ingramcontent.com/pod-product-compliance
Lightning Source LLC
Chambersburg PA
CBHW041323110526
44592CB00021B/2800